A FIELD GUIDE TO THE

Reptiles and Amphibians

OF BRITAIN AND EUROPE

Hertfordshire
COUNTY COUNCIL

Community Information

1 3 MAR 2001

2 3 JAN 2002

- 7 MAR 2002

1 5 SEP 2005

- 5 JUL 2006

2 7 MAR 2001

- 9 NOV 2009

- 7 APR 2003 2 NOV 2010

1 0 JUL 2001 2 6 APR 2005

9/12

1 8 DEC 2001 2 9 JUN 2005

Please renew/return this item by the last date shown.

So that your telephone call is charged at local rate,
please call the numbers as set out below:

	From Area codes 01923 or 0208:	From the rest of Herts:
Renewals:	01923 471373	01438 737373
Enquiries:	01923 471333	01438 737333
Minicom:	01923 471599	01438 737599

L32b

A FIELD GUIDE TO THE

Reptiles and Amphibians

OF BRITAIN AND EUROPE

E. N. Arnold and J. A. Burton

Illustrated by

D. W. Ovenden

COLLINS
Grafton Street, London

First published 1978
Reprinted 1980
Reprinted 1985
Reprinted 1992

© in the text: E. N. Arnold & J. A. Burton 1978
© in the illustrations: D. W. Ovenden 1978

ISBN 0 00 219318 3

Filmset by Jolly & Barber Ltd, Rugby
Made and printed in Great Britain by
HarperCollins*Manufacturing*, Glasgow

CONTENTS

COLOUR PLATES

Acknowledgements

Like any book containing numerous factual statements, field guides are to a large extent dependent on the published work of others. Consequently the authors owe a great debt to the numerous people who have written on European reptiles and amphibians during the last century or so. A small proportion of these are listed in the Bibliography (p. 248). Among the people who have helped us more personally are Dr J. Castroviejo and Mr P. W. Hopkins (Spanish distributions), Viscount Chaplin (Tree Frogs), Mr R. J. Clark (Greek distributions), Dr A. Dubois (French distributions), Dr I. Fuhn (Romania), Miss A. G. C. Grandison and Dr K. Klemmer (Spanish Wall Lizards), Mr G. Lanfranco (Malta), Dr T. M. Uzzell and Mr H.-J. Hotz (Green Frogs), Sir Christopher Lever (introduced species in Britain), Dr H. A. Reid (treatment of bites by venomous snakes); their help is much appreciated. We should also like to thank the Trustees of the British Museum (Natural History) for access to collections and libraries. The typing of the manuscript from barely legible drafts was undertaken by Renate Arnold.

HOW TO USE THIS BOOK

Identification

Absolute novices will find identification of reptiles and amphibians easier if they first read the Introduction (p. 13) and the preliminary remarks at the beginning of the sections on each main animal group:

Salamanders and Newts	p. 29
Frogs and Toads	p. 55
Tortoises, Terrapins and Turtles	p. 88
Lizards and Amphisbaenians	p. 101
Snakes	p. 183

Then the following approach is recommended:

★ Look quickly through the plates and try to match your animal's **appearance** as closely as possible to one of the species shown, bearing in mind that many species are rather variable.

★ Once this is done, check with the text and maps that you are within the **range** of the species concerned. This is very important. Apart from sea turtles, most reptiles and amphibians do not move about much and are only rarely found outside their normal ranges.

★ If the range fits, then compare your animal with the **description** in the Identification and Variation texts for the species. If it does not agree with these, look at the forms listed under Similar Species.

★ Should the above method fail, and the animal can be examined at close quarters, try using the **keys**. This is rather laborious but often results in more certain identification. Main keys are: Salamanders and Newts, p. 29; Frogs and Toads, p. 56; Tortoises, Terrapins and Turtles, p. 88; Lizards and Amphisbaenians, p. 103; Snakes, p. 184. There are also subsidiary keys in the text to particular groups such as Newts and Vipers.

Keys are made up of sections each containing two or more contrasted statements as in the following example:

1.	Fore-feet with four toes	2
	Fore-feet with three toes	7
2.	Toes stubby	3
	Toes not stubby	5

9

Starting at section 1, select the statement that agrees most closely with your animal. When you have done this, go to the section of the key indicated immediately after the statement, and so on until you arrive at a positive identification. For instance, in the example above, if your animal has four toes on the fore-feet, proceed to section 2. Having arrived there, check toe shape and if it is not stubby go on to section 5.

The descriptive texts

For easy reference, the text describing each species has been divided into several sections as follows.

Names. Both the scientific and vernacular names are given. The scientific name consists of two words, the first (always written with a capital letter) is the *genus*, the second the *species* name. In most cases species with the same generic name are rather similar and probably closely related. The scientific names are used by reptile and amphibian enthusiasts throughout the world, irrespective of their native language. They simplify communication and are well worth learning. Vernaculars on the other hand, although easier to remember at first, are less useful. In most languages, only the more obvious kinds of reptile and amphibian have widely accepted names and a number of species are often covered by a single term. The precise vernacular names given in books are usually recent inventions and often a confusing number of alternatives exist. They tend to be known only to people with a strong interest in the animals concerned, who are normally familiar with the scientific names anyway. Because of their limited use, foreign vernaculars have not been given for each species.

Range. The maps give a fairly detailed account of the known distribution of each species, so only a brief description is usually given in the text. However, isolated localities too small to show clearly on the maps may be mentioned here and an indication of range outside Europe is also given. See also **Distribution Maps** p. 253.

Identification. Only features necessary for positive identification are listed here. This means that descriptions are often very short for easily recognised species but longer for some of the more difficult ones. On occasions technical terms have to be used; these are explained or illustrated in the glossary or at the beginning of the relevant main sections, just before the keys (Salamanders and Newts – p. 29; Frogs and Toads – p. 55; Tortoises, Terrapins and Turtles – p. 88; Lizards and Amphisbaenians – p. 101; and Snakes – p. 183). Sizes are in centimetres (2.54 centimetres = 1 inch). In most cases total length is given, but for lacertid lizards, where the tail is usually long but often broken, the basic measurement is distance from snout to vent. For tortoises and terrapins the length of the upper shell (carapace) is given: this is a straight line measurement, not over the curve of the shell as in sea turtles.

Voice. This is only described for frogs and toads. Some other reptiles and amphibians are capable of producing usually weak grunts, squeaks and hisses but these are rarely of use as identification characters. (See also p. 18).

Habits. As much information as possible about habits is given, with particular emphasis on habitat. This is because the place where an animal is found is often characteristic of the species concerned, and as such is a useful clue to identity.

Venom. Discussion is limited to snakes with venom and distinct fangs (enlarged tubular or grooved teeth that inject the venom), the only species in Europe that might be dangerous to man. Some other snakes appear to produce saliva with toxic properties and many amphibians have poisonous skin secretions (p. 19), but these are only marginally harmful to human beings in normal circumstances. *See p. 24 for treatment of bites by dangerously venomous snakes.*

Variation. Individual and regional variation are briefly described here. (See also p. 15).

Similar Species. The species most likely to cause confusion, particularly in the field, are listed. Where convenient, distinguishing features are also mentioned but in other cases these may be discussed under **Identification.**

Family introductions. To avoid frequent repetition in the species texts, many facts common to several different animals are placed in the introductions to families or other major groups. These include the general characteristics of the members of the family or group and often some information on their habits and breeding.

Illustrations. The colour plates have been drawn from life whenever possible and should give a fairly good idea of how the animals look in the field. Individuals of nearly all species occurring in Europe are shown in colour but the sea turtles illustrated and the American Bullfrog are depicted in black and white drawings. Where they are markedly different, both sexes and juveniles are illustrated.

Because many reptile and amphibian species are very variable it is not possible to illustrate more then a selection of these differences. Where a choice had to be made, the more usually encountered variants have been shown; thus common pattern-types are illustrated in preference to rare ones and mainland and large-island forms rather than ones confined to isolated rocks and islets. Further details about variation are given in the texts. Often, the animals illustrated are not typical of any particular locality and, where possible, are 'average' specimens.

Scale. In most cases, the animals in each plate are drawn to the same scale, and unless otherwise stated are approximately life-sized.

INTRODUCTION

In Europe, west of 36°E, there are about 45 species of amphibians and 85 species of non-marine reptiles; five kinds of sea turtle have also been recorded from the area. These animals are an important and attractive part of the fauna, particularly in southern countries, yet there is no single comprehensive guide that allows them to be identified with any certainty. It is hoped that the present book will help fill this gap.

The area covered by this book takes in all of Europe west of a line joining the White Sea and the Sea of Azov. Crete and all Aegean islands are included, except for those on or near the continental shelf of Asia Minor. Similarly most other Mediterranean islands are covered but not those on or near the African continental shelf. In this book 'Europe' is used for the area defined above, not for the wider entity of the same name.

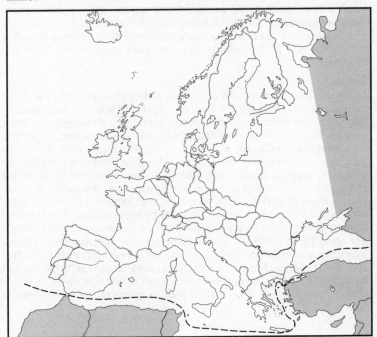

The biology of reptiles and amphibians

Reptiles (including tortoises, terrapins, turtles, lizards, amphisbaenians and snakes) can be easily recognised by their typically dry, scaly skin, whereas that of amphibians (including frogs, toads, newts and salamanders) is usually moist and lacks obvious scales. Both reptiles and amphibians are primitive vertebrates compared with mammals and birds, and differ most obviously from these in lacking both hair and feathers. They also function on a quite different energy budget. Birds and mammals usually maintain a constant high temperature (e.g. about 37°C in man). This gives them many advantages and allows them to be almost constantly active in a wide range of conditions, but it often means that a great deal of internal heat has to be produced, which requires a high food intake. Reptiles and amphibians, on the other hand, have variable temperatures and either live close to the temperature of the air or water that surrounds them or get heat by basking in the sun or sitting on sun-heated surfaces. In very cold conditions, or when sun is unavailable, activity may become impossible, but this disadvantage is balanced by the fact that little or no internal heat needs to be produced and reptiles and amphibians can therefore manage on a very low food intake. Because of this, they do very well in situations where food is sparse or intermittent, which is why they survive in spite of competition from the more sophisticated birds and mammals.

Species.
Nearly all European species of reptiles and amphibians are made up of individuals that are at least potentially capable of interbreeding successfully with each other but do not usually hybridise with members of other species. Mating between animals of different species is rare, especially under natural conditions, and when it occurs, often either few or no offspring are produced or their ability to breed or survive is curtailed. As with most generalisations, there are exceptions to this. For instance, the two species of Fire-bellied toads (p. 60) appear to interbreed in some places, although the long-term survival of such hybrids is uncertain. Also, a few species seem to have been produced by hybridisation. This is true of some relatives of the Caucasian Rock Lizard (*Lacerta saxicola*) outside our area. These consist of all-female populations that reproduce without intervention of males and arose from crosses between more normal sexual species. The Edible Frog (*Rana esculenta*, p. 86) also seems to have arisen by hybridisation: it retains both sexes but is peculiar in often being able to reproduce itself by mating with members of the parent species (see p. 84).

Variation within species.

Within a species, not all animals are exactly alike. Even excluding variation due to sex and age, members of a population can sometimes look very different. Reptiles and amphibians often show great variability in colour and pattern, which can be a source of confusion when trying to identify them. Within a population, variation may be *continuous*, so that the animals could be arranged in a series showing gradual change; or *polymorphic* in which case all individuals can be assigned to one of two or more distinct groups (*morphs*), e.g. the striped and spotted variants of the Painted Frog (p. 62), or the striped and unmarked morphs of some Wall Lizards. Morphs are often mistaken for separate species.

Most widespread species also show regional variation. For instance, in most places, the Common Wall Lizard (*Podarcis muralis*) is rather small and brown with some dark markings, but in some areas it tends to increase in size and develop a green back and heavy spotting. Many north-western Italian populations show this trend to some extent, especially in the males, but near Rome it is very marked, the Wall Lizards being extremely dark and both sexes equally affected. This sort of variation is often formally recognised by naming *subspecies*, which are indicated by adding a third word to the scientific name. The Common Wall Lizard becomes *Podarcis muralis muralis* in most areas, *P. muralis brueggemanni* in north-western Italy and *P. muralis nigriventris* near Rome.

Subspecies are geographical concepts, which means that all the animals in a particular population belong to the same subspecies, even though some of them lack its characteristic features. For example, some Wall Lizards in N.W. Italy are indistinguishable from ordinary brown *P. muralis muralis* but they would still be called *P. m. brueggemanni* like the green-backed animals among which they occur.

Subspecific names draw attention to interesting regional variation but their use may raise problems. For instance, on the European mainland, subspecies usually lack clear-cut boundaries and there may often be large intergrade areas between them where populations cannot really be assigned to one or to another. In groups of islands where there are many isolated populations, these often differ from each other and are frequently named as separate subspecies. In the west Balearic Islands over 30 subspecies of the Ibiza Wall Lizard (*Podarcis pityusensis*) have been described and well over 40 island subspecies of the Italian Wall Lizard (*Podarcis sicula*) are recognised. Memorising so many names can be difficult. The validity of a species can often be checked by seeing if it is able to interbreed freely with other forms, but no such test is available for subspecies. They tend to be far more a matter of opinion and their boundaries and number are frequently altered by specialists.

Because of these difficulties, it seems better not to list subspecies in this book (except in a few cases where they are particularly clearly defined) but to describe variation as it occurs. Many amateur herpetologists seem very concerned about subspecies but it is worth remembering that the addition of a subspecific name rarely gives much more information than a note of the locality where the animal was found.

Rare variations.
Very occasionally animals that are strikingly different from other members of their species are found. For instance, individuals sometimes turn up which completely lack pigment (albinos) or which have very odd colour patterns. These, together with two-headed terrapins and snakes and six-legged frogs, often receive a lot of attention and are of some pathological interest. But such animals are very uncommon and do not usually survive long in nature. They are therefore not included in the species texts.

Food.
The food of most European reptiles and amphibians consists mainly of live animals: the principal exceptions are tortoises, certain turtles and the tadpoles of some frogs and toads, all of which eat mostly plants. Animal food is very frequently swallowed whole after, at most, a rather cursory chewing which helps to subdue it. The kind of prey varies: most reptiles and amphibians take whatever edible animals they can overpower but snakes tend to specialise and often eat mainly one particular type – for instance Smooth Snakes (*Coronella*) usually eat lizards, while Water Snakes (*Natrix*) take amphibians and fish. Snakes eat relatively large animals for their size and often have specialised ways of reducing the activity of their prey: Smooth Snakes (*Coronella*) and Rat Snakes (*Elaphe*) hold their victim with one or more coils of their body; other species, such as vipers, inject venom which rapidly kills prey. Most reptiles and some amphibians pick up food directly with their jaws but chameleons, many frogs and toads, and some salamanders have tongues which are sticky and can be flicked forwards to catch food.

Avoiding competition.
Competition between species of snakes in the same area is often not great because many eat different kinds of prey. Most other reptiles and amphibians are not very specialised in their diet and so must avoid competing in other ways. For instance, they may hunt at different times of day and night, or take different sizes of prey, or live and hunt in different places. Differences in habitat are often very marked in closely related species. For example, in the central Balkan area, Marsh Frogs (*Rana ridibunda*) are common in lakes and slow and weedy rivers; Stream Frogs (*Rana graeca*) near springs and along cold streams; Agile Frogs (*Rana dalmatina*) in open woods, moist meadows etc. and the Common Frog (*Rana temporaria*) is the dominant species high in the mountains.

Times of activity.
As reptiles and amphibians depend on external heat for their activity, they cannot remain active when the temperature is very low, and in colder areas

they must hibernate. The winter months are passed in a state of torpor in some safe, frost-free refuge such as a hole in the ground or a deep rock crevice. Some amphibians and terrapins hibernate under water. The time of inactivity varies with local conditions: in the far North it can be up to two thirds of the year, while in southern countries, some species may not really hibernate at all. Because of this regional variability, times of hibernation are not given in the species texts. There are great differences in cold sensitivity between species: some amphibians are active in near-freezing conditions, while many reptiles require a minimum temperature of 15°C before they show themselves. Most species in southern Europe become less active in summer. This is particularly noticeable in aquatic forms which suspend activity and retreat into holes or wet mud when the water in which they live dries up. Other species tend to appear only for short periods and are usually more wary than in the spring.

Most reptiles and many amphibians are diurnal, but others are only active in the evening or at night. The diurnal ones are often most apparent in the morning and may retreat around the middle of the day to reappear in the late afternoon.

Breeding.

Most European reptiles produce eggs. In the case of tortoises, terrapins and geckoes, these are hard-shelled and often laid in dry places, while in other species they have soft, flexible shells and are usually deposited in moist sand, earth or dead vegetation. The young that hatch from these eggs are small versions of their parents, differing only in size, proportions and sometimes colouring. They are fully independent and receive no care from their parents. In a few species eggs are retained in the body of the mother who eventually gives birth to fully developed young or eggs which hatch almost immediately. This happens in most vipers, the Sand Boa (*Eryx jaculus*), the Smooth Snake (*Coronella austriaca*), the Slow Worm (*Anguis fragilis*), some skinks and the Viviparous Lizard (*Lacerta vivipara*). Most amphibians produce eggs with a gelatinous coating. They are usually laid in water where they develop into animals quite unlike their parents. These aquatic *larvae* (better known as tadpoles) spend a considerable time feeding and then change quite abruptly (metamorphose) into miniatures of their parents. Tadpoles are more fully discussed on p. 229. A minority of salamanders give birth directly to larvae or fully-formed babies, or their eggs are laid in the normal way but hatch into metamorphosed young.

Fertilisation in reptiles is internal, mating often taking place with relatively few preliminaries, although rival males may fight, or, more often, display to each other and to any females within range. Fertilisation is also internal in European newts and salamanders, but not in our frogs and toads. In these animals, males embrace the females from above but the eggs are only fertilised as they are laid. Voice is very important in the breeding behaviour of frogs and toads (see following page).

Voice.

Newts, salamanders and most reptiles are virtually silent or their voice is limited to faint grunts, squeaks or hisses. Geckoes, one or two other lizards and some tortoises produce more distinct calls but it is only frogs and toads that are highly vocal. In the breeding season, the males produce a distinct, and often loud, mating call which serves to attract females to the breeding area. The call of each species is usually highly characteristic, which enables females to present themselves to the right males. This is very important in ponds where more than one species breeds at the same time and where females are likely to be grasped by the wrong males (in many cases, male frogs and toads are not very particular about their partners and will often grab females of other species and in some cases even fish or pieces of wood etc.).

In addition to the mating call, males may have a 'release' call which is produced when they are inadvertently grasped by another male. As its name implies, this call usually results in the caller being released. Some forms have a number of other vocalisations and some, such as the Typical Frogs (*Rana*) may scream when injured or captured.

Mating calls are mainly limited to the breeding season which in most forms is in the spring, although a few may breed in the summer as well, e.g. discoglossids, Parsley Frog (*Pelodytes punctatus*) and Natterjack (*Bufo calamita*). Sporadic and isolated calling may occur at other times, especially in the autumn, and Green Frogs (p. 84) and Fire-bellied Toads (p. 60) may call throughout the warmer months of the year, even when not actively breeding.

Calls are often amplified by air-filled resonators called vocal sacs. These are soft, bag-like structures that lead off the mouth cavity and are inflated with air when calling takes place. In many species, there is a single vocal sac under the floor of the mouth. It may be relatively small and the throat-skin covering it unmodified, in which case the vocal sac is termed 'internal'. 'External' sacs are usually larger and the skin covering them is thin, wrinkled and elastic, so that when the sac is inflated, it often forms a large, translucent balloon underneath the throat. Green Frogs differ from other European species in having an external vocal sac at each corner of the mouth.

Frog and toad calls are often good field characters and are usually very easy to distinguish, once they have been heard. The easiest way to become familiar with calls is by listening to recordings of them. Records of some species are available commercially (see p. 252). The often rather gutteral sounds produced by frogs and toads can be extremely difficult to put into words, but an attempt has been made to describe them in the species texts, either by transliteration or by comparing them with more familiar sounds. It should be borne in mind that there is often individual variation in the call of a species, especially in speed, which usually varies with temperature, and in pitch, which can vary with the size of the calling individual.

There is still a great deal to find out about European frog and toad calls. At the time of writing, the calls of some species are apparently unrecorded and only known from descriptions; and, in *Alytes cisternasii* and *Pelobates syriacus* the call has apparently not even been described. Geographical variation in the calls of the more widespread species is also scarcely investigated.

Natural enemies and defence.
Most reptiles and amphibians are small, helpless and potentially edible. They consequently figure in the diets of many larger animals. Many snakes eat them and so do a variety of birds (e.g. shrikes, hawks, crows and herons) and small mammals (rats, hedgehogs, stoats, weasels, foxes, badgers etc.). Most of the warm-blooded predators take reptiles and amphibians as part of a varied diet and the only reptile specialist in Europe is the Short-toed Eagle (*Circaetus gallicus*) which eats a large proportion of snakes.

Methods of combating predators are varied. Many species have markings that make them inconspicuous in their natural habitats and they often make use of secure retreats which their enemies cannot easily enter: for instance, many rock lizards are very flattened so that they can go deep into narrow crevices. Other species depend on speed and agility to escape predators.

If cornered, many reptiles will bite, but this is only really effective in the larger species, especially the venomous snakes. Many other forms supplement their limited defensive abilities with elaborate bluffs, e.g. frogs and toads often make themselves appear larger by inflating with air, and the Common Spadefoot (*Pelobates fuscus*) will scream and jump towards its attacker. The non-poisonous Viperine Snake (*Natrix maura*) may have viper-like markings and when threatened will increase its resemblance to a venomous snake by flattening the head, hissing and striking, albeit with mouth closed. Many lizards will shed (autotomise) the tail when this is grasped, allowing them to escape and leaving the predator with a distraction. The distractive power of the tail is enhanced because it wriggles for some time after breaking off, and it is often brightly coloured as well. Most lizards rapidly grow a new tail after autotomy.

Many amphibians have noxious skin secretions which deter predators. In some cases the species concerned have black and yellow or black and red markings which have a warning function. If a predator has already suffered from attacking a brightly coloured, noxious amphibian it may associate the markings with its previous experience and be wary of a similar animal. In some instances the bright markings are always visible, e.g. on the Fire Salamander (*Salamandra salamandra*): in others they are usually hidden but are exposed by special postures in time of danger, e.g. in Fire-bellied Toads (*Bombina*) and the Spectacled Salamander (*Salamandrina terdigitata*).

Reptiles, amphibians and man

As a group, reptiles and amphibians have had relatively little effect on man although they have often entered his mythology and sometimes his digestion as well (tortoises, terrapins, turtles and their eggs, frogs and even snakes are, or have been, regular items of diet in many places). However, the effect of man on reptiles and amphibians has been considerable. The ranges of some species have been increased by human transportation, either intended or accidental. Thus, the isolated colonies of the Italian Wall Lizard, *Podarcis sicula,* in several Mediterranean countries are almost certainly the result of introduction by man.

Destruction of woodland and its replacement by cultivation has undoubtedly reduced the numbers of some forms. At the same time it has benefited those species that survive best in disturbed and more open habitats. The stone-piles and dry-stone walls that now characterise so many Mediterranean areas provide a host of refuges for reptiles and their prey and allow some species to exist in concentrations that would have been very rare in 'natural' conditions. Construction of open irrigation cisterns in dry areas has indubitably benefited many kinds of amphibians.

Other human activities are less benign. Apart from the widespread and time-hallowed practice of killing any snake-like animal encountered, there are many recent developments which are harmful to these animals. Spraying crops with pesticides often appears to have an adverse effect, either directly or by destroying their food; run-off of pesticides into pools can have a devastating result on the breeding success of amphibians. This also is true of the habit of running road drains into nearby ponds, polluting them with oil-residues from the road surface. Heavy traffic accounts for large numbers of amphibians when migrating to their breeding ponds, and also for a wide variety of reptiles, especially tortoises. Road surfaces also have a fatal attraction to many nocturnal snakes and lizards which move onto them after dark because they retain heat.

In Britain the destruction of heathland areas, removal of hedgerows and filling in of ponds have contributed to a sharp decline in several species.

Collection of animals for the pet-trade is another factor that can reduce natural populations. In most cases, its effect is probably slight, but in areas where a species has already been restricted to a few isolated populations by other factors, it could be important in extermination, at least on a local level. Conspicuous, easily caught animals, such as tortoises are most likely to suffer greatly from collecting.

Few if any European species will be completely exterminated by human activities, at least in the near future. But there are many that are in danger of being reduced from their present abundance. One of the charms of southern Europe is the large numbers of reptiles and amphibians found there. It would be a pity if this were to change.

Keeping reptiles and amphibians.
It is tempting to keep reptiles and amphibians as pets especially as they often survive for a long time even in rather poor conditions. But unless they receive a great deal of care they live a miserable travesty of their natural existence. The average semi-moribund captive tortoise bears no comparison with the alert, vigorous, herb-scented beasts that plough through the undergrowth of southern Europe. Observing wild animals is far more entertaining, and less demanding, than the drudgery of keeping them.

Watching reptiles and amphibians.
To see reptiles and amphibians in reasonable numbers, it is necessary to choose time and place carefully. In general, these animals are much easier to see and more abundant in southern countries, where they may occur almost anywhere. In the North, a high proportion of forms are restricted to a few specialised habitats, and are often rather secretive. Some idea of the sort of places that repay investigation can be gained from the **habits** section in the species texts.

Frogs, toads and newts breed communally in ponds and lakes and are much easier to see during the mating season (spring for most species) than at other times. Season is also important for other groups. In northern countries all forms hibernate during the winter months but are generally conspicuous in the spring, and remain quite active for the rest of the summer and autumn. In the Mediterranean area on the other hand, at least some species are active through most of the winter. Spring is again the season of greatest activity, but with the heat of summer many forms retreat and at most are seen only briefly or in small numbers.

For most diurnal species, sunny weather is best. They tend to be most active in the morning, and often again in the late afternoon.

You will see more reptiles and amphibians if you walk over suitable country *slowly* and *quietly*. Scan your surroundings with care, for many species are well camouflaged and depend on inactivity to avoid recognition. Any movement or rustling in vegetation may repay investigation. Breeding frogs and toads can often be located by their call, which may carry for considerable distances. Nocturnal and secretive species can be found by looking for their day-time hiding places, such as in holes, under logs and stones etc. (remember to replace stones and logs in their original position). But more can usually be seen by looking for them after dark with a broad-beamed lamp (it is not possible to illuminate enough ground with an ordinary torch). For nocturnal amphibians, the best nights are those preceded by rain.

Many species will allow an observer to get very close to them if he moves slowly (although the distance at which an animal retreats often varies with the season, time of day and many other factors). On the whole, terrapins, the larger lizards and snakes tend to be more wary than other forms. For observing the more active species, binoculars are a useful aid. High magnification is not particularly important (6× to 8× binoculars are probably best), but near-point of focusing and light-gathering power are. As many reptiles and amphibians allow a relatively close approach, it is essential to have a binocular which is still focusable at short range. Light-gathering power can be roughly assessed by dividing the diameter in millimetres of the front (object) lens by the magnification. Lens diameter is usually marked on the body of binoculars just after the magnification, e.g. 6 × 30, which would give a result of 5. Any result between about 4 and 7 is quite satisfactory.

Collecting data.
The essential requirement for any field study is a well-kept notebook. A lot of interesting information on behaviour and habits can be collected, even by an absolute beginner, provided that information is recorded in a thorough manner. At first, note-keeping may seem superfluous, it is only when a record has been kept for some time that one realises how much would have been forgotten without it. For all observations, date, locality, time of day and weather should be noted, preferably with a brief description of habitat. Only put in firm identifications if you are sure of them. In cases where there is doubt, it is much better to note that this is so.

Photography.
It is often possible to make a photographic record of reptiles and amphibians seen, and this may sometimes be helpful in identifying difficult animals. Unlike birds and mammals, they are relatively easy to photograph since many of them allow close approach, often remain still for long periods and bask in bright sun. For most purposes a 35 mm single-lens reflex camera is adequate. A standard lens, either with or without extension rings, works well for animals that can be approached very closely. Otherwise a 135 mm or 200 mm telephoto is useful, and again extension rings may help.

Preserving dead animals.
Any interesting animals found dead can be preserved. This enables doubtful identifications to be more carefully checked and may provide firm evidence of range extensions etc. Ideally, dead animals should be placed in about 8% Formalin solution (commercial Formaldehyde solution diluted with about eleven times its volume of water), or in 80% alcohol (= 140° proof spirit) for reptiles and 60% for amphibians. Larger reptiles should be liberally injected with 10% formalin or 80% alcohol first; this is also beneficial for smaller ones. In emergencies, quite good results can be obtained using distilled drinking alcohol, although this tends to be rather weak. The stronger grades of brandy, gin, anis, slivovica, tuica, rakija, schnapps, or ouzo all work quite well.

Most snakes can be identified from the head and neck alone, so these are worth preserving even when the rest of the body is badly damaged.

Handling reptiles and amphibians.

In many instances it is helpful to examine reptiles and amphibians closely when confirming identifications, but remember that these animals are delicate and even slight injury can seriously reduce the chances of their survival when released. Many species can be most easily examined by placing them in a transparent plastic bag, which should contain a little water if amphibians are to be put in it. Many amphibians produce a noxious skin mucus that is harmful to other animals, so do not use the same bag for reptiles or even other amphibian species. As plastic bags are not permeable to air, animals should not be kept in them very long.

If reptiles and amphibians have to be restrained more closely, this should be done gently. Most injuries result from holding them too tightly, often because the holder is apprehensive about being bitten. In fact, European amphibians scarcely bite at all, and although lizards and the smaller non-venomous snakes may bite, they are often incapable of breaking the skin. It is only the larger snakes that can draw blood in any but minute quantities, and provided they are held correctly this can be avoided. It should go without saying that *venomous snakes should not be handled at all*.

If amphibians are held, this should be done with a wet hand to avoid rubbing off the layer of protective mucus that covers them. Most amphibians are sensitive to excessive heat and the prolonged warmth of a human hand can harm them, so do not hold them too long. Newts and salamanders should not be gripped closely, indeed this is unnecessary as they are relatively slow moving. Frogs and toads often need some restraint, and it is easiest to hold them for short periods with the thumb and forefinger round their waist and their legs lightly gripped by the remaining fingers and palm of the hand. Lizards are most easily held with the thumb and forefinger just behind the head, and the lizard's body in the lightly closed fist; the close contact appears to make the lizard feel secure and less inclined to struggle. Never pick up a lizard by its tail: in many cases it will break off (see p. 19). Non-venomous snakes should also he held just behind the head, but the body should be supported to save putting too great a strain on the neck. Do not pull snakes out of holes or crevices by their tails; it can injure them seriously.

Snake bite and its treatment

In Europe only about a third of snake species have potent venom and the fangs necessary to inject it efficiently. They fall into two types: those with fangs at the back of the mouth (rear-fanged snakes) i.e. the Montpellier Snake (*Malpolon*, p. 190), the False Smooth Snake (*Macroprotodon*, p. 206), and the Cat Snake (*Telescopus*, p. 207); and the front-fanged Vipers. European rear-fanged snakes are generally not harmful to man; the smaller species cannot usually bring their fangs into action when biting human beings and although a bite from the larger *Malpolon* can produce symptoms, these usually pass rapidly. In contrast, the vipers are capable of delivering dangerous bites; the venom is very potent and, although less is usually injected in a defensive bite than when capturing food, severe poisoning may result. The effects are worst in children and in adults who are not in good general health.

However, provided the following precautions are taken, the chances of being bitten are very slight: do not handle venomous snakes, or wear open shoes when walking through places where they occur; watch where hands and feet are put when climbing over walls, rocks, screes, logs etc.

What to do in apparent cases of viper bite.
Do not try to kill or capture the snake, this is likely to result in further injuries. If it has already been killed, do not handle it; snakes will often bite some time after apparent death if touched.

Bear the following points in mind:

EXAGGERATION: the risks from snake bite in Europe are generally exaggerated and fatalities are very rare if correct treatment is given. However, bites should be taken seriously.

POISONING: snake-bite is not the same as viper poisoning. The snake concerned may belong to a harmless species or, if a viper, may not actually have injected venom. If no local symptoms appear within about half an hour, the chances of poisoning are not very great.

URGENCY: no time should be lost in getting treatment for viper poisoning but undue haste can be dangerous. Even a bad, untreated case of viper-bite is unlikely to cause death in less than 24 hours.

Symptoms.

1. The first and sometimes only symptom may be shock, which can also result from a bite by a non-venomous snake. The victim often just feels weak and shaky but in extreme cases can appear semi-conscious with cold, clammy skin, feeble pulse and rapid breathing.

2. If poisoning has actually occurred, then swelling starts within a few minutes at the site of the bite.

3. More general symptoms may appear later and can include sweating, vomiting, giddiness, abdominal pains and diarrhoea.

Treatment.

1. Reassure the victim. The chances of death or permanent injury are very low but anxiety and panic are harmful. Aspirin (in normal doses) can be given.

2. Wait quietly and see if swelling develops. If not, then no poison has been injected.

3. If swelling develops, keep bitten part as immobile as possible and get medical attention (preferably at a hospital). Vigorous activity will spread the venom, so the victim should remain calm and should not rush.

4. *DO NOT* cut or suck wound, or allow anyone else to do so, as this increases the risk of secondary infection and cutting is also likely to cause shock. *DO NOT* put strong disinfectants or potassium permanganate on the bitten area.

5. If medical attention is likely to be delayed for much over an hour, a firm *but not tight* ligature can be applied above the bite. This is to slow the return of blood to the body and reduce the spread of the venom. A *tight* ligature may cause severe and permanent damage.

Remember!

1. Viper bite is rarely fatal.
2. Keep calm.
3. Get help.
4. Avoid vigorous activity and *never* cut or suck a snake bite.

N.B. A few people are abnormally sensitive to venomous snake bite and may collapse almost immediately after being bitten. They need medical attention as soon as possible.

Reptiles and amphibians in the British Isles

Relatively few kinds of reptiles and amphibians are found in the British Isles. In Britain, there are only six amphibians and six reptiles that are certainly native, and in Ireland only three amphibians and one reptile are definitely known to be long established. A number of other species have been introduced, either accidentally or intentionally, and a few of these have survived and bred in England. In the following list, only those introduced species that have probably lived for at least 25 years in wild or semi-wild conditions are included. One or two others, like the Alpine Newt (*Triturus alpestris*), the Yellow-bellied Toad (*Bombina variegata*) and the Italian Wall Lizard (*Podarcis sicula*) may exist in very restricted colonies on private premises. A small introduction of the Clawed Toad (*Xenopus laevis*, family Pipidae), an African species, has recently been made on the Isle of Wight.

NEWTS

Triturus cristatus, Warty Newt	Native in Britain	p. 43
Triturus vulgaris, Smooth Newt	Native in Britain; also Ireland	p. 47
Triturus helveticus, Palmate Newt	Native in Britain	p. 51

FROGS AND TOADS

Alytes obstetricians, Midwife Toad	Introduced: isolated colonies in Bedfordshire and Yorkshire, some established over 70 years	p. 63
Bufo bufo, Common Toad	Native in Britain	p. 72
Bufo calamita, Natterjack	Native in Britain; also S.W. Ireland	p. 73
Hyla arborea, Common Tree Frog	At least one introduced colony in S. England	p. 75
Rana temporaria, Common or Grass Frog	Native in Britain; also Ireland	p. 78
Rana lessonae, Pool Frog / *Rana esculenta*, Edible Frog	Frequently introduced into S.E. England and E. Anglia; one or both may possibly have been native; small colonies still exist	p. 85, 86

26

Rana ridibunda, Marsh Frog	Introduced Romney Marsh, 1935; minor colonies elsewhere in S. England	p. 85

LIZARDS

Lacerta vivipara, Viviparous Lizard	Native in Britain; also Ireland	p. 137
Lacerta agilis, Sand Lizard	Native in England	p. 134
Podarcis muralis, Common Wall Lizard	Introduced: isolated colonies in S. England	p. 138
Anguis fragilis, Slow Worm	Native in Britain, one small introduction in Ireland	p. 175

SNAKES

Natrix natrix, Grass Snake	Native in England and Wales	p. 201
Coronella austriaca, Smooth Snake	Native in S. England	p. 204
Vipera berus, Adder	Native in Britain	p. 217

Marine Turtles may also be found on the British coast, the three species usually encountered are the Leathery Turtle (*Dermochelys coriacea,* p. 95), Loggerhead Turtle (*Caretta caretta,* p. 95) and Kemp's Ridley (*Lepidochelys kempii,* p. 98).

Channel Islands

On these islands occur some of the species found on the neighbouring French mainland but not naturally in the British Isles. These comprise the Agile Frog (*Rana dalmatina,* p. 80), and the Common Wall Lizard (*Podarcis muralis*) on Jersey, and the Green Lizard (*Lacerta viridis,* p. 131), on both Jersey and Guernsey. Other species known in the Channel Islands are Smooth Newt (*Triturus vulgaris*) on Guernsey, Palmate Newt (*T. helveticus*) on Jersey, Common Frog (*Rana temporaria*) on Guernsey, Alderney and Sark, Common Toad (*Bufo bufo*) on Jersey and Guernsey, Slow Worm (*Anguis fragilis*) on Jersey, Guernsey, Herm and Alderney, and Grass Snake (*Natrix natrix*) on Jersey and Guernsey.

Salamanders and Newts (Tailed Amphibians) – Caudata

This group includes some 300 species, 20 of which occur in our area. These all have rather long bodies, soft often moist skin without scales, and well developed tails.

The term *salamander* is used for almost all Caudata, while *newt* is often applied to various semi-aquatic species. In Europe it is best to restrict *newt* to those partly land-dwelling forms that enter water to breed and whose males have an elaborate breeding dress and courtship (i.e. members of the genus *Triturus*).

Some of the most important features for identifying newts and salamanders are shown below. Others include general proportions, skin texture and colouring. For identification of eggs and larvae, see p. 225 and p. 229.

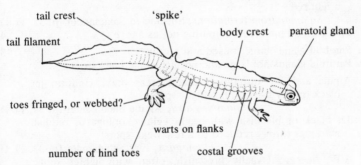

Some features to check when identifying salamanders and newts

Key to Salamanders and Newts

Newts (*Triturus*), keyed out here in section 8, have their own key on p. 41

1. E. Adriatic area only. Usually in subterranean waters. Forefeet with only three toes, hind feet with only two; very pale with pink feathery gills; eyes very small (vestigial in adults), body very elongate
Proteus anguinus, Olm (p. 54, Pl. 2)
Fore-feet with four toes, hind-feet with four or five. Eyes not very small   **2**

2. Sardinia, S.E. France, N. and Central Italy only. Feet partly
   webbed, toes appear stubby; nasolabial groove visible
   with lens (Fig., below)
                    Hydromantes spp., Cave Salamanders (p. 53, Pl. 1)
   Toes not stubby; no nasolabial groove   **3**

hind foot   nasolabial groove

Cave Salamanders (*Hydromantes*)

3. W. Italy only. Only four toes on hind feet. Small and dark
   with yellow or red mark on top of head; underside of tail
   bright red
       Salamandrina terdigitata, Spectacled Salamander (p. 35, Pl. 1)
   Five toes on hind feet; colouring not as above   **4**

4. Paratoid glands large, raised and porous   **5**
   Paratoid glands not large and porous, sometimes absent   **6**

5. Alpine and E. Adriatic mountain areas only. Uniform jet
   black (rarely brown), no bright spots
            Salamandra atra, Alpine Salamander (p. 34, Pl. 1)
   Jet black or blackish with bright yellow, orange or reddish
   markings (rarely reduced to a few weak spots)
                S. salamandra, Fire Salamander (p. 33, Pl. 1)
   S.E. Aegean. Usually brownish, often with lighter spots;
   belly pale, underside of tail orange-yellow. Males with a soft
   'spike' on upper surface of tail base
            S. luschani, Luschan's Salamander (p. 34, Pl. 2)

6. N. W. Iberia only. Very slender. Tail of adults very long,
   1½ – 2 times length of body, and not noticeably flattened.
   Eyes very prominent, costal grooves present, typically
   two copper or gold stripes on back
        Chioglossa lusitanica, Golden-striped Salamander (p. 35, Pl. 1)
   Not very slender, tail rarely much longer than body and often
   distinctly flattened from side to side   **7**

7. Iberia only. Adults large (up to 30cm); head very flat with
   small 'piggy' eyes; usually a row of prominent warts on

each flank; the ribs may protrude through these and can often be felt

Pleurodeles waltl, Sharp-ribbed Salamander (p. 38, Pl. 2)

Not like above; adults not larger than 18cm, and usually much smaller   **8**

8. Pyrenees, Corsica and Sardinia only. Usually in or near cold and often running water. Often flattened salamanders; Pyrenean species has very rough skin   **9**

Not Corsica or Sardinia. Rarely in very cold running water. Not very strongly flattened; skin never very rough in Pyrenees region *Triturus* spp., Newts (see separate key on p. 41)

9. Pyrenees only. No paratoid glands; skin very rough; males lack spurs

Euproctus asper, Pyrenean Brook Salamander (p. 38, Pl. 2)

Corsica only. Paratoid glands fairly distinct; skin not very rough; no spots on throat; males have spurs

E. montanus, Corsican Brook Salamander (p. 39, Pl. 2)

Sardinia only. Paratoid glands often not very obvious; skin not very rough; throat usually spotted, males have spurs

E. platycephalus, Sardinian Brook Salamander (p. 39, Pl. 2)

Family **SALAMANDRIDAE** *Typical Salamanders and Newts*

All but three of the European species of tailed amphibian belong to this family, which contains about 42 species and is widely distributed in the temperate regions of N.W. Africa, Europe, Asia and N. America, although only six forms are found in the latter area. In Europe a number of quite distinct kinds are present; these are: the largely terrestrial *Salamandra*, *Salamandrina* and *Chioglossa*; the more aquatic *Euproctus* and *Pleurodeles*; and the newts, *Triturus*, which are often terrestrial but spend at least the breeding season in water (see p. 40 for a detailed account of *Triturus*). Only *Salamandra* and *Triturus* are widespread, the other genera being confined to fairly small areas in S. Europe.

All salamandrids are secretive, at least outside the breeding season, and are usually only encountered during the day when turning over stones and logs and searching in crevices in moist places. Typically, they forage in the evening or at night, especially when the weather is damp.

European salamandrids vary considerably in their breeding behaviour, but in all cases the male produces a compact package of spermatozoa – the spermatophore. In *Chioglossa*, *S. salamandra* and probably *S. luschani* the male carries the female on his back for some time before depositing the spermatophore on the ground, after which he lowers the cloacal region of the female onto it. In *Salamandra atra*, the process seems to be similar but the female may be turned upside down during the preliminary stages. In *Salamandrina* contact is brief and is preceded by the partners gyrating around each other for some time. The courtship of *Pleurodeles* is essentially like that of *Salamandra salamandra*, but takes place in water. In *Euproctus* species the male clasps the female with his tail and often with his jaws as well, and the spermatophore is deposited in or close to her cloaca.

The newts, *Triturus*, differ from all other European salamandrids in their complex aquatic courtship.

With the exception of *Salamandra* species, nearly all the salamandrids lay eggs singly in water, attached to plants or stones, according to their habitat. However, *Salamandrina* and *Pleurodeles* lay their eggs in clumps. *Salamandra atra*, and apparently *S. luschani*, give birth to fully metamorphosed young. This can also occur in *S. salamandra* but in most cases well-developed larvae are produced instead.

The tadpoles of salamandrids are unlike those of European frogs and toads. They are entirely carnivorous and more like the adults in appearance, so they do not undergo such marked changes at metamorphosis; front legs are developed before the hind legs and the gills are always external. The general shape of salamandrid larvae varies with habitat – species usually living in cold running water have lower crests on the tail and body and shorter gills than those living in ponds.

Salamandrids do not normally vocalise, though they may emit squeaks and wheezes when handled.

All species are mainly invertebrate feeders, virtually any prey that can be captured by these usually rather slow moving animals being eaten.

SALAMANDRA SALAMANDRA *Fire Salamander*   Pl. 1

Range. W., central and S. Europe; also N.W. Africa and parts of S.W. Asia Map 1.

Identification. Adults up to 28 cm including tail, but usually less than 20 cm. Unmistakable; a large, often robust, rather short-tailed salamander with large paratoid glands. The only European species that usually has intense yellow, orange or reddish spots or stripes on a black ground colour (exceptionally the bright markings are reduced to a few small blotches). Underside may be entirely dark or spotted. Characteristic pattern is present even in newly metamorphosed young.

Habits. Occurs principally in forested areas, usually in mountainous or hilly country (up to 2000 m in south of range, but appears commonest under 800 m in Alps). Nearly always terrestrial in damp situations and rarely found very far from water. Strictly nocturnal and frequently encountered after rain. Very slow moving, rarely foraging more than a few metres from its daytime refuge. Exceptionally, may be aquatic at high altitudes. Protected by abundant noxious skin secretion, which irritates mouth and eyes of predators: bright body colours have warning function. Babies may be deposited fully developed at high altitudes and in much of Iberia.

Variation. Much variation in body proportions and colouring (Fig., below,

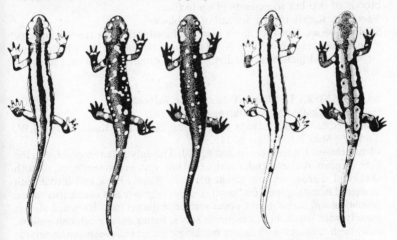

Fire Salamander (*S. salamandra*), variation in pattern

and Pl. 1); many subspecies have been described. Size, shape and number of bright markings vary considerably even within populations and entirely yellow animals sometimes occur. Individuals from most of the range tend to be spotted but striping is especially common in N. Spain, France, W. Germany and W. Switzerland; animals from W. Iberia often have reddish markings, and Italian animals may have red spots on belly.

Similar Species. Unlikely to be confused with any other species, although very dark individuals can look rather like *S. atra*; however, they usually have at least some small yellow spots. Range is also often useful in identifying these aberrant specimens.

SALAMANDRA ATRA *Alpine Salamander* Pl. 1

Range. Alps and mountainous regions of W. Yugoslavia and N. Albania. Map. 2.

Identification. Adults up to 16cm including tail. A moderately robust salamander with large paratoid glands. Generally similar to *S. salamandra* but easily distinguished by uniform, usually all-black colouring and sometimes more 'ribbed' appearance.

Habits. A montane species occurring between 400m and 3000m, but usually encountered from 800m to 2000m where it can be very abundant. Found in wooded habitats, but also above the tree-line in alpine meadows etc. Mainly nocturnal but may be seen in shady places during the day and sometimes in more open situations, especially after rain or in overcast weather. Hides beneath stones and logs, and in holes. Range does not usually overlap much with *S. salamandra* which is typically found at lower altitudes. The young are produced metamorphosed, usually in broods of two but sometimes of up to four.

Variation. Rarely brown instead of jet black.

Similar Species. Not very likely to be confused with other species but may superficially resemble Warty Newt (*Triturus cristatus* p. 43) which has no large paratoid glands, a rougher skin and usually orange or yellow on belly.

SALAMANDRA LUSCHANI *Luschan's Salamander* Pl. 2
(Sometimes called MERTENSIELLA LUSCHANI)

Range. S.E. Aegean islands (Karpathos, Saria and Kasos); also S.W. Turkey   Map 3 and Fig., p. 113.

Identification. Up to 13cm including tail. The only tailed amphibian in the S.E. Aegean. Rather slender with a thin tail, very prominent eyes, smooth skin, and narrow but prominent paratoid glands. Back and throat with scattered minute spines (feel gently), especially in males which also have a prominent soft 'spike' on the upper surface of the tail base. Brownish above, usually with small, light yellowish spots, flanks pale or whitish-yellow, belly flesh-coloured with lighter markings; throat yellowish and underside of tail orange-yellow.

Habits. Fairly quick-moving for a salamander. Often found in quite dry habitats such as pine woods and open scrub, sometimes in the vicinity of seasonal springs and streams. Apparently gives birth to fully-developed young.

Variation. Some variation in colouring.

Similar Species. None within range.

SALAMANDRINA TERDIGITATA *Spectacled Salamander* **Pl. 1**

Range. Restricted to W. Italy Map 4.

Identification. Adults between 7 and 11 cm, including tail. A small, rather slender salamander; the only European species with four toes on the hind feet. Head rather long with prominent eyes. Tail longer than head and body, cylindrical at base with a distinct dorsal ridge. Skin rather rough and prominent ribs give body 'segmented' appearance. Upperside dull blackish or brownish with prominent, roughly triangular yellow (or even vermilion) marking on head. Underside pale, with black throat and dark blotches on belly, particularly along sides. Lower surfaces of legs and tail bright red in adults.

Habits. Has very local distribution within its range, and is usually confined to well-wooded mountainsides with luxuriant undergrowth. Often lives close to clear streams, hiding among rocks and in leaf litter. Mainly nocturnal, but may occasionally emerge in early evening or even during day after rain. When captured may feign death; sometimes also curls up tail to expose brightly coloured underside. Occurs up to 1300 m.

Variation. No definite geographical trends observed.

Similar Species. Not likely to be confused with any other species.

CHIOGLOSSA LUSITANICA *Golden-striped Salamander* **Pl. 1**

Range. Confined to N.W. Iberia Map 5.

Identification. Adults up to 15 cm, usually 12–13 cm, including tail. Long, very slender body with costal grooves and long tail (if undamaged) distinguish this species from all other Iberian salamandrids. Tail unflattened and 1½ times to nearly twice as long as body in adults (shorter in young). Eyes large and prominent. Usually dark brownish above, typically with two golden or copper-coloured stripes on back, which join together at pelvic region and continue as single stripe on tail. Underside brownish or greyish. Male has a noticeably swollen base to tail and during breeding season develops rough swellings on inside of fore limbs.

Habits. A local species found in wet mountain regions up to 1300 m. Usually occurs near rocky streams and springs with dense surrounding growth of moss, shrubs and bushes. Largely nocturnal, hiding under stones and vegetation during most of the day. Rather lizard-like and can move rapidly. When disturbed scuttles away into crevices or into water, where it is a strong swimmer. During summer months often aestivates under

Plate 1　　　　　**SALAMANDERS 1**
(× ⅔)

1. **Salamandra salamandra**　*Fire Salamander*　　　　　33
· Large paratoid glands. Brilliant black and yellow to black and
reddish upper parts; pattern very variable.

　　1a. Spotted individual.
　　1b. Striped individual.

2. **Salamandra atra**　*Alpine Salamander*　　　　　34
Alps, mountains of W. Yugoslavia and Albania. Large
paratoid glands. Totally black; rarely brown.

3. **Chioglossa lusitanica**　*Golden-striped Salamander*　　　　　35
Iberia only. Very slender.

4. **Salamandrina terdigitata**　*Spectacled Salamander*　　　　　35
W. Italy only. Dark; underside of tail and legs bright red. Only
four toes on hind feet.

　　4a. Animal exposing bright 'warning' tail colour.
　　4b. Underside.

5. **Hydromantes italicus**　*Italian Cave Salamander*　　　　　53
N. and central Italy, S.E. France. Toes stubby and partly
webbed.

6. **Hydromantes genei**　*Sardinian Cave Salamander*　　　　　53
Sardinia only. Toes stubby and partly webbed: compare with
Euproctus platycephalus (**Pl. 2**), the only other salamander in
the area.

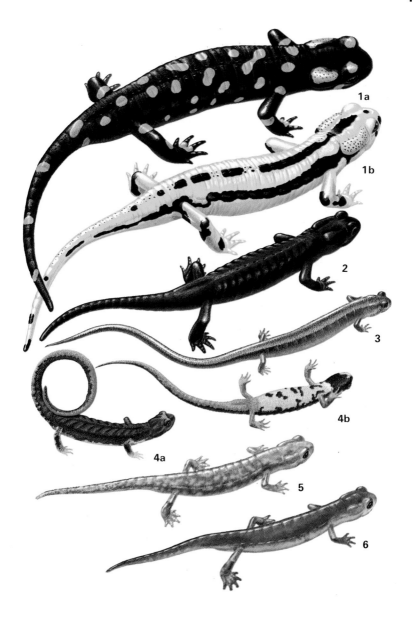

2

SALAMANDERS 2   Plate 2
(1–5 × ⅔; 6 × ½)

1. **Pleurodeles waltl**   *Sharp-ribbed Salamander*   38
   Iberia only. Large (up to 30cm). Very flat head. A row of
   warts on each flank; ribs may project through these.

2. **Euproctus asper**   *Pyrenean Brook Salamander*   38
   Pyrenees only. Very rough skin. Dull ground colour, sometimes with lighter markings.

   2a. Female: pointed vent.
   2b. Male: rounded vent.

3. **Euproctus platycephalus**   *Sardinian Brook Salamander*   39
   Sardinia only. Toes not very stubby: compare with
   Hydromantes genei (**Pl. 1**), the only other salamander in the
   area.

   3a, 3b. Two animals showing pattern variation. Males have
   blunt spurs on hind legs, females do not.

4. **Euproctus montanus**   *Corsican Brook Salamander*   39
   Corsica only. Never strongly contrasting black and yellow:
   compare with *Salamandra salamandra* (**Pl. 1**), the only other
   salamander in the area. Males have blunt spurs on hind legs,
   females do not.

5. **Salamandra luschani**   *Luschan's Salamander*   34
   S.E. Aegean islands. The only salamander in the area. Large
   paratoid glands. Brownish, often with yellow spots. Males
   have a soft 'spike' on upper tail base.

6. **Proteus anguinus**   *Olm*   54
   Subterranean waters of E. Adriatic coastal area. Elongate
   with pink feathery gills. Only two toes on hind limbs.

stones etc. Tail can be shed (autotomised); regrown tail tends to be greyer and more uniform than original. Food is caught with the tongue, which is long and sticky.

Variation. No definite geographical trends recorded.

Similar Species. Not likely to be confused with other salamanders

PLEURODELES WALTL *Sharp-ribbed Salamander* Pl. 2

Range. Iberia, but not north and north-east; also Morocco Map 6.

Identification. Adults normally between 15cm and 30cm, including tail; one of the largest tailed amphibians in Europe. A row of warty protuberances along each flank; these coincide with rib tips, which can often be felt and sometimes actually project through the skin. Head broad and very flat, with small eyes. Body heavily built and rough-skinned. Tail at least as long as the body and flattened from side to side; the amount of cresting varies, being greatest in breeding males. Upperside yellowish-grey to olive, the colour darkening with age, with dark brown often fairly regular spotting; warts on sides are orange, yellow or whitish. Belly yellow, orange, whitish or grey, usually with dark markings. Males tend to be more rufous with longer tail and when breeding have dark, rough pads on the insides of their fore-legs.

Habits. Mainly nocturnal and aquatic, being found in ditches, ponds, reservoirs, cisterns, slow moving rivers etc.; a strong swimmer. Also frequents temporary pools and streams, aestivating beneath stones and in crevices when the water dries up. Occasionally found in drier habitats, especially small individuals; here it is usually discovered under rocks, logs, etc.

Variation. Head and tail shape rather variable but no definite trends.

Similar Species. Young *Pleurodeles* can look like Pyrenean Brook Salamander (*Euproctus asper*, below), but this species is confined to the Pyrenees. It has a longer head then *Pleurodeles*, lacks rows of warts on flanks and has a protuberant vent.

EUPROCTUS ASPER *Pyrenean Brook Salamander* Pl. 2

Range. Confined to Pyrenees Map 7.

Identification. Adults normally up to about 16cm including tail, occasionally longer. Fairly robust and somewhat flattened with small eyes and only slight neck. Paratoid glands absent. Tail compressed and about as long as body. Skin very rough, much more so than other salamandrids within its range. Upperside usually muddy brownish, greyish, olive or blackish, often with some lighter, usually yellow markings. These may be completely absent or sometimes join together to form a vertebral stripe. Sides of belly with dark markings; central band is yellow or orange, sometimes unspotted. Cloacal swelling of males rounded, of females conical.

Habits. Normally found between 700 m and 2500 m, but sometimes up to 3000 m and down to 250 m. Particularly abundant around 2000 m in or near cold mountain lakes and streams with a temperature of less than 15°C. Also often encountered in damp gutters, runnels etc., or when turning stones at edge of water. Sometimes found in caves. Mainly active at night. Tends to be rare where trout – one of its main predators – are abundant. May aestivate in summer.

Variation. Considerable variation in colour and pattern.

Similar Species. Closely related to *Euproctus montanus* and *E. platycephalus*, but not likely to be confused with salamandrids within its range. Young of Sharp-ribbed Salamander (*Pleurodeles waltl,* opposite), look rather similar but are absent from Pyrenees.

EUPROCTUS MONTANUS *Corsican Brook Salamander* **Pl. 2**
Range. Restricted to Corsica Map 8

Identification. Adults up to 11·5 cm including tail, but usually not so large. Very like *E. asper* but smaller, smoother skinned, with more or less distinct paratoid glands, no dark spotting on throat and often a relatively uniform underside. Above brown or olive, sometimes with lighter greenish or yellowish markings that often form a vertebral line. Throat and belly whitish grey or brown, sometimes with white flecks. Male has spurs on hind legs and a conical cloacal swelling.

Habits. Found in or near running water often in rocky terrain from sealevel to 2100 m but most abundant between 600 m and 1500 m. Often aestivates.

Variation. Some variation in colouring.

Similar Species. Closely related to *E. asper* and *E. platycephalus*, but no really similar species within range. Fire Salamander (*S. salamandra* p. 33), the only other tailed amphibian on Corsica, is black and yellow.

EUPROCTUS PLATYCEPHALUS *Sardinian Brook Salamander* **Pl. 2**
Range. Restricted to Sardinia Map 9.

Identification. Adults up to about 14 cm including tail, but usually smaller. Very similar to *E. montanus* but head often longer and flatter, paratoid glands generally not so distinct and throat usually spotted. Above usually brown or olive often with lighter green or yellow blotches and spots and a reddish vertebral stripe. Underside often yellowish, especially in centre of belly; usually dark spotted, especially in males. Both sexes have a more or less conical cloacal swelling; males have spurs.

Habits. Very similar to other *Euproctus* species. Typically found in and near running water in mountainous areas; most abundant from 1500 m to 1800 m but may occur down to 150 m in a few places.

Variation. Considerable variation in head shape and colouring.

Similar Species. On Sardinia none. Only other Salamander on island is Sardinian Cave Salamander (*Hydromantes genei* p. 53).

NEWTS – *Triturus*

A clearly defined group of species, eight of which occur in the area covered by this book. Newts are usually terrestrial for part of the year, but they enter still or, more rarely, slow-flowing water in spring to breed. At this time the males develop a characteristic breeding dress usually consisting of bright colouring and a flexible cutaneous crest on the tail and often on the back as well. Also the toes on the hind feet may become elongated, fringed or webbed. Both sexes may develop a glandular swelling on each side of the back; these often give the body a squarish cross-section.

The courtship is elaborate, the male displaying before his largely passive mate. Display usually consists of the male vibrating his reflexed tail-tip and intermittently lashing it towards the female. Finally he emits at least one spermatophore, over which the female walks, or is led, in order to pick it up. The female usually lays her eggs singly, attaching them to aquatic vegetation or, more rarely, to stones etc. The laying period is often fairly extended.

In areas where more than one species of newt occur together, females seem to recognise their own males partly by their characteristic breeding dress. The crests, where present, are also important because they increase the surface area of the male, enabling him to take up extra oxygen from the water during his vigorous courtship.

On land newts are secretive and usually only found when turning over stones, logs and vegetation in damp places. They are more conspicuous when in the water and can often be seen as they surface to take in air. Some populations seem to be aquatic for most of the year, and in a few cases neoteny occurs – i.e. tadpoles do not metamorphose into adults, but grow to a large size and are often capable of breeding in this condition. This occurs most commonly in deep water or at high altitudes.

Newts feed on a wide variety of small invertebrates, both in and out of the water, and some, particularly the larger species, are known to prey on small fish and other amphibians and their eggs.

Identification. Because their breeding dress is partly developed as a means of clear and unequivocal recognition, breeding male newts are generally easy to identify. Non-breeding males and females – especially of the smaller species – are more difficult to run down, although with practice it is often possible to distinguish even nondescript individuals by 'jizz', as with so many problem groups. Because of the wide range of variation found in some species (seasonal and sexual differences, as well as regional variation), it is not always feasible to identify newts with certainty using only a key. Identification should therefore always be carefully checked against the relevant description of the species.

Top of newt's head

Some newts have shallow grooves on top of the head which are often helpful in identification; their usual positions are shown in Fig., above. N.B. The descriptions of breeding male newts refer to animals in full nuptial dress. When developing or losing this, they tend to have lower, less elaborate crests and less obvious tail filaments, toe fringes etc., and in some cases might be mistaken for other species, unless examined carefully. Males have a bigger cloacal swelling than females.

Key to Newts (*Triturus*)

1. S. and W. France and Iberia. Upper parts with extensive, bright green markings. Underside dull, never yellow to red, or black   *T. marmoratus*, Marbled Newt (p. 42, Pl. 3)

   Upper parts without extensive, bright green markings. Ground colour of underside pale silvery yellow to red (exceptionally black) – at least in centre of belly   **2**

2. Up to 12 cm. Belly uniform deep yellow to red; unspotted (with rare exceptions). Frequently numerous spots on flanks, often forming a complex lattice-like pattern in males No grooves or stripes on head. Upper parts usually grey to blackish or brownish, often marbled with black in males. Breeding males have smooth, low, pale crest on body, spotted or barred with black   *T. alpestris*, Alpine Newt (p. 46, Pl. 5)

   Not like *T. alpestris*. Belly often with at least some dark spots. If not, then head may have grooves, and bright colour on belly may be confined to centre   **3**

3. Absent from Iberia and S.W. France. Usually large: adults over 11 cm. Skin, often rough; moist in terrestrial animals. Underside uniform bright yellow to reddish-orange with strongly contrasting pattern of bold dark spots or blotches (exceptionally, underside entirely black). Dark above with darker blotches; terrestrial animals may seem almost entirely black. Breeding males have dark, usually spiky crests, indented at base of tail   *T. cristatus*, Warty Newt (p. 43, Pl. 3)

Not particularly large: usually under 11 cm. Skin often smooth; tends to be dry in terrestrial animals. Belly pattern less bold than *T. cristatus*, bright colour often limited to centre of belly. Head may be grooved.   **4**

4. Carpathians and Tatras only. Underside uniform yellow to reddish-orange, often unspotted in centre and on throat, spots at sides often sparse or even absent. Grooves on head, but no obvious stripes. Breeding males have almost square cross section and only poorly developed crests
T. montandoni, Montandon's Newt (p. 47, Pl. 5)

S. Italy only. Very small: most under 7·5 cm. Dark colour on side of head and neck usually has characteristic lower border (see Fig., p. 48). Underside with dark spots; throat yellow to orange, belly paler. Breeding males have no cresting on body and lack fringes on toes   *T. italicus*, Italian Newt (p. 52, Pl. 5)

W. and central Iberia only. Belly bright orange, flanked by pale streaks, with dark spots present at least at sides. Sometimes a single groove on mid-line of snout; no stripes on head. Breeding males have no crest on body and tail crest poorly developed; toes not webbed or fringed. Female has a conical cloacal swelling   *T. boscai,* Bosca's Newt (p. 51, Pl. 4)

Absent from Iberia and S. France. Underside usually spotted, including throat. Yellow to red colour on belly confined to central area; throat pale. Head usually has grooves. Breeding males usually with fairly large crests and fringed hind feet; tail ends in filament only in eastern parts of range
T. vulgaris, Smooth Newt (p. 47, Pl. 4)

W. Europe only. Spots generally small and weak on belly; absent from throat. Colour on belly confined to centre – usually rather pale – yellow or silvery-orange. Grooves present on head. Breeding males have tail ending in filament; hind feet usually dark and webbed
T. helveticus, Palmate Newt (p. 51, Pl. 4)

TRITURUS MARMORATUS *Marbled Newt*   **Pl. 3**
Range. Confined to Iberia and S. and W. France   Map 10.
Identification. Adults up to 14 cm including tail – occasionally larger. Easily distinguished from all other European newts by combination of extensive, bright green, dorsal colouring and sombre belly. A large, vivid green newt, marbled and spotted with black above. Underparts grey, brownish, or even pinkish, often mottled with black and white. Adult

females and young have an orange vertebral stripe. Terrestrial animals are brighter green than aquatic ones and have dry, velvety skin.

Breeding males develop a smooth-edged dorsal crest, indented at tail-base and regularly barred with black; a light streak present on side of tail.

Habits. Very similar to *T. cristatus*, but rather less aquatic and may be sometimes found in fairly dry woods and heathland. More restricted to low altitudes than *T. cristatus*.

Variation. Fairly uniform throughout its range, although in the south it tends to be smaller. In France may occasionally hybridise with *T. cristatus* where the two species co-exist. Hybrids (originally described as a separate species, *T. blasii*) are intermediate between the parent forms.

Similar Species. Unlikely to be confused with any other European newt or salamander.

TRITURUS CRISTATUS *Warty Newt* Pl. 3

Range. Most of Europe but not S. and S.W. France, Iberia, S. Greece, Ireland and Mediterranean islands. Also eastwards to Caucasus and central Asia Map 11.

Identification. Adults usually up to 14 cm including tail; females may occasionally reach 18 cm. A large, dark, usually coarse skinned newt, always lacking green of *T. marmoratus*. Typically brownish or greyish above with darker spots. Belly usually yellow, orange, or reddish-orange, almost invariably boldly patterned with blackish or dark grey spots or blotches. Terrestrial animals have a moist skin and may appear almost jet-black above, contrasting strongly with the usually bright underside.

Breeding males develop a high, usually spiky crest, indented at base of tail, which has whitish or bluish streak along its side.

Habits. An often fairly aquatic newt that may be encountered in water throughout the year, although in many parts of its range it is terrestrial outside the breeding season. Prefers still, or (notably in Danube Delta) slow-flowing water, with good weed growth. On land, may be found close to breeding ponds and in woods, etc. hiding beneath stones and logs. Occurs from sea level to about 2000 m, becoming more montane in south of its range.

Variation. A very variable species, several fairly well defined subspecies having been described, based mainly on variations in size, proportions, skin texture and colour pattern:

T.c. cristatus. The most widely distributed form, occurring over most of the northern parts of the species range. Large, rough-skinned, with white stippling along flanks. Belly yellow or orange with very variable pattern of dark spots or dark blotches, sometimes completely black in Scandinavia.

T.c. carnifex. Italy, north to Alps, parts of Austria and N. Yugoslavia. Rather smoother-skinned than previous subspecies, with little or no white stippling. Belly often more orange and has large, well-defined, dark

Plate 3   **LARGE NEWTS**
                               (× ⅔)

1. Triturus cristatus *Warty Newt*   **43**
   Not S.W. Europe. Dark above, belly usually bright yellow or
   orange, with dark spots. Skin often rough.

   1a. Breeding male: high spiky crest and pale tail flash.
   1b. Female.
   1c. Underside.
   1d. *T.c. carnifex,* male. Italy and neighbouring areas.

2. Triturus marmoratus *Marbled Newt*   **42**
   S.W. Europe only. Green and black above; belly sombre.

   2a. Breeding male: smooth, barred crest and pale tail flash.
   2b. Female: orange vertebral stripe.
   2c. Underside.

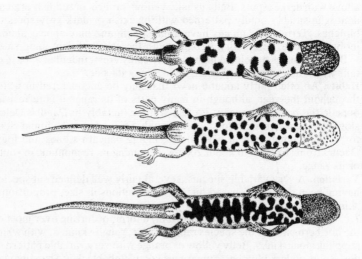

Warty Newt, some variations in belly pattern

1a

1b

1c

1d

2a

2b

2c

4

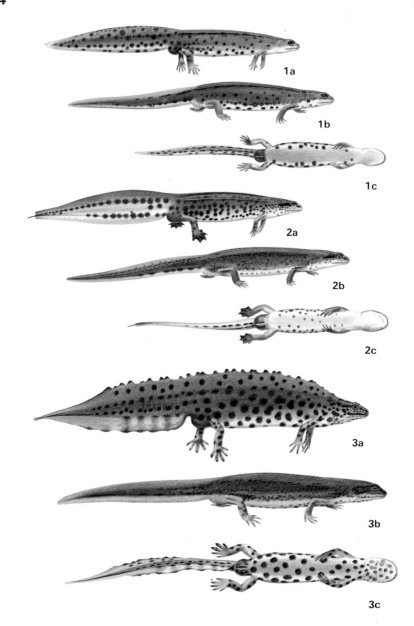

1a

1b

1c

2a

2b

2c

3a

3b

3c

SMALLER NEWTS 1   Plate 4
(× ⅘)

1. Triturus boscai *Bosca's Newt*   **51**
W. and central Iberia. *T. helveticus* and *T. alpestris* are also present but only in north of range. Bright orange dark-spotted belly with pale streaks at sides.

  1a. Breeding male: crest only on tail; no toe fringes.
  1b. Breeding female: pointed cloacal swelling.
  1c. Underside.

2. Triturus helveticus *Palmate Newt*   **51**
W. and S.W. Europe but not S. Iberia. Non-breeders can easily be confused with *T. vulgaris*. Delicately coloured: belly with silvery-orange or yellow streak and weak spots; throat pale, unspotted often pinkish.

  2a. Male: low crest; tail filament; dark, webbed feet.
  2b. Female.
  2c. Underside.

3. Triturus vulgaris *Smooth Newt*   **47**
Not S.W. Europe. In west, can be confused with *T. helveticus* but usually has more spots on belly and some on throat.

  3a. Breeding male *T.v. vulgaris* (N. and W. Europe): undulating crest; fringes on hind toes.
  3b. Female.
  3c. Underside of breeding male; spots are often smaller in females.

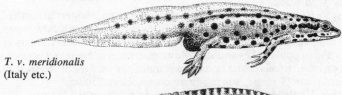

T. v. meridionalis
(Italy etc.)

T. v. graecus
(S. Balkans)

Smooth Newt, variation in male breeding dress

greyish spots; sometimes completely black. Female often has yellow vertebral stripe.

T.c. karelinii. The more south-easterly parts of range, in Balkans and S.W. Asia. Quite smooth-skinned, with little stippling along flanks and normally rather small spots on belly. May have bluish sheen. Throat pale with dark spots.

T.c. dobrogicus. Danube plain and Danube Delta. Often intergrades with *T.c. cristatus* and *T.c. karelinii*. Rather small with very coarse skin, small head and little or no stippling on flanks. Brown or even reddish above. Belly often reddish-orange with blackish-brown spots which may join together to form one or two bands. Female often has yellow vertebral stripe. For hybrids with *T. marmoratus* see p. 43.

Similar Species. Not likely to be confused with any other species, except possibly *T. alpestris* (below) if ventral spotting is very reduced, or with Alpine Salamander *Salamandra atra* p. 34, if belly completely black.

TRITURUS ALPESTRIS *Alpine Newt* **Pl. 5**

Range. More widely distributed than its name suggests. From extreme W. Russia westwards to N. and E. France and from S. Denmark south to N. Italy and central Greece. An isolated population exists in N.W. Spain (Cantabrian Mountains). Doubtfully recorded from central Spain Map 12.

Identification. Females up to about 12 cm including tail, males smaller. A medium-sized newt, usually identifiable by distinctive colouring: dark above, with uniform deep yellow to red belly. Head rather flat, without grooves. Males grey to blackish above, usually with darker markings, females often browner and more uniform. Frequently numerous, small spots along the flanks, often set on a light ground in males, giving a lattice-like effect. Flanks may occasionally have a white stipple. Throat often plain, but can be spotted; belly almost always unmarked (rarely with a few small spots, e.g. some animals from S. Balkans and Italy, and exceptionally elsewhere). Skin of terrestrial animals velvety (smooth or granular in water).

Breeding males have low, smooth-edged, yellowish crest, barred or spotted with black.

Habits. Very aquatic and nearly always found in or near water. In north of range occurs in wide variety of habitats, even including shallow, open water in lowlands, but is commoner in cold, almost plantless ponds in woods and in pools, lakes and slow-flowing streams in mountain regions. When on land, usually found in very cool, moist places. Strictly montane in southern parts of range, where it may occur above 2500 m.

Variation. Neotenous, or partly neotenous, populations (i.e. animals that retain some of the larval characteristics, but are able to breed: see p. 230) occur, particularly in Yugoslavia. Often, these have more or less adult colouring, but may also have gills. There is some variation in size and shape of head. Animals from N. Italy, west and south of the Po Valley, and

extreme S. E. France have heavily spotted throats and bright red bellies.
Similar Species. Quite distinctive, but might be confused with *T. cristatus*
(p. 43), or *T. montandoni* (below).

TRITURUS MONTANDONI   *Montandon's Newt*   **Pl. 5**
Range. Carpathian and Tatras Mountains. Small introduction in
Bavaria   Map 13.
Identification. Females up to 10 cm including tail, males less. A relatively
small newt, with three grooves on the head. Upper parts yellowish-brown,
greenish-brown or olive, usually with darker spots or mottling. Underside
almost entirely yellow to reddish-orange, often with some small, black
spots at sides; occasionally, these spots are more widespread, but they are
often absent from the throat. Terrestrial animals usually have a noticeably
granular skin (rather smoother in water).

Breeding males have crest on tail, which ends in a filament, but only a
ridge along the centre of the back. Body is very square in cross section and
hind toes are not obviously fringed. Tail has pale streak each side and
lower edge is orange with black spots.
Habits. A montane species that breeds in a wide variety of waters, including lakes, slow-moving streams, ditches and even puddles and wheel-ruts.
It prefers clear, cold, acid ponds, but is also found in many other situations, even polluted water. On land, often lives near breeding ponds and
in wooded country under rocks, fallen trees, etc. Usually between 500 m
and 1500 m, but may occur from 200 m to almost 2000 m. Frequently found
alongside *T. alpestris*.
Variation. No marked geographical variation recorded. Hybrids with
T. vulgaris have been reported and are presumably intermediate in appearance between the two parent species.
Similar Species. *T. alpestris* (opposite), is larger, usually darker and
lacks grooves on head; *T. vulgaris* (below), has distinctive ventral
pattern and often a striped head or at least a vague dark streak on each
side.

TRITURUS VULGARIS   *Smooth Newt*   **Pl. 4**
Range. Widely distributed; occurring over most of Europe, but not
S. France, Iberia, S. Italy and most Mediterranean islands. Also occurs in
W. Asia   Map 14.
Identification. Adults up to 11 cm including tail, but in some areas (especially S. Balkans) considerably smaller; males tend to be slightly larger
than females. Very widespread and the commonest newt over much of its
range. Small and smooth-skinned, often with a characteristic ventral
pattern; three grooves usually visible on head. Terrestrial animals and
breeding females yellow-brown, olive or brown above, often with small,
dark spots (which may fuse into two lines on back, especially in females)
and a vague stripe on side of head. Belly typically with well developed

48

Plate 5   **SMALLER NEWTS 2**
(× ⅔)

1. Triturus italicus *Italian Newt*   **52**
S. Italy. Only likely to be confused with *T. vulgaris* (**Pl. 4**). Throat yellow or orange; belly paler. Head pattern usually characteristic (see Fig. below).

    1a. Breeding male: crest low; toes unfringed.
    1b. Female.
    1c. Underside.

2. Triturus alpestris *Alpine Newt*   **46**
Absent from most of S.W. Europe. Underside uniform deep yellow to red; belly usually unspotted (rare exceptions). No grooves on head.

    2a. Breeding male: smooth crest with dark spots.
    2b. Female.
    2c. Neotenous individual.
    2d. Underside: throat may be spotted.

3. Triturus montandoni *Montandon's Newt*   **47**
Carpathians and Tatras. Only likely to be confused with *T. alpestris* or *T. vulgaris*. Underside yellow to reddish-orange, often with spots especially at sides. Grooves on head.

    3a. Breeding male: low crest, toes unfringed, body section very square.
    3b. Female.
    3c. Underside.

Italian   Smooth

Small newts in Italy, head patterns

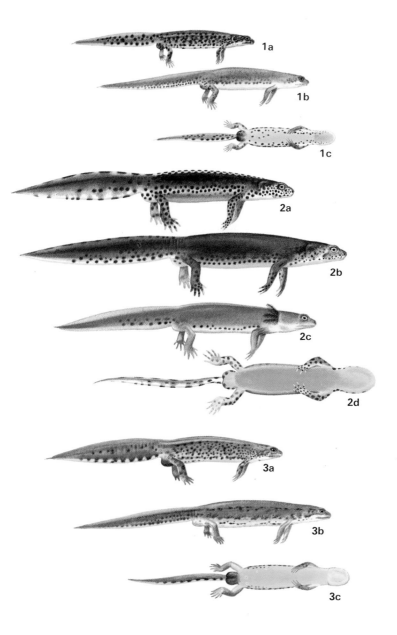

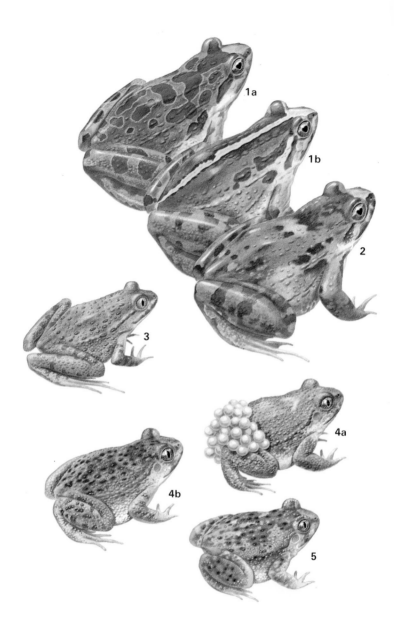

PAINTED FROGS, PARSLEY FROG Plate 6
and MIDWIFE TOADS
(× ¾)

1. **Discoglossus pictus** *Painted Frog*   **62**
   Iberia, Sicily, Malta etc. Rather like Typical Frogs (*Rana*,
   Pls. 10, 11 and **12**) but pupil not horizontal.

   1a, 1b. Colour variants: may be spotted or striped.

2. **Discoglossus sardus** *Tyrrhenian Painted Frog*   **62**
   Corsica, Sardinia, Iles d'Hyères etc. Distinguish from
   D. pictus by range. Head may be broader than *D. pictus*. Often
   a pale blotch on back; never striped but may be uniform.

3. **Pelodytes punctatus** *Parsley Frog*   **71**
   S.W. Europe only. Small (up to 5 cm), slender, long-legged;
   vertical pupil. Green or olive spots on back.

4. **Alytes obstetricans** *Midwife Toad*   **63**
   Western Europe only. Small (up to 5 cm), plump, short-
   legged. Vertical pupil. Males may carry eggs. *Three* tubercles
   on hand (Fig., p. 63).

   4a. Male with eggs: typical northern animal.
   4b. Female: typical southern animal.

5. **Alytes cisternasii** *Iberian Midwife Toad*   **66**
   W. and central Iberia only. Like *A. obstetricans* but only *two*
   tubercles on hand (Fig., p. 63).

dark spots or blotches which usually extend onto throat; bright orange, yellow or even red pigment present; but confined to a central stripe. Terrestrial animals have dry, velvety skin.

Breeding males develop large dark spots above, clear head stripes, a continuous crest on tail and body and fringes on toes of hind feet; lower edge of tail usually orange with light bluish streak above it. For other details of breeding dress see below.

Habits. More terrestrial than many other species of European newts. On land occurs in a wide variety of damp habitats, including cultivated land, gardens, woods, field edges, stone piles etc. Usually found by turning over stones or logs or by searching in crevices, leaf-litter etc. Breeds in still, often shallow water, preferring weedy ponds, ditches etc. and avoiding heavily shadowed and very exposed sites. Tends to be a lowland species, but extends to over 1000 m (even 2000 m) in southern parts of range.

Variation. Considerable variation in size amount of spotting on belly (see Fig., below) and male breeding dress. Several subspecies have been described, the more distinctive of which are mentioned below; intermediates between them are known.

T.v. vulgaris. N. and W. Europe. A large form with a relatively high, notched or undulating crest. However this is almost smooth-edged when developing or when being resorbed after breeding season.

T.v. meridionalis (Fig., p. 45). Italy and N. Yugoslavia. Crest on body fairly low, with an almost smooth upper edge; body rather square in cross section; tail ends in filament. Some N.W. Romanian animals are also rather like this.

T.v. graecus (Fig., p. 45). S. Balkans. Rather small: often under 7.5 cm. Central body crest low, but an additional crest or ridge often present on each side of it. Tail ends in filament. Centre of belly orange or reddish. Females quite heavily spotted.

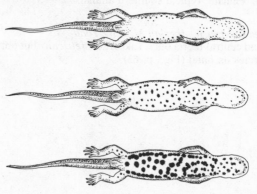

Smooth Newt, some variations in belly pattern

T.v. schreiberi. Only around Zadar, Yugoslavia. Small; crest on body low and straight. Tail ends in filament. Belly unspotted.
Similar Species. *T. vulgaris* occasionally lacks spots on throat and such animals can be confused with *T. helveticus* (below), especially when subadult. *T. montandoni* (Carpathians – p. 47); *T. italicus* (S. Italy – p. 52).

TRITURUS HELVETICUS *Palmate Newt* Pl. 4
Range. W. Europe, south to N. Iberia and north to Scotland; absent from Ireland   Map 15.
Identification. Adults up to 9 cm including tail, usually less; males smaller than females. A small smooth-skinned newt, with three grooves often visible on head, which may be rather short and rounded. Olive or pale brownish above, frequently with small spots which may form two lines on the back, especially in females; often a dark stripe on side of head. The belly may be almost immaculate but some spots usually present though often small. Bright colour on underside always restricted to a central stripe on belly and usually yellow or silvery orange. *Throat unspotted, often translucent pinkish.* Skin dry and velvety in terrestrial animals.

Breeding males have a very low smooth-edged crest on body and well developed smooth-edged crest on tail, which is truncated and ends in a dark filament; hind feet dark and strongly webbed. Head and body have usually heavy dark markings. Central band on side of tail orange, bordered by two rows of large spots.
Habits. Fairly terrestrial, but usually more aquatic than *T. vulgaris*. Breeds in a wide variety of still (occasionally running), often shallow water including puddles, ponds, heath and woodland pools, edges of mountain lakes and even brackish pools near sea. Tends to prefer clearer, less rich, and more acid water than *T. vulgaris*. Adults secretive like other newts and found in a wide variety of habitats near breeding ponds. Often found in hilly country, up to 1000 m in Alps and 2000 m in Pyrenees.
Variation. In some Iberian populations the hind feet of breeding males are not fully webbed.
Similar Species. *T. boscai* (below). *T. vulgaris* (p. 47) – in areas of overlap aquatic males easily separated by characteristic colour and pattern (see Pl.4) and traces of these may remain on land. Terrestrial *T. helveticus* and aquatic females are often recognisable by more delicate colouring of belly and usually pinker unspotted throat.

TRITURUS BOSCAI *Bosca's Newt* Pl. 4
Range. Confined to W. and central Iberia   Map 16.
Identification. Adults up to 10 cm including tail, but often smaller; females larger than males. Sometimes a single longitudinal groove on snout. Colour rather variable: from fairly pale yellow-brown to grey-brown above, usually with more or less distinct dark spots or marbling. No stripe on side of head. Underside with bright orange-yellow to orange-red colouring,

this pigment confined to a broad central stripe down belly, the sides being paler or whitish. Nearly always dark, often large, spots on belly; these may form an irregular row on each side and sometimes extend onto throat. Lower edge of tail orange, often with dark spots. Females have conical cloacal swelling. Skin may be smooth or granular.

Breeding males not very different from females; no crest on body and crest on tail low. Tail may end in short filament; toes not webbed or fringed.

Habits. Breeds in small clear streams, small ponds and even waters in open caves. Usually spends some time on land but may occasionally be completely aquatic.

Variation. No subspecies recognised but shows considerable variation in adult size, colouring and habits.

Similar Species. The only *Triturus* species over most of its range, but may be confused with *T. helveticus* (p. 51) or *T. alpestris* (p. 46) in the north-west. At all seasons *T. helveticus* is more delicately coloured and pigment on belly is yellow to pale silvery orange, not bright orange. Spots on underside of *T. helveticus* tend to be finer and never extend to throat, three grooves are often visible on head, and there may be dark stripe through eye. *T. alpestris* is larger and underside is uniform orange, nearly always lacking spots; spots along flanks are usually much finer and more numerous. In both these species, the shape of the female cloaca differs from *T. boscai*.

TRITURUS ITALICUS *Italian Newt* Pl. 5
Range. Restricted to S. Italy Map 17.
Identification. Adults rarely larger than 7·5 cm including tail, males smaller than females. A diminutive newt easily distinguished from *T. vulgaris*, the only other species of small newt extending into its range, by size and colouring – especially throat pigmentation, pattern on side of head, and breeding dress. Head without obvious grooves or striping. Brownish above, flanks often lighter but usually with dark spots which may join to form a line between the fore and hind legs. Underside with dark spots; ground colour of throat orange or yellow, belly is paler (throat of *T. vulgaris* is paler than belly). Light colour usually extends upwards as a prominent narrow band towards eye, and dark dorsal colouring extends well down on side of head (see Fig. on p. 48 for typical pattern).

Breeding animals have no crest on body, but tail is crested and may end in short filament; toes not fringed. Both sexes develop gold spots on flanks and a gold blotch behind the eye during breeding season.

Habits. In breeding season found in still ponds, cisterns etc. On land leads a secretive life in damp places, like other newts. Occurs from sea level to 1500 m.

Variation. Animals from higher altitudes tend to be larger; partly neotenous individuals may be common in permanent water.

Similar Species. Only likely to be confused with *T. vulgaris* (see above).

Family **PLETHODONTIDAE** *Cave Salamanders*

European Cave Salamanders belong to an essentially North American group, the Plethodontidae or Lungless Salamanders. They are members of the genus *Hydromantes* the other representatives of which live in California. Unlike other European tailed amphibians, Cave Salamanders are quite agile climbers and can be recognised easily by their feet which are partly webbed with short blunt toes. Because of their rather specialised habitat, Cave Salamanders tend to occur in isolated populations that differ slightly in appearance.

During courtship the male grasps his mate from above, putting his legs round her neck and body and precedes this by stroking her with his chin (which bears a specialised gland). Females lay small clutches of eggs in crevices and may stop close to them until they hatch, which can take a year.

HYDROMANTES GENEI *Sardinian Cave Salamander* **Pl. 1**
Range. Sardinia only (mainly south and east). Map 18.
Identification. Up to 13.5 cm including tail, but usually smaller. A moderately built salamander with broad, flat head, smooth skin and prominent eyes. Best identified by feet, which are partly webbed, so that the usually square-tipped toes appear rather short and stubby. A nasolabial groove is visible with lens, Fig., p. 30). Reddish brown to dark brown above with varying amounts of light spotting and dappling (often yellowish or olive), although this is sometimes absent. Underside pale, often yellowish or pinkish, occasionally with fine dark speckling.
Habits. Usually encountered in cool (under 17°C) caves with high humidity; typically but not always in limestone areas up to 1000 m. Climbs well, even on vertical surfaces, and appears to use the tail as well as the feet. Food is caught with the sticky tongue, which is mushroom-shaped and very extensible. Some animals have an aromatic smell.
Variation. Considerable variation in colouring, and some in size and proportions.
Similar Species. None within range. Only other salamander in Sardinia, *Euproctus platycephalus* (p. 39), has unmodified feet and different general appearance.

HYDROMANTES ITALICUS *Italian Cave Salamander* **Pl. 1**
Range. N. and central Italy, south of Po Valley, also extreme S.E. France Map 19.
Identification. Up to 12 cm including tail, but usually smaller. Similar to *Hydromantes genei* (see above), but *H. italicus* tends to be not as large, with relatively smaller feet, more rounded toe-tips, and there may also be some indication of canthi (see p. 243) on the snout. Dorsal pattern is often, although not always, more contrasting, with yellow, light brown or pink-

ish spots or blotches; and the underside is usually fairly dark, often with whitish marbling.

Habits. Very similar to *H. genei*. Also occurs on wet cliffs and rock faces and in moist shady places under stones, logs, vegetable refuse etc. In these open situations it is entirely nocturnal and retreats deep into crevices in dry conditions.

Variation. Considerable variation in colouring, and some in size and proportions.

Similar Species. None within range.

Family **PROTEIDAE** *Olm*

This family consists of only one cave-dwelling species in Europe and four open-water species in the eastern USA. All of them are permanent larvae with characteristic feathery gills. However, unlike normal salamander larvae, they can breed in this state. The European species feeds on small aquatic invertebrates. It produces eggs (12 to 70 per brood) but, rarely, these are retained in the body and in such cases usually two fully developed young are produced.

PROTEUS ANGUINUS *Olm* Pl. 2

Range. Cave systems along E. Adriatic seaboard, as far north as Istrian region and as far south as Montenegro. An isolated colony exists in N.E. Italy   Map 20.

Identification. Adults about 20–25cm including tail, occasionally 30cm. Essentially cave-dwelling and unmistakable; a very large aquatic salamander, always pale with large obvious salmon-pink gills. Body elongate and cylindrical, with compressed tail. Limbs poorly developed with three toes on fore-limbs and two on hind-limbs. Eyes very small. Neotenous (see p. 230), retains gills throughout life. Usually whitish, though occasionally greyish, pinkish or yellowish, with faint blotches, particularly in young animals.

Habits. Lives exclusively in underground streams and lakes in limestone caves; normally found in waters with a temperature ranging between 5° and 10°C. Often occurs far underground. Most readily seen in 'tourist' caves such as those open to the public at Postojna, Yugoslavia. May occasionally be swept into open streams by floods.

Variation. A rather variable animal.

Similar Species. Not likely to be confused with any other species.

Frogs and Toads (Tailless Amphibians) – Anura

There are about 4000 species of frogs and toads of which only 25 are found in the area covered by this book. They are all tailless, with a short body, quite long hind legs and usually moist skin without scales.

The English terms *frog* and *toad* originally referred to the two basic types of anurans found in Britain, Typical Frogs (*Rana*) and Typical Toads (*Bufo*), but they are now used for members of other groups in a rather arbitrary way. *Frog* is usually employed for the more graceful animals with wetter, smoother skins, while *toad* is used for the drier, warty, stouter forms. As animals of these two general types are found together in a number of separate families, neither *frog* nor *toad* indicates a closely related group of animals.

Identification. Some of the most important features for identifying frogs and toads are shown in the figure below and in the key and texts. Other useful points to look for are general proportions, especially leg-length, skin texture and colour. When checking the leg-length of frogs, the leg should be gently turned forwards along the body, and the 'hump' in the back carefully pressed down (see Fig., p. 56). For identification of eggs and larvae, see p. 225 and p. 229.

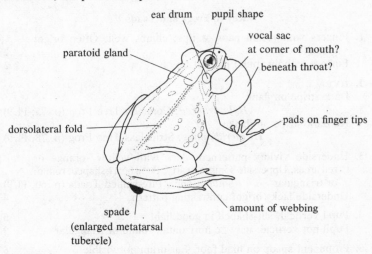

Some features to check when identifying frogs and toads

55

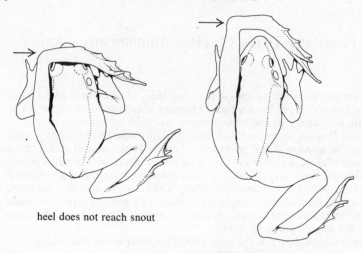

heel does not reach snout

heel extends beyond snout

Checking leg-length of frogs and toads

Key to Frogs and Toads

1. Fingers with round pads at tips; climbs well. Often bright
   green   2
   Fingers without round pads at tips   3

2. HYLA
   Dark stripe on flank
               Hyla arborea, Common Tree Frog (p. 75, Pl. 9)
   No dark stripe on flank
             H. meridionalis, Stripeless Tree Frog (p. 78, Pl. 9)

3. Underside vividly patterned: dark with yellow, orange or
   red areas. Upperside sombre, warty. Pupil heart-shaped, round,
   or triangular   *Bombina* spp., Fire-bellied Toads (p. 60, Pl. 9)
   Underside lacks bright contrasting pattern   4

4. Pupil vertical, slit-shaped in good light   5
   Pupil not vertical: may be horizontal, round or triangular   9

5. Prominent spade on hind foot. Ear-drum not visible   6
   Lacks spade on hind foot. Ear-drum usually visible, though
   sometimes not very obvious   7

6. PELOBATES

Spade on hind foot black. S.W. Europe only
P. cultripes, Western Spadefoot (p. 67, Pl. 7)
Spade on hind foot pale. Webbing between hind toes indented
(Fig., p. 64). Back of head relatively flat. E. Europe only
P. syriacus, Eastern Spadefoot (p. 70, Pl. 7)
Spade on hind foot pale. Webbing between hind toes not in-
dented (Fig., p. 64) or only slightly. Head behind eyes
domed *P. fuscus*, Common Spadefoot (p. 67, Pl. 7)

7. Rather slender with small green or olive spots. Heel reaches
beyond eye when hind limb is laid forward along body. Body
length nearly three times width of head
Pelodytes punctatus, Parsley Frog (p. 71, Pl. 6)
Plump. Heel does not reach beyond eye when hind limb is
laid forward along body. Body length only just over twice
width of head **8**

8. ALYTES

Three tubercles on palm of hand (Fig., p. 63)
A. obstetricans, Midwife Toad (p. 63, Pl. 6)
Two tubercles on palm of hand (Fig., p. 63)
A. cisternasii, Iberian Midwife Toad (p. 66, Pl. 6)

9. Warty with large, obvious paratoid glands **10**
Smooth-skinned, or not particularly warty; no paratoid
glands **11**

10. BUFO

Paratoid glands oblique (Fig., p. 72). Colour not green; often
lacks clear patterning. Tubercles under longest hind toe
usually paired. Eye usually deep gold or copper coloured
B. bufo, Common Toad (p. 72, Pl. 8)
Paratoids roughly parallel. Often olive, grey or greenish; usually without very distinct pattern except for a yellow vertebral
stripe (only rarely absent). Tubercles under longest hind toe
usually paired (Fig., p. 73). Eye pale gold. Not much of E.
Europe, Italy etc. *B. calamita*, Natterjack (p. 73, Pl. 8)
Paratoids roughly parallel. Upperside usually boldly marked
with greenish, often dark-edged 'islands' on pale background;
rarely has yellow vertebral stripe. Tubercles under longest
hind toe normally single (Fig., p. 73). Eye pale gold. Not most
of W. Europe *B. viridis*, Green Toad (p. 74, Pl. 8)

11. Pupil not horizontal, often more or less round, or triangular.
   Ear-drum usually not clearly visible.
                    Discoglossus spp., Painted Frogs (p. 62, Pl. 6)
   Pupil horizontal. Ear-drum usually fairly obvious   **12**

12. RANA
   No continuous dorsolateral fold, but short fold just behind ear.
   Ear-drum as large as eye (females) or much larger (males).
   Introduced into N. Italy.
                    R. catesbeiana, American Bullfrog (p. 87)
   Continuous dorsolateral folds always present. Ear-drum
   smaller than eye   **13**

13. Eyes close together (Fig., below). Often green or greenish.
   Males have vocal sacs at corners of mouth   **14**
   Eyes well separated (Fig., below). No bright green in dorsal
   colouring. Dark facial mask nearly always present. Males
   lack external vocal sacs   **15**

eyes close together    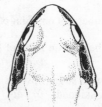 eyes well separated

          Green Frog   Brown Frog

14. GREEN FROGS
   Back of thigh marbled dark and whitish, olive or grey – not
   yellow. Metatarsal tubercle small, rather soft, and blunt (Fig.,
   p. 86). Vocal sacs grey   *R. ridibunda*, Marsh Frog (p. 85, Pl. 12)
   Back of thigh often marbled with yellow or orange and brown or
   black. Metatarsal tubercle larger, harder and usually sharp-
   edged (Fig., p. 86). Vocal sacs often whitish.
                    Rana esculenta, Edible Frog (p. 86, Pl. 12)
                    Rana lessonae, Pool Frog (p. 85, Pl. 12)

15. BROWN FROGS
   The species of Brown Frogs are all very similar and rather variable which makes it difficult to produce a key that will identify
   them all with certainty. The following couplet will not
   always place frogs correctly, so if a frog is taken through the

key but does not fit the relevant description, return to this point and follow the other branch of the couplet.

Legs short: heel usually does not extend beyond snout, Fig. on p. 56. Dorsolateral folds close together (distance between them, measured just behind forelimbs, goes 5½−7 times into length of animal). **16**

Legs long: heel usually extends to, or beyond, snout. Dorsolateral folds well separated (distance between them, measured just behind forelimbs, goes not more than 5, rarely 5½, times the length of animal). **17**

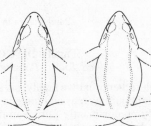

close together   well separated

Dorsolateral folds

16. Metatarsal tubercle small and soft (Fig., p. 79); snout often blunt. Almost never striped above.
R. temporaria, Common Frog (p. 78, Pl. 10)

Metatarsal tubercle large, hard, and sometimes sharp-edged – ½–⅔ length of first hind toe; snout usually pointed. Often striped above. *R. arvalis,* Moor Frog (p. 80, Pl. 10)

17. Underside usually unmarked or with only stippling at sides of throat in dark individuals. Ear-drum large and usually very close to eye. Metatarsal tubercle rather prominent.
R. dalmatina, Agile Frog (p. 80, Pl. 11)

Throat usually spotted or marbled, and often belly as well. Ear-drum not very close to eye. **18**

18. Iberia only. Small frog, frequently with dark throat, weak metatarsal tubercle and often a pinkish flush on belly.
R. iberica, Iberian Frog (p. 83, Pl. 11)

N. Italy only. Often pink flush beneath. Distance between nostrils less than distance between nostril and eye (Fig., p. 82). Ear-drum prominent.
R. latastei, Italian Agile Frog (p. 81, Pl. 11)

Italy and Balkans. No pink on underside. Distance between
nostrils more than distance between nostril and eye. Ear-
drum not prominent.   *R. graeca*, Stream Frog (p. 82, Pl. 11)

round-   heart-shaped   vertical,   horizontal
triangular   cat-like

Pupil shapes in frogs and toads

Family DISCOGLOSSIDAE
Fire-bellied Toads, Painted Frogs and Midwife Toads

A small, rather primitive family, six species of which are found in Europe
and neighbouring areas and three in E. and S.E. Asia. Discoglossids are
the only predominantly European family of amphibians or reptiles. All
species have a disc-shaped tongue that cannot be protruded to catch prey
as it can be in many other frogs and toads. The three main types of
discoglossid found in Europe differ considerably in appearance and
habits, but are alike in having relatively subdued voices and being able to
breed two or three times a year.

Fire-bellied Toads (*Bombina*) and Painted Frogs (*Discoglossus*), are
largely aquatic and breed in water, the males grasping the females around
the loins during amplexus. Unlike the Midwife Toad (*Alytes*), the males of
these species have nuptial pads. These are present on the fingers but also
occur in other areas (chin, belly and toe web of Painted Frogs, forearm of
Fire-bellied Toad, forearm and toes of Yellow-bellied Toad). Fire-bellied
Toads lay large eggs in small groups, often on weed; each female probably
produces fewer than 100 per brood. Painted Frogs lay up to 1000 small eggs
singly. These may form a single layer on the pool bed, or be attached to
weed. In contrast Midwife Toads mate on land and the large eggs (up to
about 60 per female) are produced in strings that the male carries wrapped
around his hind legs. He keeps the eggs moist by visiting pools and streams
until they are ready to hatch when he deposits them in shallow water. The
newly metamorphosed young of Painted Frogs are small, but those of
other European discoglossids are quite large. They all reach maturity
rapidly.

BOMBINA VARIEGATA *Yellow-bellied Toad*   **Pl. 9**
Range. Most of central and S. Europe, except Iberian area, S. Greece,
much of Sicily and most other islands   Map 21.
Identification. Adults usually less than 5 cm. A small warty, aquatic toad

with flattened body, a round, heart-shaped or triangular pupil, and brightly coloured underside: typically yellow or orange with blue-grey or blackish markings, sometimes enclosing white dots. Yellow or orange colour usually present on finger-tips and may also extend as a patch onto back of thigh. Back grey, brown, yellowish or even olive, with prominent warts, often ending in black, spiny points. No vocal sac.

Voice. Calls in chorus, both by day and night, although often heard most obviously in the evening. Song a rather musical 'poop . . . poop . . . poop . . . . .', brighter and faster than the call of *B. bombina*. Usually about one or two calls a second, sometimes slower.

Habits. Largely diurnal, although often also active at night. Found in a variety of usually shallow water: edges of rivers and streams, ponds, small pools in marshes, drainage ditches, even wheel ruts and temporary puddles. Very aquatic and often sociable, many animals being found together in small areas of water. A lively, active toad, often seen floating, with legs spread on surface of water. If molested, will arch back and throw up limbs to show bright belly and may even turn itself upside down. This is a warning device, since skin secretion of *Bombina* is distasteful to many potential predators. Where it occurs with *B. bombina*, *B. variegata* tends to be found in the more mountainous or hilly areas.

Variation. Nearly all the characteristic features of this species are subject to occasional exceptions. This is especially true for colour and pattern: for instance the underside may sometimes be almost entirely black. Italian individuals often have dark throats and breasts and predominantly yellow or orange bellies. Balkan animals frequently have many dark points which are often spiny and may extend onto belly.

Similar Species. Likely to be confused with the closely related *B. bombina* Range is often useful in identifying untypical animals.

BOMBINA BOMBINA *Fire-bellied Toad*   **Pl. 9**

Range. E. Europe as far west as Denmark and S. Sweden (where probably extinct), and south to N. Yugoslavia and Bulgaria   Map 22.

Identification. Adults usually less than 5cm. Very like *Bombina variegata* (above): a small, warty, aquatic toad with characteristically flattened body and brilliantly coloured underside; pupil usually round or triangular. Differs from *B. variegata* in often having a predominantly black ground-colour on belly with small white dots and bright red-orange or red markings; finger-tips may be dark or pale but not usually brightly coloured; *B. bombina* tends to be less robust than *B. variegata*, with a narrower head; back often darker or sometimes green or with green spots; warts are smaller and smoother, sometimes rough tipped but usually not really spiny. Internal vocal sac present.

Voice. Calls usually in chorus, by night and day but heard most clearly in evening. A rather musical, although mournful, 'oop . . . oop . . . oop

. . . .'. Call speed varies, but usually slower than *B. variegata*, often about one call every 1½–4 secs.

Habits. Very similar to *B. variegata* but tends to be exclusively a lowland animal.

Variation. As with *B. variegata*, nearly all the characteristic features of this species are subject to occasional exceptions: in some animals, the amount of black on the belly is reduced. In areas where both *B. bombina* and *B. variegata* occur, animals with intermediate characters are often found. In some places such individuals result from hybridisation where the two species meet, and typical *B. variegata* and *B. bombina* may occur nearby. At other localities, whole populations may be intermediate in appearance and 'pure' animals of one or both species are absent.

Similar Species. Only likely to be confused with *B. variegata* (p. 60). Range is often useful in identifying untypical animals.

DISCOGLOSSUS PICTUS   *Painted Frog*   Pl. 6

Range. Iberia (except N.E.), S. France (Pyrénées Orientales only), Sicily, Malta. Also N.W. Africa   Map 23.

Identification. Adults 6–7 cm. A medium-sized, shiny, plump frog, usually with a pointed snout. Most likely to be confused with Typical Frogs (*Rana*), but easily distinguished by pupil shape which is usually roundish or triangular, not horizontal. Also ear-drum is inconspicuous in most cases, and tongue is disc-shaped. Colour extremely variable: grey, olive, yellowish, brownish or even red above, with darker, often light edged spots. Some specimens have a light stripe on back. Belly whitish, sometimes with brown speckling.

Voice. A rather quiet, rolling 'laugh'; a feeble, rapid, growling 'rar-rar-rar . . .'.

Habits. Usually found in or around still or running water. Prefers shallow areas in pools, streams, cisterns and river-edges. Active by day and night. Often seen sitting with just head above water. Sometimes found in marshes and brackish water. May occur with Green Frogs (p. 84).

Variation. Considerable variation in pattern and shape.

Similar Species. Some similarity to Typical Frogs (*Rana*). See also *D. sardus* (below).

DISCOGLOSSUS SARDUS   *Tyrrhenian Painted Frog*   Pl. 6

Range. Corsica, Sardinia, Giglio. Monte Cristo and Iles d'Hyères Map 24.

Identification. Usually up to about 7 cm, sometimes larger. Very similar to *Discoglossus pictus*, but tends to be more robust with a broader head. Pattern often consists of dark spots (frequently less well defined than in *D. pictus*) and there is usually a pale blotch on back; some animals are uniform, but none are striped. Some of these features are subject to exception, so locality is very important in the identification of atypical animals.

Voice. Very like previous species.
Habits. Found up to 1200 m. Very similar to *D. pictus*. Often occurs with *Rana esculenta* on Corsica.
Variation. Some variation in shape and pattern.
Similar Species. Could be confused with Edible Frog (*Rana esculenta*, p. 86), but pupil not horizontal.
Note. The exact status of this form is still uncertain.

ALYTES OBSTETRICANS *Midwife Toad*   Pl. 6
Range. W. Europe as far south as the Alps and Iberia, and eastwards to Germany. A few small introductions have been made in England Map 25.
Identification. Adults normally less than 5 cm. A small, plump toad with prominent eyes and vertical pupil. Colour variable, but usually grey, olive or brown with some small darker, often greenish markings. Separated from Spadefoots (*Pelobates*) by lack of spade on hind foot, and from Parsley Frog (*Pelodytes*) by shorter legs and plumper body. In Iberia can be distinguished from closely related and very similar *A. cisternasii* by presence of three tubercles on the palm of hand (*A. cisternasii* has only two; see Fig., below). In summer, males may be seen with strings of yellowish eggs wound around the hind limbs.
Voice. Calls by night, often away from water. A high-pitched, plosive, musical 'poo . . . poo . . . poo . . .' about one call every 1–3 secs; usually higher and shorter than *Bombina*. Individuals may vary considerably in pitch, and often sound as if they are responding to each other. Single individuals could be confused with Scops Owl (*Otus scops*).
Habits. Found in woodlands, gardens, dry-stone walls, quarries, rock slides and a variety of similar habitats at altitudes of up to 2000 m (in southern parts of range). Mainly nocturnal; frequently calls from cover and can be very difficult to locate. By day hides in crevices, under logs, stones, and in burrows which it may excavate using the forelimbs.
Variation. Iberian specimens tend to be smoother with more distinct markings.
Similar Species. *Alytes cisternasii* (p. 66); Spadefoots (*Pelobates*, p. 67); Parsley Frog (*Pelodytes*, p. 71).

Midwife   Iberian Midwife

Midwife Toads, palms of hands

Plate 7   **SPADEFOOTS**
                                 (× ⅔)

Plump toads with big eyes and vertical pupils; a prominent
'spade' on the hind foot.

1. **Pelobates cultripes**   *Western Spadefoot*   67
   S.W. Europe only. Spade black.
   Two animals, showing variation in pattern.

2. **Pelobates fuscus**   *Common Spadefoot*   67
   Not most of S. Europe. Spade pale; lump on top of head,
   behind eyes. Extensive webbing on hind feet. Two animals,
   showing variation in pattern.

3. **Pelobates syriacus**   *Eastern Spadefoot*   70
   E. and S. Balkans only. Spade pale. No lump on head. Webbing on hind feet indented (see Fig., below).

Western   Common   Eastern

Spadefoots, hind feet

1a

1b

2

3

TYPICAL TOADS   Plate 8
(× ⅔)

Often large toads with warty skins, large paratoid glands and
horizontal pupils.

1. Bufo bufo *Common Toad*   72
Large (up to 15 cm). Rather uniform. Paratoid glands oblique
(Fig., below). Eye often copper coloured.

   1a. Southern female.
   1b. Northern male.

2. Bufo calamita *Natterjack*   73
Not S.E. Europe or Italy. Usually a yellow stripe on back.

3. Bufo viridis *Green Toad*   74
Not S.W. Europe. Distinctive marbled pattern.

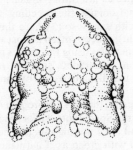   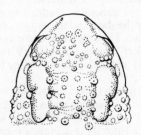

Common   Natterjack, Green
oblique   parallel

Typical toads, paratoid glands

ALYTES CISTERNASII *Iberian Midwife Toad* **Pl. 6**
Range. Restricted to W. and central Iberia Map 26.
Identification. Adults up to 5 cm, but usually smaller. Very similar to preceding species, but easily distinguished at close quarters by presence of two (not three) tubercles on palm of hand (Fig., p. 63). In general, tends to be smaller, plumper, and browner than Iberian *A. obstetricans*, with a comparatively large head and shorter legs. Often a series of pale warts on the upper eyelid.
Voice. Apparently unrecorded.
Habits. As far as is known, similar to *A. obstetricans*, but tends to live in sandy localities, where it burrows, digging with forelimbs.
Variation. No obvious variation recorded.
Similar Species. *A. obstetricans* (p. 63); Western Spadefoot (*Pelobates cultripes*, opposite); Parsley Frog (*Pelodytes*, p. 71).

Family **PELOBATIDAE** *Spadefoots and Parsley Frog*

A rather primitive family with representatives in Europe and neighbouring areas of N.W. Africa and Asia, in southeast Asia, and in North America. Four species are found in Europe: three Spadefoots (*Pelobates*) and the Parsley Frog (*Pelodytes punctatus*). Spadefoots are relatively short-limbed animals which have a superficial resemblance to Typical Toads (*Bufo*), but differ in having a very robust skull, vertical pupils, and a very prominent, flattened, sharp-edged 'spade' (modified metatarsal tubercle) on the hind foot. All three European species are rather similar.

Spadefoots are quite strictly nocturnal outside the breeding season. They are generally confined to areas with sandy soil, where they hide during the day (and in periods of drought) in deep, often almost vertical burrows. They dig these burrows for themselves using the spades on their hind feet alternately. In very sandy soil, Spadefoots sink out of sight quickly and the upper part of the burrow usually collapses, covering them completely.

The fourth European member of the family, the Parsley Frog (*Pelodytes punctatus*), is much more frog-like than the Spadefoots, lacks spades and almost all webbing on the hind feet, and does not dig much. The name derives from its appearance – speckled with green as if garnished with parsley.

Pelobates and *Pelodytes* breed in the spring, often in quite deep pools and at this time of the year may be active during the day. Spadefoots have no nuptial pads, but these are present in mating *Pelodytes*, which, unlike the others may often breed more than once a year. Males of all of them grip the females just in front of the hind limbs. The eggs are laid in a thick, rather short band, usually wound round the stems of water plants; the tadpoles may grow very large (often 10 cm in Spadefoots, and occasionally up to 17.5 cm).

PELOBATES CULTRIPES *Western Spadefoot* **Pl. 7**

Range. Iberia, W. and S. France. A closely related species occurs in N.W. Africa. Little, if any, actual overlap with *P. fuscus* Map 27

Identification. Adults up to 10cm, larger than *P. fuscus*. A big, plump, smooth-skinned toad with large eyes, a vertical pupil and a black spade on the hind foot; top of head is not obviously domed. Upperside greyish, yellowish, or whitish with dark brown or greenish blotches, spots, or speckles – rarely forming longitudinal bands. Often greener than *P. fuscus*, and less frequently has orange spots. Eye silvery or greenish. Sexual differences similar to *P. fuscus*.

Voice. Breeding males produce a rapid 'co-co-co' which sounds rather like a clucking hen.

Habits. Generally like other Spadefoots. Often found in large numbers on sandy coasts; also in open marshy areas by shallow water. Occasionally to be seen in vast numbers after rain. Sometimes less nocturnal than *P. fuscus*. Said not to have 'threat' display found in this species. Numbers fluctuate: in some areas, extremely abundant in some years but rare in others.

Variation. Considerable variation in colour and pattern, but no definite trends noted.

Similar Species. *P. fuscus* (below) has domed head and pale spade. Typical Toads (*Bufo*, p. 72), have horizontal pupil and lack spade. Midwife Toads (*Alytes*, p. 63), also lack a spade.

PELOBATES FUSCUS *Common Spadefoot* **Pl. 7**

Range. Lowland W., central and E. Europe. Also east to Urals, Kirghiz Steppes and Aral Sea. Map 28

Identification. Adults up to about 8 cm, usually smaller. A plump, smooth-skinned toad with large eyes and vertical pupils, a large pale-coloured spade on the hind foot which is more or less fully webbed, and a well marked lump (dome) on top of the head just behind the level of the eyes. Colour of upperside extremely variable: grey, pale brown, yellowish, or whitish, with darker brownish markings, which may form blotches, marblings, speckles, or stripes. Sides and sometimes back often have small orange spots. Eye golden, orange, or coppery. Often smells strongly of garlic. Males tend to be smaller than females, and have large, raised, oval gland on upper arm, and also have pearly granules on lower arm and hand during breeding season.

Voice. Breeding males produce, under water, a repeated clicking 'c'lock – c'lock – c'lock'. Females grunt or produce a more rasping 'tock – tock – tock'. Alarm call: shrill cry rather like that of a kitten.

Habits. Generally similar to other European Spadefoots – see family introduction. Often found in cultivated areas at low altitudes; especially where asparagus is grown. Nocturnal, not emerging until after sunset; particularly active in wet weather. Usually progresses in a series of short

Plate 9　　　**FIRE-BELLIED TOADS**
(× ⅔)

Small, flattened toads with warty skins and brightly coloured
bellies.

1. **Bombina variegata**　*Yellow-bellied Toad*　　　**60**
Belly usually yellow or orange with darker markings;
finger-tips also often brightly coloured.

2. **Bombina bombina**　*Fire-bellied Toad*　　　**61**
Not W. or much of S. Europe. Belly usually largely black
with red-orange or red markings; finger-tips rarely brightly
coloured.

TREE FROGS
(× ⅔)

Small, often bright-green frogs with round pads on finger and
toe tips. Colour can change rapidly.

3. **Hyla meridionalis**　*Stripeless Tree Frog*　　　**78**
No stripe on flank.

4. **Hyla arborea**　*Common Tree Frog*　　　**75**
Distinct stripe along flank.

　　4a. Typical form: stripe with upward branch.
　　4b. Typical form calling: vocal sac expanded.
　　4c. *H.a. sarda*: stripe without upward branch. Only on
　　Corsica, Sardinia, Elba and Capraia.

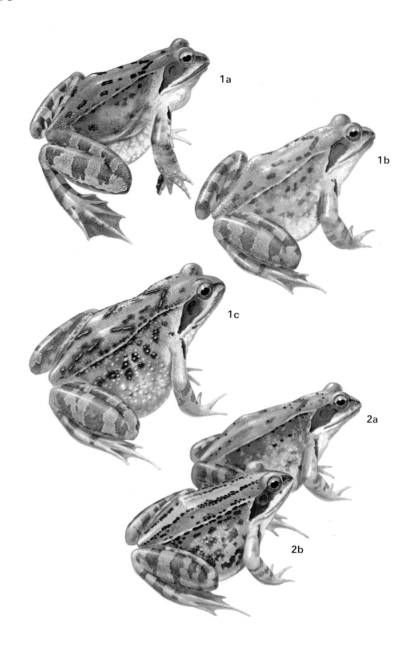

1a

1b

1c

2a

2b

BROWN FROGS 1   Plate 10
(× ⅔)

Frogs with horizontal pupils, dorsolateral folds and a dark 'mask'. Often not very aquatic outside breeding season.

1. Rana temporaria   *Common Frog*   **78**
Very variable in colour and pattern but not obviously striped. Dorsolateral folds close together (Fig., p. 59). Legs usually rather short.

  1a. Breeding male: bluish throat, thick arms, large nuptial pads; extensive foot webs.
  1b. Male outside breeding season.
  1c. Breeding female: very plump; pearly granules on flanks.

2. Rana arvalis   *Moor Frog*   **80**
Often very short-legged. Large hard metatarsal tubercle on hind foot. Snout usually pointed. Sometimes striped (both sexes).

  2a. Male. Breeding animals are often wholly or partly blue.
  2b. Female.

  N.B. In south of range, more long-legged individuals occur and these might be confused with *R. dalmatina* (**Pl. 11**).

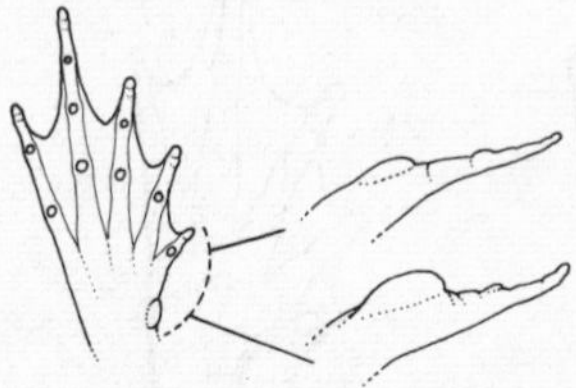

Common Frog, small and soft

Moor Frog, large and hard

Brown Frogs, metatarsal tubercle

jumps. When attacked or alarmed has impressive but harmless 'threat' display: squeals repeatedly, inflates body, stands high on legs, and may jump at intruder with mouth open. During breeding season is partly diurnal, and found in deep pools and ditches.

Variation. Considerable individual variation in colour and pattern, but no obvious geographical trends.

Similar Species. *P. cultripes* (p. 67); *P. syriacus* (below). Typical Toads (*Bufo*, p. 72) have horizontal pupil and no spade. Midwife Toads (*Alytes*, p. 63) lack spade.

PELOBATES SYRIACUS *Eastern Spadefoot*   Pl. 7

Range. S.E. Romania, S. Yugoslavia, Bulgaria and parts of Greece. Also S.W. Asia   Map 29.

Identification. Adults up to 9 cm. Similar to other spadefoots, but distinguished by combination of undomed skull, pale spade, and indented webbing on hind feet (Fig., below). Skin often has scattered, very small warts. Upperside is yellowish, greyish, or whitish, usually with large dark greenish or brownish blotches (often dark edged) or, more rarely, irregular stripes. Sides and back often have small yellow, pink or dark red spots. Males not noticeably smaller than females, but have large glands on upper arm.

Voice. Apparently not described.

Habits. Similar to other Spadefoots. Usually breeds in clear, deep (often temporary) water, with relatively little vegetation.

Variation. Some variation in colour pattern, but no obvious trends in Europe.

Similar Species. *Pelobates fuscus* (p. 67) has domed skull and more fully webbed feet. Green Toad (*Bufo viridis* p. 74) has horizontal pupil, fairly obvious eardrum, and no real spade (though metatarsal tubercle often fairly large).

Western   Common   Eastern

Spadefoots, hind feet

PELODYTES PUNCTATUS *Parsley Frog* **Pl. 6**
Range. Iberia, France, W. Belgium and extreme N.W. Italy Map 30.
Identification. Rarely more than 5 cm. Small, agile and rather long-limbed, with flat head and prominent eyes, which have vertical pupils. Hind toes almost completely unwebbed, or with a thin flange of webbing on each toe, and skin of back is fairly warty – the larger warts often forming irregular lines. Ear-drum indistinct, but often visible. Usually pale greyish to light olive above, with small darker olive to bright 'parsley' green spots; often a light X-shaped mark on upper back. Warts along sides may be orange. Often smells of garlic. Male has shorter body, thicker forelimbs, and darker throat than female and nuptial pads are present in breeding season.
Voice. Breeding males produce a sonorous 'co-ak' under water, to which the female replies with a rather feeble 'coo'. Out of water a medium pitched, weak 'cre-e-e-ek' – rather like a squeaky shoe or a low-pitched version of the squeak produced by a cork being drawn from a bottle.
Habits. Mainly nocturnal and terrestrial outside breeding season. Generally found in slightly damp habitats, e.g. among bushes, in vegetation at the base of walls, and sometimes by small streams. Quite agile and moves by jumping. By day can be found under stones and in shallow burrows which it digs itself. A good swimmer. Can climb smooth surfaces using belly as 'sucker'. Sometimes found sitting in bushes and on top of stones and rocks at night. In breeding season more diurnal, occurring in or near still water, usually with vegetation.
Variation. Some variation in colour, but not obvious geographical trends.
Similar Species. Typical Frogs (*Rana*, p. 78), Painted Frog (*Discoglossus pictus*, p. 62); *Pelodytes* easily distinguished by vertical pupils and by almost complete lack of webbing on hindfeet. Midwife Toads (*Alytes*, p. 63), are more robust and have shorter hind legs: heel does not reach eye in *Alytes*, extends beyond in *Pelodytes*.

Family **BUFONIDAE** *Typical Toads*

A large, widespread family found throughout much of the world but not most of the Australian region. The three European species all have warty skins, large paratoid glands and horizontal pupils. They are all largely nocturnal and terrestrial, but in the breeding season assemble in ponds and slow streams, often in large numbers. Males develop dark nuptial pads on the three inner fingers and call in chorus at night. In amplexus, females are grasped just behind the forelimbs. Each female may produce several thousand eggs which are laid in long strings. The tadpoles are among the smallest in Europe. The Natterjack (*Bufo calamita*) has a more extended breeding season than the other species.

BUFO BUFO *Common Toad* **Pl. 8**

Range. Found over most of Europe except Ireland, Corsica, Sardinia, the Balearics, Malta, Crete, and some other smaller islands. Also N.W. Africa and across Palaearctic Asia to Japan   Map 31.

Identification. Adults up to 15 cm long, but there is geographical variation in size and females are larger than males. The largest European toad, heavily built with a horizontal pupil, very warty skin and prominent paratoid glands that are slightly oblique (Fig., below). Colour usually brownish, but varying from sandy to almost brick-red, rich dark brown, greyish or occasionally olive. Tends to be fairly uniformly coloured, but may have darker blotches and patches, especially in south. Underside usually whitish or grey, often with darker marbling. Eye deep gold or copper-coloured. No external vocal sac.

Voice. Calls at night, the male 'release' call being most often heard. This is a not very powerful, rather high-pitched rough 'qwark-qwark-qwark', about 2–3 syllables a second, or more. The actual mating call is slower and the syllables are longer; it is rarely heard.

Habits. One of the most ubiquitous European amphibians, found in wide variety of often fairly dry habitats. Mainly nocturnal, hiding by day usually in one particular spot and emerging around dusk. Normally walks, but hops when alarmed. When approached by predators may assume characteristic posture: head down, hindquarters raised.

Variation. Animals from the south are often larger and may have spinier skins. Very rarely, may hybridise with other European *Bufo* species.

Similar Species. *B. calamita* (opposite) has lighter eye, usually a yellow stripe on back and parallel paratoid glands. *B. viridis* (p. 74) has lighter eye, distinctive pattern and parallel paratoid glands. Spadefoots (*Pelobates*, p. 67).

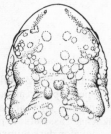

Common
oblique

Natterjack, Green
parallel

Typical toads, paratoid glands

BUFO CALAMITA *Natterjack* Pl. 8

Range. W. and Central Europe, eastwards to W. Russia. Also Britain where it is declining and S.W. Ireland   Map 32

Identification. Up to 10cm but normally about 7 or 8cm; females larger than males. A robust, relatively short-limbed toad with prominent paratoid glands that are roughly parallel (Fig., opposite), horizontal pupil and typically a bright yellow stripe down centre of back (occasionally weak or absent). General colouring usually brownish, grey or greenish with darker markings that are rarely as distinct as in *B. viridis*. Eye silvery gold. Tubercles under longest hind toe are usually paired (Fig., below). External vocal sac present in males.

Voice. Sings mainly at night, usually in chorus, beginning shortly before sunset. Call is a loud rolling croak like a ratchet, which is repeated a number of times. Each croak begins and ends fairly abruptly and often lasts for about 1 or 2 seconds. On still, quiet evenings, a chorus can often be heard over 2km or more.

Habits. Nocturnal. In north of range, typically found in sandy areas, even in dunes and often near the sea, where it may breed in brackish water. Elsewhere, can occur in a wider range of habitats and in Iberia may reach altitudes of 2000m. Tends to run in short bursts, not walk or hop. Frequently burrows in loose soil using forelegs and, occasionally, hind legs as well. When alarmed inflates body and raises rump, like *B. bufo*. Sometimes suddenly abandons established breeding ponds and migrates to new area.

Variation. Some variation in colour and intensity of pattern. Iberian animals may grow particularly large and often lack clear stripe. Occasionally hybridises with *B. viridis* and very rarely with *B. bufo*.

Similar Species. *B. bufo* (opposite); *B. viridis* (p. 74); Spadefoots (*Pelobates*, p. 67).

tubercles paired

tubercles single

Typical Toads, undersides of hind feet

BUFO VIRIDIS *Green Toad* **Pl. 8**

Range. A mainly eastern species, extending as far north as S. Sweden and as far west as W. Germany, extreme E. France, Italy, Corsica, Sardinia and the Balearic Islands. Doubtfully reported from N.E. France. Also N. Africa and eastwards to central Asia Map 33.

Identification. Up to 10 cm but usually smaller; females larger than males. A robust toad with prominent paratoid glands that are roughly parallel and a horizontal pupil. Similar in general appearance to *B. calamita* but differs in following features: dorsal pattern usually much more contrasting (pale with bold, clearly defined greenish markings often with dark edges); nearly always no bright yellow stripe (although a weak stripe occasionally present); hind limbs rather longer; tubercles under longest hind toe unpaired. External vocal sac present in males.

Voice. Sings at night in chorus. Call rather like a high pitched trilled liquid 'r-r-r-r-r-r...'. Starts quietly and often lasts up to about ten seconds. Not likely to be confused with other amphibians, but could possibly be mistaken for an insect song (e.g. crickets).

Habits. Mainly nocturnal, although sometimes active by day. In Europe, usually found in lowland areas, often but not invariably in dryish and sandy habitats. Frequently seen around human habitations and may be extremely numerous especially in south of range where it often enters villages and hunts insects around the base of street lamps etc.

Variation. Disposition and size of markings is very variable, but no obvious geographic trends. Hybrids with *B. calamita* occur occasionally in area of overlap. Hybrids with *B. bufo* are very rare.

Similar Species. *B. bufo* (p. 72); *B. calamita* (p. 73). Eastern Spadefoot (*Pelobates syriacus*, p. 70) has vertical pupil and very prominent spade on heel.

Family **HYLIDAE** *Tree Frogs*

A very large and successful group of frogs occurring over much of the tropical and temperate world except parts of S. Asia and most of Africa. The Australasian 'hylids' are now sometimes placed in a separate family. The two European species are typical members of the genus *Hyla*, a mainly American group. They are small, plump, smooth-skinned frogs with horizontal pupils, long legs, and disc-shaped adhesive pads on the tips of their fingers and toes. Both species are climbing frogs, usually found in trees or other vegetation, and only rarely come to the ground. They feed mainly on flying insects which they capture with great agility.

Breeding takes place at night in ponds, cisterns etc. The males develop small nuptial pads on the thumbs and they embrace the female just behind the forelegs. The pale eggs are laid in floating, walnut-sized clumps containing 800–1000 eggs. The tadpoles, which tend to be solitary, have a deep tail fin extending far forwards onto the back and swim with fast fish-like movements.

The two European species are closely related but quite distinct. They differ most obviously in call, colour pattern, and shape of the vocal sac.

HYLA ARBOREA *Common Tree Frog* Pl. 9

Range. Most of Europe except north but absent from the Balearic Islands and from parts of S. France and Iberia. Introduced into at least one very restricted locality in England. Also found in Asia Minor and southern USSR east to Caspian Sea. A related form occurs in S.W. Asia Map 34.

Identification. Adults up to 5 cm. Unlikely to be confused with any other frog except *Hyla meridionalis*. Small, long-limbed and smooth-skinned with characteristic disc-like adhesive pads on tips of fingers and toes. Colour variable, usually bright uniform green, but may vary from yellow to blotchy dark brown (Tree Frogs can change colour quite rapidly). In mainland Europe, a dark stripe extends from eye, through ear-drum, and along flanks to groin and just before this it nearly always branches upwards and forwards. This stripe is often edged with cream, and there are prominent stripes on the limbs as well. Green colour does not extend onto throat. Males have a large, obvious yellowish or brownish vocal sac beneath chin, at least in breeding season. This is spherical when blown up, and when deflated does not usually form longitudinal folds.

Voice. During breeding season, at night, a strident, rapid 'krak, krak, krak . . .', about 3–6 pulses a second. Call tends to accelerate at the beginning and slow down at end. It is repeated at intervals. Choruses are very noisy and from a distance can sound like quacking ducks. Outside the breeding season, may occasionally call briefly during the day, especially in late summer.

Habits. Mainly nocturnal. Usually found in well-vegetated habitats, and shows a marked preference for areas with bushes, trees, or reed-beds. Tree Frogs are the only European amphibians to climb very extensively (*Pelodytes* climb only occasionally). They are frequently found far off ground, but young animals often occur low down in herbage. Sometimes seen sitting fully exposed in sun.

Variation. Some regional variation in limb length: legs tend to be rather longer in south. Occasional individuals from S.E. Europe have upward branch of side stripe very narrow or even absent.

Corsica, Sardinia, Elba and Capraia. Tree Frogs on these islands differ from mainland *H. arborea* in a number of ways: they tend to be smaller with a shorter snout, the flank stripe is poorly developed and always lacks an upward branch, at times the back bears distinct spots (dark green when the frog is light green), and the hind legs may have cross-bars. The call, however, is very like mainland *H. arborea* although often slightly faster and at present it is usual to treat these island frogs as a very distinct subspecies of *H. arborea*: *H. arborea sarda*.

Similar Species. *Hyla meridionalis* (p. 78).

Plate 11 BROWN FROGS 2

(× ⅔)

Frogs with horizontal pupils, dorsolateral folds and a dark 'mask'. Often not very aquatic outside breeding season.

1. **Rana iberica** *Iberian Frog* 83
   W. and central Iberia. Most likely to be confused with *R. temporaria* (**Pl. 10**). Dorsolateral folds well separated. Two animals, showing variation in colouring.

2. **Rana dalmatina** *Agile Frog* 80
   Legs often very long. Snout rather sharp. Ear-drum large and very close to eye. Yellow on groin; throat pale, or stippled at sides only.

3. **Rana latastei** *Italian Agile Frog* 81
   N. Italy and S. Switzerland etc. Like *R. dalmatina* but ear-drum smaller, often a pinkish flush on underside and throat dark. Distance between nostrils less than distance from nostril to eye.

4. **Rana graeca** *Stream Frog* 82
   Balkans and Italy. Often yellow under hind legs; throat dark. Snout may be rounded; distance between nostrils greater than distance from nostril to eye. Usually near running water. Two animals, showing variation in colouring.

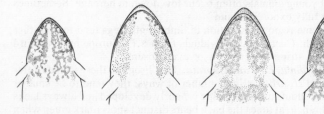

Iberian Agile Italian Agile Stream

Typical throat patterns: there is great variation in some forms and the Common Frog (**Pl. 10**) may have all the patterns shown.

GREEN FROGS Plate 12
(× ½)

Frogs with horizontal pupils, dorsolateral folds, no obvious 'mask', eyes set close together, and vocal sacs at the corners of the mouth in males. Often aquatic and noisy. Colouring very variable.

1. **Rana ridibunda** *Marsh Frog* 85
   Absent from parts of W. Europe and much of Italy. Often very large (up to 15 cm). Back of thighs without yellow or orange colouring. Vocal sacs of male grey. Metatarsal tubercle small (Fig., p. 86).

   1a. On land.
   1b. In water, calling.

2. **Rana esculenta** *Edible Frog.* 86
   Absent from S. Balkans and Iberia. Back of thighs often with yellow or orange colouring. Vocal sacs of male often white. Metatarsal tubercle large (Fig., p. 86).

3. **Rana lessonae** *Pool Frog.* 85
   Similar distribution to Edible Frog and similar range of colouring including that of back of thigh and vocal sacs, but often smaller and metatarsal tubercle very large (Fig., p. 86).

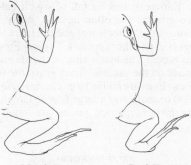

Marsh Frog   Pool Frog

Green Frogs, differences in leg proportions.

HYLA MERIDIONALIS *Stripeless Tree Frog* **Pl. 9**
Range. S. Iberia, S. France, N.W. Italy (Liguria), Balearic Islands. Also
N.W. Africa, the Canaries and Madeira   Map 35.
Identification. Adults up to about 5cm. Very similar to *H. arborea*, but
otherwise unmistakable; a small, smooth-skinned, long-limbed frog with
obvious disc-shaped climbing pads on fingers and toes. Like *H. arborea*
most usually bright green, but may be brownish or yellowish, sometimes
with small dark spots. At night perhaps more translucent then *H. arborea*.
Easily distinguished from this species by lack of clear stripe along flanks.
Other differences include larger average size, green usually extending
onto sides of throat, stripes on limbs not very obvious, back of thighs often
yellow, pale orange, or with dark mottling. Males possess a larger and
broader vocal sac than *H. arborea*, and it is longitudinally folded when
deflated.
Voice. A slow, fairly deep, resonant 'cra-a-ar', repeated not much faster
than once per second and typically more slowly.
Habits. Very similar to *H. arborea* but tends to be found at lower altitudes
where the two species occur together.
Variation. Very little recorded in Europe: dark stripe may extend a short
distance onto flank in young animals. Blue individuals occur occasionally.

Family **RANIDAE** *Typical Frogs*

A large family common over most of the world but not in much of
Australasia and S. South America. All European species are slim-waisted,
long-legged frogs with fairly smooth skins. With the exception of the
American Bullfrog (*Rana catesbeiana*), which has been introduced, they
can all be distinguished from other European frogs and toads by possessing both horizontal pupils and clear dorsolateral folds (Fig., p. 55). All are
agile and progress on land by leaping. In water, they are often powerful
swimmers. Native European species (all of which belong to the genus
Rana) fall into two groups: the often aquatic, noisy Green Frogs (*R.
ridibunda, R. lessonae* and *R. esculenta*) and the more terrestrial, quieter
voiced Brown Frogs (i.e. all other species). Typical Frogs often assemble
in large numbers to breed. The males sing in chorus and develop prominent dark nuptial pads on the thumbs. They grasp the female around the
body behind the arms. Eggs are laid in large clumps, a female Brown Frog
producing up to 2000 or more and a large female Green Frog as many as
10,000. The newly metamorphosed young are small and are usually
difficult to identify.

BROWN FROGS

RANA TEMPORARIA *Common or Grass Frog* **Pl. 10**
Range. Widely distributed throughout Europe, but absent from most of
Iberia, much of Italy, and the S. Balkans. Also eastwards to Urals   Map
36.

Identification. Adults up to 10 cm, but usually smaller. The most wide-spread Brown Frog in Europe and, in many areas, the commonest species. Usually robustly built with relatively short hind limbs (heel only rarely extends beyond snout-tip), closely spaced dorsolateral folds, and weak metatarsal tubercle. Old specimens tend to be round-snouted, but younger animals vary considerably in head shape. Ear-drum usually fairly distinct.

Extremely variable in colour. Grey, brown, pink, olive or yellow above, usually with dark blotches (sometimes these are orange or red), and often a dark ∧-shaped mark between the shoulders. Scattered black spots frequently occur on the back – these may be extensive (more so than in any other Brown Frog). Flanks are usually spotted or marbled. Underside white, yellow, or even orange, typically marbled, spotted, or speckled with darker pigment. Throat sometimes has light central stripe. Breeding males have very strong forelimbs, and are 'flabby' with a bluish tinge, especially on throat. Nuptial pads black.

Most like *R. arvalis*, *R. temporaria* usually has less pointed snout, is almost never striped (*R. arvalis* often is), and has a small soft metatarsal tubercle. Most other Brown Frogs tend to have longer legs (see these species for other differences). *R. temporaria* with long legs (heel extending just beyond tip of snout) do rarely occur, but are usually recognisable by their close dorsolateral folds.

Voice. A dull rasping 'grook...grook...grook', usually produced under water.

Habits. Largely terrestrial and often only found in water during breeding season or hibernation. Occurs in a very wide variety of habitats and may be encountered in almost any moist place within its range except in permanently frozen areas. Often found at high altitudes, even up to snow line, especially in south where it avoids lowlands.

Variation. Shows considerable variation over its range, but few consistent geographical trends. Animals from the N.W. of Spain and the Pyrenees may have reduced webbing on the hind feet. Some lowland Pyrenees animals are very long legged and have been mistaken for *R. iberica* and perhaps *R. dalmatina*.

Similar Species. Is likely to be confused with almost all other Brown Frogs, but especially *R. arvalis* (p. 80).

Common Frog, small and soft

Moor Frog, large and hard

Brown Frogs, metatarsal tubercle

RANA ARVALIS *Moor Frog*   **Pl. 10**
Range. From N.E. France eastwards; north to Sweden and Finland and south to Alps, N. Yugoslavia and N. Romania. Also across Asia to Siberia   Map 37.
Identification. Adults up to about 8 cm. A robust frog that often has very short legs (heel does not extend to snout-tip), closely spaced dorsolateral folds, a pointed snout and a large, hard, sometimes sharp-edged metatarsal tubercle. Dorsal pattern often striped and belly usually almost unmarked. Ear-drum well separated from eye.

Animals from the south of the range (i.e. Austria, Czechoslovakia, Hungary, Romania, N. Yugoslavia etc.) tend to be larger and slimmer and have longer hind legs (heel may reach just beyond snout). These animals are often separated as *R. arvalis wolterstorffi*.

Colour very variable: grey, yellowish or brownish. Sometimes uniform but usually with dark blotches and some black spots, which may be numerous. Many populations include animals that have a broad, pale vertebral stripe, often with a darker border. Sides usually blotched or marbled. Underside usually whitish; often yellow on groin. Throat may be spotted or flecked and may have light central stripe. Breeding males can be bright blue; nuptial pads are blackish.

R. arvalis is easily distinguished from *R. temporaria* by its usually more pointed snout, larger metatarsal tubercle, and frequently striped pattern. Long-legged animals in the south of the range can be confused with *R. dalmatina* but they are more robust, usually shorter limbed with closer dorsolateral folds, and the ear-drum is smaller and further from the eye.
Voice. Rather quiet, often described as being like a blade being repeatedly and abruptly whipped through the air, or like air escaping from a submerged bottle. Difficult to transcribe but could be rendered as 'waup, waup, waup. . .' At a distance, often sounds like a small dog barking.
Habits. Found in damp fields, meadows, fens, sphagnum bogs etc. Often in the same area as *R. temporaria*, but shows a preference for wetter habitats. Often breeds in temporary waters. Rarely occurs at high altitudes.
Variation. Considerable variation in size, proportions and colour. Dark bellied individuals are known.
Similar Species. Most likely to be confused with *R. temporaria* (p. 78) and *R. dalmatina* (below).

RANA DALMATINA *Agile Frog*   **Pl. 11**
Range. Widely distributed, but absent from most of Iberia and N. Europe. Isolated colonies in N. Germany, Denmark and S. Sweden   Map 38.
Identification. Adults up to 9 cm, but usually smaller. An elegant, delicately coloured (sometimes slightly translucent) Brown Frog. Hind limbs long (heel extends beyond snout tip in adults – often considerably), dorsolateral folds well separated, snout pointed, ear-drum large and close to

eye, and underside pale (dark animals may have throat dark-stippled at sides, nearly always leaving broad pale central area). Metatarsal tubercle quite large.

Colour not very variable or strongly contrasting; usually yellow-buff or pinkish brown above (often described as dead-leaf coloration) but can change to a darker colour. Faint vertebral stripe may be present, and back often marked with scattered darker blotches including a ∧ between the shoulders. Occasionally, a few jet black spots, especially on dorsolateral folds. Legs conspicuously banded. Sides often unmarked and groin frequently sulphur yellow. Nuptial pads greyish.

R. latastei and *R. graeca* are nearly always easily separated by their characteristic throat patterns. *R. temporaria* is more robust, usually with shorter legs, closer dorsolateral folds, and a weak metatarsal tubercle. See also *R. arvalis* (opposite).

Voice. A rather quiet, fast 'quar-quar-quar-quar-quar-quar', that tends to increase in loudness.

Habits. Found in woods, swampy meadows etc; usually only in fairly damp habitats. An extremely agile frog capable of very long leaps. May take to water when pursued, but is rather poor swimmer.

Variation. No obvious geographical trends. Very rarely, throat may be rather dark with a narrow light central stripe.

Similar Species.
All other Brown Frogs, but especially southern *R. arvalis* (opposite). Not likely to occur with *R. iberica*, but overlaps with all other *Rana* species.

RANA LATASTEI *Italian Agile Frog*   Pl. 11
Range. N. Italy and S. Switzerland, possibly also neighbouring areas of S.E. France and N.W. Yugoslavia   Map 39.
Identification. Adults up to about 7.5 cm. A graceful Brown Frog with rather long hind legs (heel reaches beyond snout) and well separated dorsolateral folds. Throat dark with a narrow light central stripe and frequently a pink flush on limbs and underparts. Snout often fairly pointed, but may be quite blunt. Ear-drum prominent, though not very large, and well separated from eye.

Colouring rather variable: upperparts greyish or reddish brown, often with some darkish blotches – especially a bar between eyes and a ∧-shaped mark between shoulders. No lichenous pattern on back or heavy blotches on flanks. Throat pattern (see above) is constant; dark marbling usually extends onto belly, at least anteriorly. Nuptial pads of breeding males dark brown.

Most likely to be confused with *R. dalmatina* and *R. graeca*. Differs from *R. dalmatina* in throat pattern, smaller ear-drum well separated from eye, less prominent metatarsal tubercle, and often pink flush on limbs and underparts. (*R. dalmatina* usually has yellow on groin). For distinction from *R. graeca* see this species. *R. temporaria* is more robust than

R. latastei, with shorter legs, more closely spaced dorsolateral folds, and usually no pink flush beneath.

Voice. Said to be a feeble but rapid 'keck-keck-keck-keck-keck'.

Habits. Tends to be a lowland species, not often found above 800 m. Frequently occurs in moist woods. Generally similar to *R. dalmatina* and, like this frog, is very agile.

Variation. Some variation in colouring and snout shape, but no obvious geographical trends.

Similar Species. Other Brown Frogs, especially *R. dalmatina* (p. 80) and *R. graeca* (below).

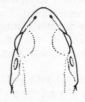

Italian Agile Frog

Stream Frog

Brown Frogs, snouts

RANA GRAECA *Stream Frog*   Pl. 11

Range. Balkan peninsula from central Yugoslavia and S. Bulgaria southwards; Italy and perhaps S. Switzerland   Map 40.

Identification. Adults up to 7.5 cm, occasionally larger. A rather flattened, fairly long-legged Brown Frog with often rounded snout, widely separated nostrils and well-spaced dorsolateral folds. Throat dark with a light central stripe. Ear-drum small and not very distinct.

Colour variable; often greyish above, but can be brownish, coffee-coloured, reddish, yellowish or olive. May have small scattered black spots, especially on dorsolateral folds, or may have obscure dark blotches including a ∧-shaped mark between the shoulders. Frequently has lichenous pattern of soft-edged pale spots. Sides of snout often dark; flanks not normally marbled. Throat dark with pale, narrow central line and pale spots, especially at jaw edge. Belly usually pale, often a yellowish flush under hind legs. Breeding male has powerful forelimbs and blackish-brown nuptial pads.

Has longer legs (though not invariably), less distinct ear-drum, and more widely separated dorsolateral folds than *R. temporaria*. *R. dalmatina* is more delicately built than *R. graeca*, and has a large prominent ear-drum and different throat pattern (Fig., p. 76). In Italy *R. graeca* may be confused with *R. latastei*, but *R. graeca* has the nostrils more widely separated (distance between nostrils is greater than distance between nostril and eye, Fig., above), a more extensive area of pearly granules on back of thighs, often little marbling on belly, and a less distinct ear-drum. Also the dark line running along outer side of hind leg is less clear in *R. graeca*.

Voice. A very rapid 'geck-geck-geck-geck-geck . . . . . .' .

Habits. Nearly always associated with cool running water, and most often found in mountain areas, but may follow water courses to lower altitudes. Typically encountered in or near streams, springs, wet caves, and flowing irrigation channels. Usually seen on bank or rocks in streams from which it leaps into water when disturbed to swim strongly and hide beneath bank, in vegetation or under stones.

Variation. Italian specimens are often smaller and shorter legged than Balkan animals.

Similar Species. All other Brown Frogs; particularly *R. temporaria* (p. 78), *R. dalmatina* (p. 80), and *R. latastei* (p. 81).

RANA IBERICA *Iberian Frog* Pl. 11

Range. Confined to Portugal, N.W. and central Spain. Also said to occur in the Pyrenees but this is unconfirmed and may be due to confusion with long-legged *R. temporaria* occurring there   Map 41.

Identification. Adults up to about 7 cm. A rather small, usually plump Brown Frog with widely separated dorsolateral folds.

Colouring very variable, upper parts often greyish brown, reddish-brown, olive, or sand coloured, with or without darker markings. Back sometimes has yellowish blotches and back and flanks may be dark-spotted. Hind limbs with or without clear barring. Underside can be uniformly pale but often with dark marbling or spotting; if so, a light central line often present on throat. Underparts may have a pinkish flush, especially in males. Nuptial pads of breeding males greyish.

Easily distinguished from *R. temporaria* by sometimes longer hind legs, widely separated dorsolateral folds (Fig., p. 59) and, in N.W. Spain by fuller webbing on toes (often reduced in *R. temporaria* here, see Fig. below).

Iberian Frog
webbing usually extensive

Common Frog
webbing often reduced

Brown Frogs in N.W. Spain, hind feet

Voice. Said to be a rapid 'cock-cock-cock-cock . . . .'.

Habits. Typically a montane frog occurring up to at least 2000 m. Usually encountered not far from cold, moving water being found in or near mountain streams, springs, etc. in woods, moors and meadows. However may sometimes live in polluted conditions. Very agile, jumping into water and swimming strongly if disturbed.

Variation. Considerable variation in colour, but no obvious geographical trends.

Similar Species. Other Brown Ranas, especially *R. temporaria* (p. 78), see above.

GREEN FROGS

Green Frogs are often noisy, frequently aquatic and usually gregarious. They contrast with the quieter, more often terrestrial Brown Frogs and can be distinguished from these by their more closely set eyes, the absence of a dark mask on each side of the head and the presence in males of external vocal sacs at the corners of the mouth.

In Europe, there are three main kinds of Green Frog: the Marsh Frog (*Rana ridibunda*), the Pool Frog (*Rana lessonae*) and the Edible Frog (*Rana esculenta*). Together they form one of the most complex groups among our amphibians and reptiles and their relationships have still not been fully worked out. The recognition of the Pool Frog as a distinct species is fairly recent. Previously, it was not clearly distinguished from the Edible Frog and it has often been included in statements about the latter. Marsh and Pool Frogs sometimes interbreed and the offspring so produced are Edible Frogs. Such hybridisation is almost certainly the ultimate source of this form. Unlike the great majority of populations of hybrid origin, some Edible Frogs are capable of breeding very successfully with one or other parent species. Matings with the parent species usually produce not intermediates but more Edible Frogs. In fact Edible Frogs appear to exist in at least four forms, although these cannot be certainly distinguished in the field. One often breeds successfully with the Pool Frog and another with the Marsh Frog; the other two are triploid, that is they have an extra set of chromosomes. Members of some of these forms can breed together and the results of such unions are mainly Edible Frogs, but Marsh or Pool Frogs are sometimes produced as well.

This odd situation, in which a form of hybrid origin can reproduce itself by breeding with one of its parent species seems to be connected with a peculiar chromosome mechanism. All Edible Frogs have at least one set of Marsh Frog chromosomes and at least one of Pool Frog origin, as would be expected in a first generation hybrid. But surprisingly, the genes in the two sets do not become mixed up (by the chromosomes 'crossing over') when the Edible Frog forms its reproductive cells. Instead its eggs and sperm often contain the chromosomes of only one of the two parent species. For instance, in Edible Frogs that breed with Marsh Frogs, the reproductive

cells often have only Pool Frog chromosomes, so that the offspring produced from such matings will have one Pool Frog and one Marsh Frog set
and are consequently Edible Frogs.

RANA RIDIBUNDA *Marsh* or *Lake Frog*   **Pl. 12**
Range. Two separate areas in Europe: one in the south-west (Iberia and
S. France) and the other in the east (Germany eastwards to Russia, and
south to the Balkans). Introduced into England (first to Romney Marsh
area – hence the English name 'Marsh Frog') and Italy (Imperia
province)   Map 42.
Identification. Adults up to 15 cm; the largest native European frog. Big,
robust and sometimes rather warty with a pointed snout, often some green
or olive on back and dark spots. Usually vocal sacs are grey and backs of
thighs are marbled dark and whitish, pale grey or olive; hind legs are long
(Fig., p. 77) and metatarsal tubercle is typically soft and small, about ¼ to
⅖ the length of first hind toe (Fig., p. 86).
Voice. Sings by night and day. Most noisy during breeding season, but
continues throughout summer. One of the most varied songs of the European amphibians: a wide variety of resonant croaks and chuckles – some
of which can be rendered as 'croax-croax' and a vigorous 'bre-ke-ke-ke-
ke-ke-kek'; also a metallic 'pink-pink'. The chorus often fluctuates errati-
cally.
Habits Usually gregarious, diurnal, and very aquatic; but also active at
night and animals occasionally found some distance from water, especially in south. Over much of its range *R. ridibunda* occurs in nearly all
types of water including small ponds, ditches and streams, but where it
overlaps with *R. esculenta* and *R. lessonae* it tends to be confined to lakes
and rivers. Frequently suns itself on bank, where often inconspicuous
until it leaps into water with a characteristic 'plop'. Often seen on lily pads
or floating among water weeds with only head exposed. Usually hibernates in water.
Variation. Animals from central and eastern Europe (which includes the
English populations as these originated from Hungarian stock) are rather
sombre and often largely brownish with dark spots. Southern animals are
more variable and often have bright green on the back.
Similar Species. Most species of *Rana*, but especially *R. esculenta* (p. 86)
and *R. lessonae* (below). Easily separated from Brown Frogs by closely
set eyes and vocal sacs at corner of mouth in males.

RANA LESSONAE *Pool Frog*   **Pl. 12**
Range. From France eastwards through central Europe to W. Russia,
north to S. Sweden and south to Italy and N. Balkans. Some existing
Green Frog colonies in S. England usually known as Edible Frogs
(*R. esculenta*) may involve this species which was possibly native but has
also been introduced   Map 43.

Identification. Adults up to about 9 cm. Generally similar to *R. ridibunda* but differs in following features: usually considerably smaller; vocal sacs often whitish and back of thigh typically marbled yellow or orange and brown or black; hind legs quite short (Fig., p. 77); metatarsal tubercle large, hard and usually sharp-edged, up to ⅔ length of first hind toe (Fig., below). Colouring is highly variable: some animals are largely green and others predominantly brown. Dark spots are usually present and there is often a pale (sometimes green or yellow) stripe along centre of back; dorsolateral folds are also often pale. Some breeding males have a yellow head and back.

Voice. Calls are similar to those of *R. ridibunda* but less resonant. The equivalent of the 'bre-ke-ke-ke-ke-ke-kek' call is more even and purring.

Habits. Often found in and around relatively small bodies of water but may sometimes be quite terrestrial outside the breeding season. However, occasionally lives in larger ponds and lakes. Often hibernates on land. Like *R. ridibunda*, it is largely diurnal and sun-loving.

Variation. Great variation in colouring and some in the size of metatarsal tubercle.

Similar Species. *R. ridibunda* (p. 85) and especially *R. esculenta* (below); *R. catesbeiana* (opposite).

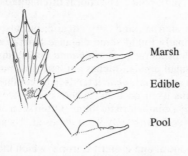

Marsh

Edible

Pool

Green Frogs, hind foot showing typical sizes of metatarsal tubercle

RANA ESCULENTA *Edible Frog* Pl. 12

Range. Apparently more or less the same as the previous species, but may exist alone on Corsica and at some other localities. Some small colonies in southern England; possibly all introduced Map 43.

Identification. Up to 12 cm. but usually smaller. Range of body colouring is similar to that of *R. lessonae* and, as in this species, vocal sacs are usually whitish and the back of the thigh typically marbled brown or black and yellow or orange. Males in some areas have yellow heads and backs in the breeding season. Differs from *R. lessonae* in having longer hind legs (Fig., p. 77) and a smaller metatarsal tubercle, ⅓ to ½ length of first hind toe (Fig., above).

Voice. Tends to be intermediate between *R. ridibunda* and *R. lessonae*.

Habits. Usually very aquatic and can occur in a wide range of waters, often in the company of one of the two other kinds of Green Frog and even occasionally with both. Like these, it is frequently active by day and often basks in the sun. In spite of its name, it is not peculiar in being edible, other Green Frogs and Brown Frogs being eaten in some areas.

Variation. Extremely variable and sometimes looks very similar to other Green Frogs, especially *R. lessonae*. Some variation in size of metatarsal tubercle.

Similar Species. *R. ridibunda* (p. 85); separation from this species is often quite easy. *R. lessonae* (p. 85) is usually distinguishable where it occurs in colonies with *R. esculenta* and a number of animals can be compared, but certain identification of single-species colonies can present problems.

RANA CATESBEIANA *American Bullfrog* Fig. below

Range. Originally eastern North America, but now introduced into many other places including parts of N. Italy (in Lombardy, Mantua, and Pavia) Map 44.

Identification. Adults up to 15 cm, occasionally longer. A very large aquatic frog unlikely to be confused with any native species except perhaps *Rana esculenta* and *R. lessonae*. Easily distinguished from European *Rana* by its lack of dorsolateral folds and by its very large ear-drum (as large as eye in females and larger in males). Vocal sac is beneath chin, not at sides of mouth as in *R. esculenta* and *R. lessonae*. *R. catesbeiana* tends to be more uniformly coloured than these species; it is usually green, olive-green, or brown above, sometimes mottled with grey or darker brown. Head often light green and legs usually banded; belly whitish, mottled grey, and there is often a yellowish flush on throat.

Voice. Quite different from native European species. A very deep groaning call: a slow 'br-wum,' sometimes described as 'jug-o-rum'.

Habits. Very aquatic. Found in lakes, ponds, cisterns, and small rivers. Prefers bodies of water with good growth of vegetation at edges. Active by day and night, but more often heard calling at night.

Similar Species. *Rana esculenta* (opposite) and *R. lessonae* (p. 85).

American Bull frog (*Rana catesbeiana*)

Tortoises, Terrapins and Sea Turtles – Testudines

There are some 300 species in this group which is characterised by its members possessing a bony shell that encloses the body and is covered by horny plates or, less commonly, tough skin. In Europe there are three land species and two that are semi-aquatic in fresh or brackish water; as many as five marine species have also been recorded.

In Britain, no one vernacular name exists that covers all members of the group. *Tortoise* is used for the strictly land-dwelling forms, *terrapin* for the semi-aquatic ones and *turtle* for the marine species and sometimes for one or two other very aquatic groups. In the United States, *tortoise* is used more or less as in Britain, but *turtle* can cover all aquatic and semi-aquatic forms and may sometimes be used for all shelled reptiles.

Key to Tortoises, Terrapins and Sea Turtles

N.B. *Carapace* is the domed, upper part of the shell; *plastron* the flatter, lower section, and the area on each side joining these two regions is the *bridge*.

1. Carapace strongly domed; no webbing between toes; terrestrial ... 2

   Carapace rather low; webbing present between toes; semi-aquatic in fresh or brackish water ... 3

   Carapace low; limbs form very flat, paddle-shaped flippers; marine ... 4

2. TORTOISES

   A large, well-defined horny scale on tail-tip; no spurs on backs of thighs; usually two supracaudal plates present (Fig., p. 91)

   > *Testudo hermanni*, Hermann's Tortoise (p. 91, Pl. 13)

   No large, well-defined scale on tail-tip; spurs often present on backs of thighs; usually only one supracaudal plate present (Fig., p. 91)

   > *Testudo graeca*, Spur-thighed Tortoise (p. 91, Pl. 13)
   > *Testudo marginata*, Marginated Tortoise (p. 92, Pl. 13)

3. TERRAPINS

   Neck usually with light spots and streaks but no stripes; no

88

inguinal plates (Fig., p. 97); plastron hinged in adults (front part moves slightly)

> *Emys orbicularis*, European Pond Terrapin (p. 93, Pl. 14)

Neck with distinct stripes; inguinal plates present (Fig., p. 97); plastron not hinged in adults.

> *Mauremys caspica*, Stripe-necked Terrapin (p. 93, Pl.14)

4. SEA TURTLES

Carapace covered by skin, with five or seven prominent ridges.

> *Dermochelys coriacea,* Leathery Turtle (p. 95, Fig., p. 99)

Carapace covered by horny plates, with at most one well-developed, central ridge   **5**

5. Five costal plates on each side; nuchal in contact with first of these   **6**

Four costal plates on each side; nuchal separated from first of these   **7**

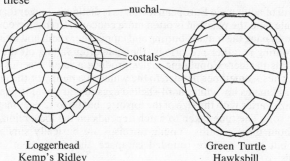

Loggerhead
Kemp's Ridley

Green Turtle
Hawksbill

Sea Turtle carapaces

6. Carapace clearly longer than broad; plastron with three infra-marginal plates (if more, then numbers on each side tend to be different); no pores in inframarginals (Fig., p. 98)

> *Caretta caretta*, Loggerhead Turtle (p. 95; Fig., p. 99)

Carapace often almost as broad as long, or broader; plastron with four (rarely three) pairs of inframarginal plates, each with a pore (Fig., p. 98)

> *Lepidochelys kempii*, Kemp's Ridley (p. 98)

7. Plates on carapace do not overlap; one pair of prefrontal scales on snout (Fig., p. 100)

> *Chelonia mydas*, Green Turtle (p. 100)

Plates on carapace usually do overlap; two pairs of prefrontal scales on snout (Fig., p. 100)

> *Eretmochelys imbricata*, Hawksbill Turtle (p. 100)

Family **TESTUDINIDAE** *Tortoises*

This group contains nearly all the mainly herbivorous shelled-reptiles that are modified for life in dry or fairly dry habitats. There are about 40 species distributed throughout most of the warm parts of the world except the Australian region. Only three species occur in Europe and these are restricted to the south.

European tortoises occur in a wide variety of habitats varying from meadowland to almost barren hillsides. They can often be detected by the constant rustling they make as they push through the undergrowth (quite unlike the intermittent noise made by lizards or the more even, continuous sound of a moving snake). They tend to be active in the morning and evenings, spending the remainder of the day resting. Although mainly herbivorous, tortoises eat varying amounts of carrion, faeces and invertebrates.

The tail of adult male European tortoises is distinctly longer than that of the female, and the plastron is often more concave. Courtship consists of the male chasing the female, butting and tapping her shell, and biting at her limbs. Mating is rather precarious, the male often falling off the smooth shell of his partner. Copulating males produce a regular series of high-pitched cries, sometimes likened to the whine of a puppy or the miaowing of a cat. Females lay white, hard-shelled eggs that are oval in shape. The clutch size varies with the size of the tortoise, but up to 12 eggs may be laid in loose soil. The time taken to hatch depends on the local climate but is often about three months. Young tortoises are basically similar to the adults, but have a more rounded carapace and more clearly defined markings.

In the past, there has been considerable confusion of the vernacular names of the two more widespread species of tortoise in Europe. Both *Testudo graeca* and *T. hermanni* have been known as the 'Greek' Tortoise: *T. graeca* on account of its scientific name, even though it has a very restricted distribution in Greece, and *T. hermanni* because it is the most widespread species in that country. It seems best to abandon the name 'Greek' in favour of 'Spur-thighed' for *T. graeca* and 'Hermann's' for *T. hermanni*.

Mediterranean populations have suffered severely from over collecting, either for the pet-trade or, less commonly, for food. Tortoises are also frequently killed on roads and in scrub and forest fires, especially in late summer.

Tortoises are usually quite easy to identify but confusion may arise because people often transport European species to places outside their normal ranges and other forms are commonly imported into Europe and frequently escape.

TESTUDO HERMANNI *Hermann's Tortoise* **Pl. 13**
Range. S. Europe: Balkans (mainly south of Danube), Ionian islands,
S. and W. Italy, Sicily, Elba, Pianosa, Corsica, Sardinia, Balearics,
S. France and possibly E. Spain. Introductions have also been made
elsewhere   Map 45.
Identification. Carapace length of adults usually up to about 20 cm (larger
individuals are rare). Carapace strongly domed, sometimes rather lumpy.
Shell yellowish, orange, brownish or greenish, overlaid with varying
amounts of dark pigment. Differs from other European tortoises in having
following combination of features: large scale on tail tip, no spurs on
thighs, usually two supracaudal plates (Fig., below), scaling on front of
fore limbs tends not to be very coarse.
Habits. Restricted to areas with hot summers. Found in a variety of moist
and dry habitats: lush meadows, cultivated land, scrub-covered hillsides,
light woodland, stabilised dune areas and even rubbish dumps. Prefers
places with dense vegetation.
Variation. Considerable variation in colour and shape. Old animals may be
very dark and are often scarred, producing a gnarled appearance. Western
animals have some tendency to be smaller, and more rounded than eastern
ones.
Similar Species. *T. graeca* (below) and *T. marginata* (p. 92).

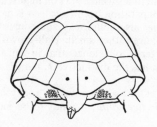
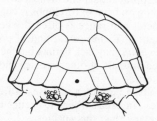

Herman's
often two supracaudals,
large scale on tip of tail

Spur-thighed
often one supracaudal,
spurs on thighs

Tortoises, back views

TESTUDO GRAECA *Spur-thighed Tortoise* **Pl. 13**
Range. E. Balkans south of Danube to Macedonia, European Turkey and
the islands of Thasos, Samothrace (?) and Euboa; Sicily and neighbouring
Italy, Sardinia (?), Balearics and S. Spain. Also N. Africa, Asia Minor
and Middle East to Iran. Introductions have also been made elsewhere
Map 46.

Identification. Carapace length of adults sometimes up to 25 cm or even larger. Very like *T. hermanni* although shell rarely lumpy; differs in having obvious spurs on thighs, typically a single supracaudal plate (Fig., p. 91) and frequently coarser scaling on the front of the fore-legs; there is no large scale on tail-tip.

Habits. Generally similar to *T. hermanni*.

Variation. Considerable variation in colour and shape. Adults in eastern parts of range are said to have a broader, flatter shell than those in west, but this difference is not very constant. Old animals may have the back of the shell slightly flared, but not as much as in *T. marginata*.

Similar Species. *T. hermanni* (p. 91); *T. marginata* (below).

TESTUDO MARGINATA *Marginated Tortoise* Pl. 13

Range. Greece from Mount Olympus southwards, some small offshore islands, Skyros and Poros in the Aegean, and Sardinia (where almost certainly introduced). May possibly be introduced elsewhere Map 47.

Identification. Carapace length of adults often up to 25 cm but sometimes as much as 30 cm. Mature animals very distinctive: carapace long and strongly flared at rear, mainly black except for a characteristic light orange or yellow patch on each large plate. Hatchlings look very like young of other species, as they are rounded and lack flaring and distinctive colouring. They can usually be separated from *T. hermanni* because there is only one supracaudal plate in most cases, sometimes weak spurs on thighs, and scaling on front of forelimbs is coarse. Separation from *T. graeca* is more difficult and range is often the best clue; also spurs may sometimes be absent in *T. marginata* and, if present, are rather small. Half-grown *T. marginata* may lack flaring, but the shell tends to be longer than in similarly sized animals of other species and often has the distinctive *T. marginata* pattern.

Habits. Like other tortoises. Often found on scrub-covered, rocky hillsides. In areas where it occurs with *T. hermanni*, it tends to be more montane than this species.

Variation. Not very variable. Some old animals entirely black.

Similar Species. *T. graeca* (p. 91); *T. hermanni* (p. 91).

Family **EMYDIDAE** *Terrapins*

A mainly aquatic or semi-aquatic family with about 80 species occurring in the warmer areas of the world except Australia, Madagascar, and most of Africa. There are only two species in Europe, both of which live in or near water. Unlike the tortoises they are mainly carnivorous, feeding on a wide variety of aquatic animals (especially fish, amphibians and large invertebrates), and carrion. Differences between the sexes and mating behaviour are generally similar to those of tortoises. 3–16 hard-shelled elongate eggs are laid in soft ground, *Emys* usually producing rather more eggs than

Mauremys. Juveniles, especially those of *Mauremys*, are much more brightly marked than adults and also much rounder in outline. As with tortoises, exotic escapes are common.

EMYS ORBICULARIS *European Pond Terrapin* **Pl. 14**
Range. Most of Europe except N. and parts of centre. Introductions beyond natural range are fairly common. Also W. Asia and N.W. Africa Map 48.
Identification. Carapace of adults usually up to 20 cm but occasionally to 30 cm. Black, blackish or brownish, usually with pattern of light, often yellow, spots and streaks. Readily distinguished from tortoises by more flattened shell. Only likely to be confused with Stripe-necked Terrapin but differs in colour, lacks distinct stripes on neck, and inguinal plates (Fig., p. 97). Shell more or less oval in outline, slightly wider behind, with a central keel in young but not in old specimens. Plastron rather flexible in young; more rigid in adults but a transverse hinge allows the front section to move up and down slightly. Hatchlings very small (shell often less than 2 cm), more rounded in outline, longer tailed and more brightly marked than adults.
Habits. Usually found in still or slow moving water with a good growth of aquatic plants and overhanging vegetation. Also occurs in ditches, swamps and brackish areas. Typically seen when basking on stones or logs at water's edge. Sometimes only head and neck visible, sticking up above surface. Rather timid and dives when disturbed.
Variation. Some variation in colouring but no obvious geographic trends.
Similar Species. Stripe-necked Terrapin (*Mauremys caspica*, below).

MAUREMYS CASPICA *Stripe-necked Terrapin* **Pl. 14**
Range. Iberia and S. Balkans (north to S.W. Yugoslavia and S. Bulgaria). Also N.W. Africa and S.W. Asia. Possibly introduced elsewhere Map 49.
Identification. Carapace of adults usually up to about 20 cm, sometimes longer; typically grey-brown or greenish. Young animals are often warm brown with clear red or yellowish markings. Flattened shell quite unlike that of tortoises; only likely to be confused with European Pond Terrapin (*Emys orbicularis*, above). Differs in having usually less dark colouring, conspicuous stripes on neck, and inguinal plates (Fig., p. 97). Shell with distinct central keel (best developed in young but visible at least at rear of shell in adults). Plastron rather flexible in young but rigid in older animals, without a hinge. Hatchlings 2–3 cm long, longer tailed, more brightly coloured and more rounded in outline than adults. Some animals have algal infection of shell which makes it flaky and often results in the horny plates sloughing off.
Habits. Very like *Emys* but sometimes found in larger, more open waters,

big rivers etc. In small pools and streams, tends to aestivate when they dry up. Very tolerant of brackish or polluted water. May produce musky odour when disturbed.

Variation. Eastern and western populations were once regarded as separate species: *M. caspica* and *M. leprosa*. S.E. European animals tend to be more uniformly dark underneath than Iberian ones.

Similar Species. European Pond Terrapin (*Emys orbicularis*, p. 93).

Families **DERMOCHELYIDAE** and **CHELONIIDAE**
Sea Turtles

There are two distinct types of Sea Turtle: the Cheloniidae contains six species having a shell made up of large bones and covered by horny plates, while the Dermochelyidae comprises a single form, the Leathery Turtle (*Dermochelys coriacea*) in which the shell consists of many small bones and is covered by skin.

Sea Turtles are superb swimmers and spend virtually all their lives in water, only the females coming ashore occasionally to lay their eggs; they may, however, be thrown up on beaches when sick, damaged or dead. All species have streamlined shells, incompletely retractable heads and flat paddle-like fore limbs (flippers). When swimming the forelimbs are flapped slowly up and down like the wings of a bird, so that the turtle virtually flies through the water. Sea Turtles are essentially warm-water animals but some kinds reach cooler seas and may be found in the N.E. Atlantic as well as the Mediterranean. There is some evidence that many, if not all, of the turtles encountered off N.W. Europe swim or drift from the W. Atlantic with the Gulf Stream. Females produce large clutches of soft-shelled eggs which are usually buried on sandy beaches of warm seas, the young entering the water as soon as they hatch.

Turtles suffer considerably from exploitation and other human activities. They and their eggs are eaten in many areas, the horny plates of mainly one species provide 'tortoiseshell', and others are often butchered to make souvenirs, soup etc. The opening up of originally deserted sandy beaches for tourism can have a catastrophic effect on the breeding of turtles.

When stranded, or egg-laying, turtles should present no real problems of identification, even though they may sometimes be encrusted with sea-weed and barnacles. At sea, where clear views are much harder to obtain, turtles can be difficult to identify.

In the following descriptions, the carapace lengths given are taken over the curve of the shell.

DERMOCHELYS CORIACEA *Leathery Turtle* Fig., p. 99
Range. Atlantic (even recorded from Arctic waters) and Mediterranean, where it is known to breed. Also Pacific and Indian Ocean.
Identification. Carapace length up to 180cm or more in adults, but only 6cm in hatchlings. Adults may weigh over 350kg and are said to reach 500kg. A huge dark turtle with five or seven very prominent ridges on the carapace, which is covered by thick leathery skin; ridges are sometimes notched. Skin black or dark brown above, usually with lighter flecks. Upper jaw has two distinct tooth-like points at front.
Habits. Often seen in very deep waters. Carnivorous: feeds principally on floating salps and jellyfish but will take other animals. Sometimes sticks head and neck right out of water, when it may look quite unturtle-like.
Variation. Some in colour.
Similar Species. Unlikely to be confused with any other turtle if a clear sighting is obtained.

CARETTA CARETTA *Loggerhead Turtle* Fig., p. 99
Range. Atlantic, Black Sea and Mediterranean, where it breeds. Also Pacific and Indian Ocean.
Identification. Carapace up to about 110cm in adults, but usually smaller, and only about 5cm in hatchlings. A large horny-shelled turtle, with an oval, often rather long carapace, five costal plates (Fig., p. 89) and usually three inframarginal plates on each side, which always lack pores (Fig., p. 98). Inframarginals may exceed three but numbers on each side then tend to be different. Young have keeled vertebral plates that each end in a projection, giving the animal a 'saw-backed' appearance. Red-brown above, dark streaked in young.
Habits. Occurs in deep water but often found relatively near shore. In N.E. Atlantic (i.e. French coast northwards) most animals encountered are immature. The commonest turtle in Mediterranean. In deep water tends to feed especially on salps and jellyfish, but in shallows takes crabs, sea urchins, molluscs etc.
Variation. Some in colour, which also varies with amount of barnacle and plant-growth.
Similar Species. Juveniles may look superficially like Kemp's Ridley (*Lepidochelys*, p. 98). Adults have some resemblance to Green Turtle (*Chelonia*, p. 100). See also Hawksbill (*Eretmochelys*, p. 100).

Plate 13   **TORTOISES**
(× ½)

1. **Testudo hermanni**   *Hermann's Tortoise*   91
   Large scale on tail-tip. Usually two supracaudal plates (Fig., below).

2. **Testudo graeca**   *Spur-thighed Tortoise*   91
   Spurs on back of thighs. Usually one supracaudal plate (Fig., below).

3. **Testudo marginata**   *Marginated Tortoise*   92
   Greece and Sardinia only. Rather like *T. graeca* but shell usually strongly flared in adults. See text for younger animals.

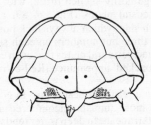

Herman's
often two supracaudals,
large scale on tip of tail

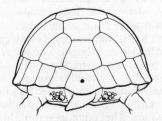

Spur-thighed
often one supracaudel,
spurs on thighs

Tortoises, back views

1

2

TERRAPINS   Plate 14
(× ½)

Tortoise-like animals usually found in or near water.

1. **Emys orbicularis**   *European Pond Terrapin*   93
Usually dark with yellowish spots and streaks.

2. **Mauremys caspica**   *Stripe-necked Terrapin*   93
Neck with obvious stripes.

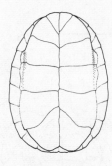
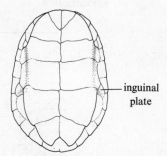

inguinal
plate

European Pond   Stripe-necked

Terrapins, undersides of shells

SEA TURTLES
(not to same scale)

1. Dermochelys coriacea *Leathery Turtle*   **95**
   Adult. Shell to 180 cm or more, skin-covered with five or
   seven prominent ridges.

2. Caretta caretta *Loggerhead Turtle*   **95**
   Subadult. Shell about 80 cm. See text and key (p. 89) for
   identification.

3. Lepidochelys kempii *Kemp's Ridley*   below
   Young animal. Shell about 30 cm. Adults do not occur in
   European waters. 'Saw-backed' appearance also found in
   young Loggerhead Turtles. See text and key for
   identification.

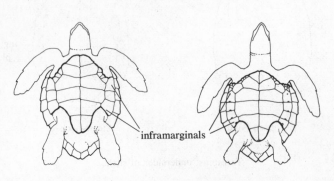

inframinals

Loggerhead   Kemp's Ridley

Sea Turtles, undersides

LEPIDOCHELYS KEMPII *Kemp's Ridley*   Fig., opposite
Range. Atlantic but rare in European waters; no certain records for
Mediterranean.
Identification. Carapace of adults up to 65 cm (sometimes more), but only
young specimens recorded from European waters. A small, very broad-
shelled turtle. Young have keeled vertebral plates that each end in a

projection giving a 'saw-backed' appearance. Look rather like young Loggerheads (*Caretta*); but shell distinctly wider, usually four infra-marginals on each side, and these have pores (Fig., opposite). Colour is not reddish but varies from blackish to brownish, grey, or olive, often with weak streaking.

Habits. Appears to be an essentially shallow water species that sometimes drifts across the Atlantic from Gulf of Mexico, where it breeds. Feeds principally on crabs.

Variation. Some in colour.

Similar Species. Loggerhead (p. 95) is superficially similar. Further south in the Atlantic, another Ridley, the Pacific Ridley (*Lepidochelys olivacea*) occurs, which can be recognised by having 6–9 costals on each side instead of 5. It has not been recorded from European waters.

CHELONIA MYDAS *Green Turtle*

Range. Very rare in European waters but records exist from Atlantic and Black and Mediterranean Seas. Has been said to breed in the Mediterranean. Also Indian and Pacific Oceans.

Identification. Carapace length of adults up to 140 cm. A large turtle with an oval shell; only four costal plates on each side (Fig., p. 89) and one pair of prefrontals on snout (Fig., below). Shell usually brown or olive, often with darker mottling, streaks or blotches. Scales on top of head have light edges.

Habits. Largely in warm, shallow water with a good growth of seaweed, but capable of long transoceanic migrations. Adults eat mainly plant material, but babies are largely carnivorous. Has been heavily exploited as food.

Variation. Some in colour.

Similar Species. Loggerhead (*Caretta*, p. 95) is sometimes mistaken for Green Turtle, but tends to be reddish-brown and has five (not four) costal plates on each side. See also Hawksbill (*Eretmochelys*, below).

ERETMOCHELYS IMBRICATA *Hawksbill Turtle*

Range. May occur in European waters but extremely rare. Found mainly in tropical areas of Atlantic, Pacific and Indian Oceans.

Identification. Carapace of adults up to 90 cm (sometimes more). A moderately small, turtle, usually easily distinguished from all others by the distinctly *overlapping* horny plates on its carapace. Old adults may lack this feature but can be separated from Green Turtles because they have two pairs (not one) of prefrontal scales on the snout, and a nuchal scale (Fig., p. 89) of which the front border is only about half the length of the hind one.

Habits. An essentially tropical turtle. Omnivorous, but takes mainly animal food. Is main source of tortoiseshell.

Variation. Considerable variation in shape: adults have narrower shells than young animals.

Similar Species. Old adults can be confused with Green Turtles (*Chelonia*, above)

Sea Turtles, snouts

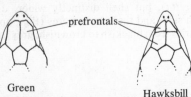

prefrontals

Green

Hawksbill

Lizards and Amphisbaenians –
Sauria and Amphisbaenia

Perhaps 3000 lizard species exist of which 51 occur in Europe. All these have scaly skins, relatively long tails and in most cases, closable eyelids and two pairs of legs. However, three more or less limbless species are found in the area covered by this book (for separation from snakes, see p. 183). Amphisbaenians of which there are about 150 species in all but only one in Europe, are also nearly all legless but differ from both snakes and limbless lizards in having ring-like grooves on their bodies.

Identification. Some of the features important for identifying lizards are shown in Fig., p. 103 and in the keys. Typical lizard head scaling is illustrated in Fig., p. 102. As with other groups, body proportions, colour and pattern are also helpful in confirming identifications. A hand lens (8× or 10×) is very useful for checking details of lizard scaling.

COUNTING BODY SCALES. Where these are all roughly the same size, a count is made round the body, midway between the fore and hind legs (or halfway between the head and vent in limbless species). If ventral scales are distinctly and abruptly larger than the others (as in lacertid lizards), ventral and dorsal scales are counted separately.

Ventral (belly) scales. The number of longitudinal rows of enlarged scales at midbody is counted. At the sides, any scale that is as long as the other ventral scales is included, even if it is narrower than the rest.

Dorsal scales. A count is made, in as nearly a straight transverse line as possible across the back from the outermost belly scale on one side to the outermost belly scale on the other.

Pattern. Some common features of lizard dorsal patterns, especially of lacertid lizards, are shown in Fig., below.

Mid-back of lizard showing common positions of stripes or rows of spots

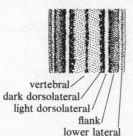

vertebral
dark dorsolateral
light dorsolateral
flank
lower lateral

SOME FEATURES TO CHECK WHEN IDENTIFYING LIZARDS

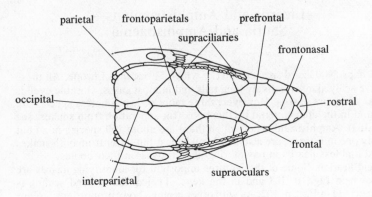

parietal · frontoparietals · supraciliaries · prefrontal · frontonasal · occipital · rostral · frontal · interparietal · supraoculars

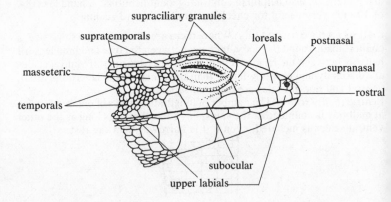

supraciliary granules · supratemporals · loreals · postnasal · masseteric · supranasal · temporals · rostral · subocular · upper labials

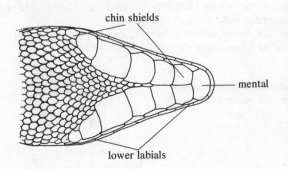

chin shields · mental · lower labials

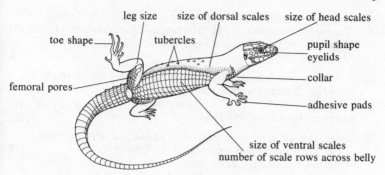

leg size size of dorsal scales size of head scales
toe shape tubercles pupil shape
eyelids
femoral pores collar
adhesive pads
size of ventral scales
number of scale rows across belly

Key to Lizards and Amphisbaenians

1. Worm-like, with regular ring-like grooves on body
   Blanus cinereus, Amphisbaenian (p. 182, Pl. 33)
   Not worm-like; if legless, then without ring-like grooves **2**

2. Pupil a vertical slit in bright light **3**
   Pupil not slit-shaped in bright light **5**

3. GECKOES
   Toes with flat adhesive pads **4**
   Toes without adhesive pads; strongly kinked (Fig., below)
   Cyrtodactylus kotschyi, Kotschy's Gecko (p. 110, Pl. 15)

4. Toes with flat adhesive pads only at tips (Fig., below); no
   tubercles on back
   Phyllodactylus europaeus, European Leaf-toed Gecko
   (p. 109, Pl. 15)
   Toes with undivided, flat adhesive pads along their whole
   length (Fig., below); claws only on third and fourth toes of
   each foot *Tarentola mauritanica*, Moorish Gecko (p. 108, Pl. 15)
   Toes with flat adhesive pads divided on lower surface, and
   not extending to toe tips (Fig., below)
   Hemidactylus turcicus, Turkish Gecko (p. 109, Pl. 15)

Kotschy's   European Leaf-toed   Moorish   Turkish
(side)   (underside)   (underside)   (underside, side)

Gecko toes

5. Body strongly flattened from side to side; eyes very bulging
Chamaeleo chamaeleon, Mediterranean Chameleon (p. 111, Pl. 16)
Body not strongly flattened from side to side, eyes not very
bulging   **6**

6. S. Balkans and Aegean islands only. Scales on head all small;
a large, flattened, rather spiny lizard
Agama stellio, Agama (p. 110, Pl. 16)
Scales on head relatively large   **7**

7. Scales on back small or, if large, then keeled and often pointed;
legs and femoral pores present (Fig., below)   **8**
Scales on back large, often more or less smooth and shiny;
legs sometimes absent or reduced; no femoral pores (Fig.,
below)   **19**

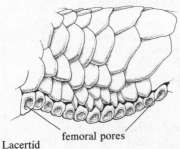 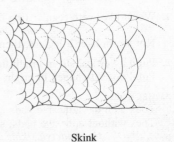

Lacertid   femoral pores   Skink

Lizard thighs from beneath

8. Well defined collar present (Fig., below)   **9**
No collar, or at most a poorly defined one; dorsal body scales
relatively large and keeled   **17**

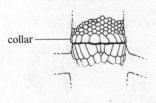 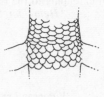

collar

collar present   collar absent

Lizard necks from beneath

9. Dorsal body scales large, larger than those on tail **10**
   Dorsal body scales small, smaller than those on tail **13**

10. ALGYROIDES
    Scales on back blunt, much larger than flank scales **11**
    Scales on back pointed, about the same size as flank scales **12**

11. E. Adriatic area. Back scales strongly keeled
    Algyroides nigropunctatus, Dalmatian Algyroides (p. 115, Pl. 18)
    Spain. Back scales flattish and feebly keeled
    Algyroides marchi, Spanish Algyroides (p. 118, Pl. 18)

12. Corsica and Sardinia. Very small; about 15–19 scales across
    mid-back.
    Algyroides fitzingeri, Pygmy Algyroides (p. 118, Pl. 18)
    S. Greece and Ionian islands. Not very small; 20 or more
    scales across mid-back.
    Algyroides moreoticus, Greek Algyroides (p. 118, Pl. 18)

13. Iberia, E. Romania and neighbouring USSR. No occipital
    scale (Fig., p. 102), subocular scale does not reach lip, or
    only very narrowly (Fig., below) **14**
    Occipital scale nearly always present, subocular reaches lip
    extensively **15**

14. E. Romania, neighbouring USSR. First upper labial scale
    well separated from nostril (Fig., below); belly scales in
    14–20 longitudinal rows *Eremias arguta*, Eremias (p. 122, Pl. 17)
    Iberia. First upper labial scale borders or is close to nostril
    (Fig., below); belly scales in ten (rarely eight) longitud-
    inal rows
    Acanthodactylus erythrurus, Spiny-footed Lizard (p. 122, Pl. 17)

subocular   first upper labial
    Eremias   Spiny-footed Lizard

15. Collar more or less smooth-edged (Fig., p. 106)
    Small Lacertas (p. 136)
    Collar strongly serrated (notched) **16**

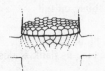
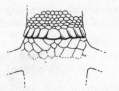

collar smooth-edged   collar serrated (notched)

Lacertid necks from beneath

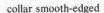

16. Large (7–21 cm from snout to vent), robust, belly scales very
strongly overlapping. Often green, at least on back or flanks.
Often two postnasals, and supratemporals large
Green Lizards (adults, p. 126)
As above, but small; often not green; frequently with characteristic pattern (Pl. 22). Typical baby lizard shape: very large
rounded head and big eyes   Green Lizards (juveniles, p. 126)
Small (up to 8 cm from snout to vent), often brown, with darker
flanks, often one postnasal. If green, then supratemporals
shallow (Fig., below)   Small Lacertas (p. 136)

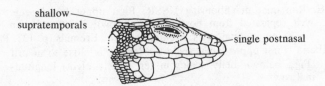

shallow
supratemporals

single postnasal

17. S. Balkans. Eye without obvious eyelids (touch eye to see
if it closes); first upper labial separated from nostril (Fig.,
p. 102)
Ophisops elegans, Snake-eyed Lizard (p. 119, Pl. 17)
S.W. Europe. Eye with normal eyelids; first upper labial
reaches nostril   **18**

18. PSAMMODROMUS
Adults less than 5.5 cm snout to vent, weak collar present,
scales on side of neck small and granular (Fig., p. 121),
Psammodromus hispanicus, Spanish Psammodromus
(p. 121, Pl. 17)
Adults up to 8.5 cm snout to vent, no collar, scales on
side of neck strongly overlapping and keeled (Fig., p. 121)
Psammodromus algirus, Large Psammodromus (p. 120, Pl. 17)

19. Legs absent, or only a minute hind pair **20**
   Two pairs of legs present, although these may be very small **22**

20. Balkans only. A prominent groove on either side of the body
   Ophisaurus apodus, European Glass Lizard (p. 175, Pl. 33)
   No groove on either side of the body **21**

21. Head blunt (viewed from above); 23 or more rows of scales
   round mid-body; over 20 cm when adult
   Anguis fragilis, Slow Worm (p. 175, Pl. 33)
   Greece only. Head pointed (viewed from above); 18 (occasionally 20) rows of scales round mid-body; rarely over
   20 cm. *Ophiomorus punctatissimus,* Greek Legless Skink
   (p. 181, Pl. 33)

22. S.E. Europe only. Diminutive; head and body less than 6 cm
   long. Eye without obvious eyelids and will not close if
   gently touched
   Ablepharus kitaibelii, Snake-eyed Skink (p. 178, Pl. 32)
   Head and body of adults over 6 cm long. Eye with normal
   lids **23**

23. CHALCIDES
   Snake-like; legs minute with only three toes on feet; 22–24
   scales round body
   Chalcides chalcides, Three-toed Skink (p. 180, Pl. 32)
   Thick-bodied; limbs not extremely small, with five toes;
   24–38 scales round body **24**

24. Spain and Portugal only. Loreal borders second labial scale
   (Fig., p. 179); 24–28 scales round body
   Chalcides bedriagai, Bedriaga's Skink (p. 180, Pl. 32)
   Sardinia, Malta, Sicily, Naples area, Greece and Crete
   Loreal borders second and third labial scales (Fig., p. 179);
   28–38 scales round body
   Chalcides ocellatus, Ocellated Skink (p. 179, Pl. 32)

Family GEKKONIDAE *Geckoes*

There are about 650 species of geckoes distributed throughout the warmer
parts of the world, only four of which reach Europe. Typically they are
small, plump lizards with large heads and eyes and a soft, granular skin
that may have scattered tubercles. In Europe geckoes differ from other
lizards in having a vertical pupil (most obvious in good light).

Most geckoes are basically nocturnal, although they may sometimes
be active by day, especially in temperate regions (e.g. Europe). Unlike

many other night-active animals, they hunt largely by sight – hence their very large eyes. These are usually covered by a transparent 'spectacle', as in snakes, and cannot be closed. In fact, geckoes have eyelids but in most species they are fused together and the spectacle develops as a very large window in the lower lid. Nearly all geckoes differ from most other lizards in having a voice which varies from a thin squeak in some small species to a strident bark in the 35 cm long *Gekko gecko* of S.E. Asia. Many geckoes are superlative climbers and, in addition to claws, have sophisticated adhesive pads on the toes. These are covered beneath by a mass of hairlike structures (setae) that frequently branch several times. It is the ends of these setae being brought into contact with minute crevices and irregularities that allows many geckoes to climb with ease on apparently smooth surfaces.

Many species enter buildings and hunt on the walls and even on ceilings. Like agamas and chameleons, geckoes can change colour quite rapidly, although this is mainly confined to lightening or darkening the basic pattern.

Most species lay hard-shelled eggs that are attached to the walls of crevices etc. Usually there are only two eggs to a clutch, sometimes only one.

Because they enter buildings etc., geckoes are often accidentally transported in cargo and may turn up a long way from their original range, especially in port areas.

TARENTOLA MAURITANICA *Moorish Gecko*   Pl. 15

Range. Mediterranean area, including islands, from Iberia east to Ionian islands, neighbouring parts of the mainland and Crete. Also Canaries and N. Africa   Map 50.

Identification. Up to about 15 cm including tail, but often smaller. A robust, plump gecko with a flattened body and head. Obvious, broad, adhesive pads are visible in the field and extend along length of toes, being widest near their tips (Fig., p. 103). Claws are present only on third and fourth toes of each foot. Body and tail have prominent tubercles giving a rather spiny appearance. Colour variable but usually brownish or brownish-grey with dark bands that are best developed on tail and in young animals. Regenerated tail is uniform and lacks tubercles.

Habits. Found mainly in warm, dry, lowland coastal areas but extends inland in some regions, especially Iberia. Often occurs on dry-stone walls, ruins, boulders, cliffs, wood piles and the outside walls and tiled roofs of buildings, which it enters. May be seen near lights, catching insects attracted to them. Frequently active at night, if temperature is above 15°C, but also diurnal, particularly in cooler parts of year. In some places it seems to take over the niche usually filled in Europe by rock-dwelling Small Lacertas. Climbs with great agility, even on overhanging rock-faces; body is kept close to surface and legs project sideways. Toes may

be curled upwards to protect adhesive pads when these are not in use.
Variation. Little in Europe.
Similar Species. Might possibly be confused with other geckoes.

HEMIDACTYLUS TURCICUS *Turkish Gecko* Pl. 15

Range. Mediterranean coastal area including islands. Also N. Africa and
S.W. Asia, east to India; introduced into parts of N. and central
America   Map 51.
Identification. Up to about 10 cm. A rather slender gecko with tubercles on
the back and tail and flat adhesive pads that do not extend right to the tips
of the toes (Fig., p. 103). Often pale and rather translucent, rarely so dark
and opaque as other European geckoes. Back usually marked with irregular blotches but tail banded, especially in young.
Habits. Mainly in warm, coastal areas including some very small islands.
Found on dry-stone walls, cliffs, caves, on boulders, rocky hillsides, tree
boles, between the leaves of *Agave* plants, and among their fallen remains,
among rubbish and in both empty and occupied houses. May catch insects
attracted to lights. Largely crepuscular and nocturnal but sometimes
active by day. Very fast and agile, an excellent climber, although sometimes occurs on the ground. Has mournful, mewing cry.
Variation. Some variation in colour. A striped population occurs on
Addaya Grande, near Minorca.
Similar Species. Other geckoes.

PHYLLODACTYLUS EUROPAEUS *European Leaf-toed Gecko* Pl. 15

Range. Largely confined to islands in the Tyrrhenian area: occurs on
Corsica and Sardinia, on islands off the coast of S.E. France and N.W.
Italy, and at one or two places on the Italian mainland. Also islands off the
coast of N. Tunisia   Map 52.
Identification. Adults up to about 8 cm including tail, but usually about
6 cm. The smallest European gecko and the only one without tubercles on
the back. Head broad and flat, body rather long so that limbs appear fairly
short; tail often swollen, especially when regenerated. Toes have flattened
adhesive pads only at their tips (Fig., p. 103). Colour rather variable: often
brownish or greyish with yellowish marbling or spotting, or may be
predominantly yellowish.
Habits. A rather secretive, mainly nocturnal gecko. Often found under
stones and under bark of dead trees and logs in degraded scrub habitats,
olive groves etc. Also on dry-stone walls and sometimes in outbuildings
but does not usually enter houses.
Variation. Some variation in colour.
Similar Species. Other geckoes.

CYRTODACTYLUS KOTSCHYI   *Kotschy's Gecko*   Pl. 15
Range. S. and E. Balkans, Ionian and Aegean islands, S. Crimea and S.E. Italy. Also S.W. Asia   Map 53.
Identification. Up to 10cm including tail. Has characteristic gecko shape but is rather slender with fairly slim tail and limbs – at a distance can look almost like a Small Lacerta. Tubercles present on back, and tail (if not regenerated); toes lack adhesive pads but have characteristic 'kinked' shape (Fig., p. 103). Colour variable: usually grey or grey-brown with dark, pale-edged, V-shaped cross bands. Some animals are more or less uniform. Underside often yellow.
Habits. Typically found in rather dry rocky or stony places: on ground among stones, on dry-stone walls, outsides of buildings, cliffs and sometimes tree-boles. Does not enter houses very often. Climbs less, and less high, than *Tarentola* (p. 108) and *Hemidactylus* (p. 109), but very agile in spite of having no adhesive pads. When disturbed, may run onto underside of rocks and cling on upside down, or may retreat into holes, or bases of bushes. Often at least partly nocturnal in summer, but regularly active by day in the cooler parts of the year, particularly in morning and evening. Often abundant where it occurs, and frequently encountered alongside Wall Lizards.
Variation. In Aegean islands, some variation in proportion, colour, details of scaling, size of tubercles etc.
Similar Species. None really similar but has superficial resemblance to other geckoes and to some Small Lacertas.

Family AGAMIDAE   *Agamas*

Agamid lizards are mainly confined to the warmer regions of Africa, Asia and Australia, being replaced in America, Madagascar and Fiji by the closely related Iguanids. There are about 280 species in the family, only one of which reaches Europe. This belongs to the genus *Agama* which is widely distributed in Africa and S.W. Asia. It contains plump, short-bodied lizards with thin tails, triangular heads and long legs; they have no very large scales on the head or belly. Agamas are capable of some colour change. Food consists mainly of insects but some vegetable matter, such as flowers and soft fruit is also taken. The European species lays clutches of about 6–8 eggs.

AGAMA STELLIO   *Agama*   Pl. 16
Range. Small colonies in Greece and the Greek islands (area round Thessaloniki, Corfu, Mykonos, Delos, Paros, Antiparos and Naxos). Also S.W. Asia and N.E. Africa   Map 54 and Fig., p. 113.
Identification. Adults up to about 30cm including tail. Unmistakable. A large, robust lizard with conspicuously flattened, relatively short body, rather flat triangular head, well-defined neck and fairly long legs and tail.

Noticeably spiny, particularly on neck, with transverse rows of tubercles on body that are especially well developed on flanks. Scales on head small. Colour variable (can change quite quickly): usually light or dark brown or grey, with a series of roughly diamond-shaped, often yellowish markings along middle of back. Tail may be conspicuously barred. Throat often dark flecked. Dominant males tend to be very brightly coloured.

Habits. A diurnal, sun-loving lizard found in a variety of dry habitats. Frequents walls, rocky hillsides and olive groves, where it climbs well both on trees and rocks. Hides in holes and crevices. Characteristically bobs head vertically. Often quite abundant where it occurs.

Variation. Considerable variation in colouring. Animals from Mykonos island usually have pale yellowish heads and unspotted throats.

Similar Species. Not likely to be confused with any other species.

Family **CHAMAELEONTIDAE** *Chameleons*

This family contains about 85 species, all rather similar to each other. Chameleons are slow-moving lizards that nearly all climb in bushes, trees and other vegetation. The headquarters of the family is in Africa and Madagascar, but a few species are found on islands in the Indian Ocean and in S.W. Asia and one just reaches Europe. Chameleons can change colour quite rapidly and are able to move each eye independently of the other. The body is flattened and leaf-shaped which, with ability to change colour, gives good camouflage. The toes are arranged so that the feet can grip twigs firmly and the tail is strongly prehensile. The mainly insect prey is caught on the sticky tongue which can be shot forwards for more than the length of the body. Accurate aim of the tongue depends on good sight and the eyes are large, bulging and capable of being turned forwards to give binocular vision. A few species give birth to living young, but the majority produce eggs (often 20–30 in the European species) that are laid in the ground.

CHAMAELEO CHAMAELEON *Mediterranean Chameleon* **Pl. 16**
Range. S. Iberia and Crete; possibly introduced elsewhere. Also Canaries, S.W. Asia, N. Africa   Map 55.
Identification. Adults up to about 30 cm, including tail, but usually smaller. Quite unmistakable. Slow movements, laterally flattened body, prehensile tail, and bulbous eyes that can be moved independently make this species unique in Europe. Colour very variable and capable of quite rapid changes: typically green but can be blackish, brown or whitish. May have two light bands along each flank, and some darker blotches. Often pale at night.
Habits. Nearly always found climbing in bushes, often in quite dry habitats. Usually moves slowly and catches prey with sticky extensible

I12

Plate 15   **GECKOES**
                        (× ⅔)

Soft-skinned lizards with large eyes and vertical pupils. All
four European species are agile climbers and often nocturnal.

1. Tarentola mauritanica   *Moorish Gecko*   **108**
Robust. Adhesive pads extend along whole length of toes
and are undivided beneath. Claws on third and fourth toes
only of each foot.

2. Hemidactylus turcicus   *Turkish Gecko*   **109**
Adhesive pads do not extend to toe-tips and are divided
beneath. Often pale brown above.

3. Phyllodactylus europaeus   *European Leaf-toed Gecko*   **109**
Tyrrhenian area only. Small. No tubercles on back. Adhesive
pads limited to toe-tips.

   3a. Animal with intact tail.
   3b. Animal with regenerated tail.

4. Cyrtodactylus kotschyi   *Kotschy's Gecko*   **110**
S.E. Europe. No adhesive pads, but toes characteristically
kinked.

Moorish   Turkish   European Leaf-toed   Kotschy's
(underside)   (underside, side)   (underside)   (side)

Gecko toes

AGAMA and CHAMELEON   Plate 16
(× ½)

1. **Agama stellio** *Agama*   110
   Isolated areas in Greece and Aegean. Spiny and rather
   flattened. Small scales on head and belly. Often bobs head.

2. **Chamaeleo chamaeleon** *Chameleon*   111
   Body flattened from side to side. Eyes bulging. Feet adapted
   for grasping.

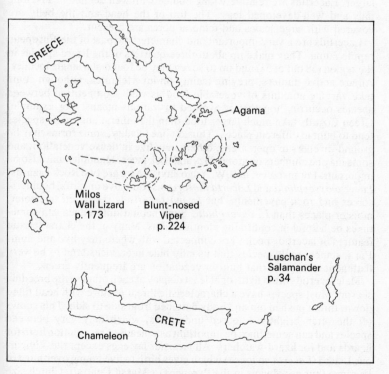

Some Aegean specialities

tongue. Only rarely descends to ground – for instance when depositing eggs. When disturbed, inflates itself with air, opens mouth and often becomes very dark.

Variation. No geographical trends recorded in Europe.

Similar Species. None.

Family **LACERTIDAE** *Lacertids or Typical Lizards*

There are about 180 species of lacertids. The family occurs throughout much of Europe, Africa and Asia. All its members are alert, active, diurnal lizards most of which measure less than 8 cm from snout to vent, although a few species, including the European Green Lizards (p. 126) grow much larger. Lacertids are relatively long-bodied with well defined heads, long tails and well-developed legs. The top of the head and the belly are covered with large scales and femoral pores are present.

Lacertids are a very important and characteristic part of the European reptile fauna. They make up about three quarters of the lizard species in the region (38 out of 51) and up to seven may be found at a single locality. All are active hunters, preying mainly on invertebrates, although some take varying amounts of vegetable food as well. Competition between species occurring together is avoided by various means. For example, Green Lizards take much larger food than the others, and many species tend to hunt in different places. Thus, at one locality, some forms may be ground-dwellers in open areas, others may live in dense vegetation, and some may be climbers on stone piles and rock faces. Humidity may also be important. For instance, in S.W. Yugoslavia, there are two Rock Lizards, *Lacerta oxycephala* and *Lacerta mosorensis*; both live on cliffs, boulders, screes and rock-pavements, but *L. mosorensis* is restricted to cooler, moister places than *L. oxycephala*. Such habitat differences can sometimes be helpful in confirming identifications. Many of the characteristic features of lacertid species are connected with where they live and hunt. For instance, rock species that usually hide in crevices tend to be very flattened, and forms that hunt in vegetation are frequently green.

Male lacertids often fight, or at least display at each other in the breeding season. Most species have a characteristic threat posture with head tilted down, throat pushed out and body flattened from side to side. This shows off the often brightly coloured underparts, which may vary between species and can sometimes be important as a means of recognition both for lizards and for lizard-watchers. All lacertids lay eggs except the Viviparous Lizard (*Lacerta vivipara*) which gives birth to live young over most of its range (but not always in the Pyrenees or Massif Central). Clutch size varies. In small species it is often 1–4 eggs but in larger forms the number is greater (up to 23 in some large Green Lizards). Some smaller lacertid species are also relatively large-brooded, e.g. *L. vivipara* produces up to 11 young and clutches can reach six or more in *L. monticola*, *Psammodromus algirus* and *Acanthodactylus erythrurus*. The time taken to hatch is rather variable but may be about six weeks in small species. The bigger lacertids are often long-lived: *L. lepida* has survived 20 years in captivity.

In general, male lacertids have bigger heads than females, shorter bodies and better developed femoral pores (Fig., below). Also, the base of the tail is often swollen in the breeding season. Young animals have relatively larger, more rounded heads, relatively larger eyes and shorter tails than their parents.

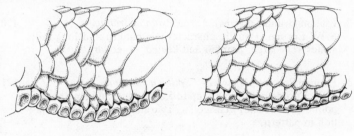

Male   Female

Lacertid lizards,
underside of thighs showing sexual difference in femoral pore size

ALGYROIDES NIGROPUNCTATUS *Dalmatian Algyroides* Pl. 18

Range. E. Adriatic coastal region, from Istria in north to N.W. Greece and Ionian islands in south   Map 56.

Identification. Adults up to 7 cm snout to vent; tail usually twice as long. A small, dark lizard about the size and build of a Wall Lizard but easily distinguished from these and other Small Lacertas by rough appearance of back scales and sombre colouring above. Back scales are large, blunt and strongly keeled, flank scales are much smaller. Typically dark grey-brown to reddish-brown above, often with scattered black spots. Adult males have intense blue throat and eye, and belly is orange to red, the colour often extending onto flanks.

Habits. Seen in a wide variety of habitats, but usually in degraded scrub, on hedges, walls, and bushes between fields and olive groves etc. A good climber. Most conspicuous when perched on pale walls, boulders etc., but also occurs commonly on tree-trunks and in bushes. Tends to prefer shady or partly shaded areas and is rather secretive. On Corfu, where there is no climbing Small Lacerta to do so, it enters towns and villages.

Variation. No obvious geographical trends recorded.

Plate 17   MISCELLANEOUS LACERTIDS

1. **Acanthodactylus erythrurus**   *Spiny-footed Lizard*   122
   Iberia only.

   > 1a. Adult: usually with some striping; no occipital scale
   > (Fig., p. 102); subocular narrowed (Fig., p. 105).
   > 1b. Juvenile: black with pale stripes; red tail.

2. **Psammodromus algirus**   *Large Psammodromus*   120
   S.W. Europe. Usually characteristic pattern and long tail;
   scales very large, pointed and keeled; no collar.

3. **Psammodromus hispanicus**   *Spanish Psammodromus*   121
   S.W. Europe only. Small (up to 5.5 cm snout to vent); scales
   pointed and keeled; weak collar. Two animals, showing variation in pattern.

4. **Eremias arguta**   *Eremias*   122
   Black Sea coastal area only. Robust. 14–20 rows of scales
   across belly.

5. **Ophisops elegans**   *Snake-Eyed Lizard*   119
   S. Balkans only. No collar. Eye without obvious eye-lids (will
   not close when touched).

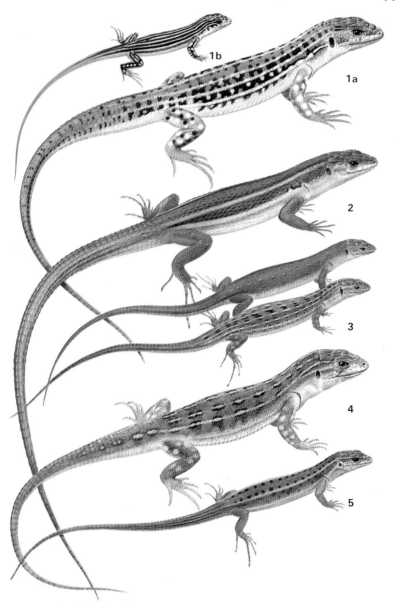

ALGYROIDES   Plate 18

Small lizards with large, keeled scales and a distinct collar.
Often found in or near semi-shaded places.

1. **Algyroides nigropunctatus** *Dalmatian Algyroides*   115
   E. Adriatic coast to Ionian islands. Back scales large, strongly
   keeled and blunt; flank scales granular. Male with orange
   to red belly and brilliant blue throat.

2. **Algyroides moreoticus** *Greek Algyroides*   118
   S. Greece and Ionian islands. Back and flank scales all large,
   strongly keeled and pointed.

   2a. Female: largely uniform.
   2b. Male: dark, light-spotted sides.

3. **Algyroides marchi** *Spanish Algyroides*   118
   S.E. Spain. Scales on back large, blunt and weakly keeled;
   flank scales granular.

4. **Algyroides fitzingeri** *Pygmy Algyroides*   118
   Corsica and Sardinia. Very small (about 4 cm snout to vent or
   less). Scales on back and flanks all strongly keeled and
   pointed.

Similar Species. *A. moreoticus* (below): only likely to be confused in Ionian islands; back and flank scales are all large, pointed and keeled.

ALGYROIDES MOREOTICUS *Greek Algyroides*   Pl. 18

Range. S. Greece (Peloponnese) and Ionian islands (Cephalonia, Ithaca, and Zante) Map 57.

Identification. Adults up to 5 cm from snout to vent, tail about 1½–2 times as long. A small lizard easily distinguished from Small Lacertas in its range by the large, pointed and keeled scales on its back and flanks. Typically dark brown or reddish-brown above; females more or less uniform, but males have darker flanks with light spots and a pale dorsolateral streak on each side. Underside is whitish, sometimes flushed yellowish-green, often with a few black spots.

Habits. A rather secretive, inconspicuous animal and, like other *Algyroides*, usually prefers semi-shaded situations. Quite often found on north-facing slopes and near water. Occurs in piles of brushwood, in hedge bottoms, among leaf litter at base of bushes etc. May occasionally be seen on tree-trunks and walls where it can be conspicuous, but these are not really typical habitats.

Variation. No obvious geographical trends recorded.

Similar Species. *A. nigropunctatus* (p. 115). Snake-eyed Lizard (*Ophisops elegans*, opposite) has no obvious eyelids (eye does not close if gently touched) and no collar.

ALGYROIDES FITZINGERI *Pygmy Algyroides*   Pl. 18

Range. Restricted to Corsica and Sardinia Map 58.

Identification. Adults usually less then 4 cm from snout to vent; tail about twice as long. A very small lizard, easily distinguished from young Small Lacertas occurring on Corsica and Sardinia by its uniform, often dark, colouring and coarse scaling on back and flanks (the scales being large, keeled, and pointed). Head and body rather flattened; tail long and often fairly stout. Normally dull brown, olive, or even blackish above, sometimes with a vertebral streak or scattered black spots. Underside of males may be yellowish or orange.

Habits. An inconspicuous species usually seen in or near degraded scrub habitats especially on rocky slopes. May also occur on dry-stone walls, and sometimes climbs in brushwood or on tree boles (particularly bases of oak and olive). Will hide under loose bark etc. and is like other *Algyroides* in preferring semi-shaded places. Normally found below 1100 m.

Variation. No obvious geographical trends recorded.

Similar Species. Not likely to be confused with any other species in range.

ALGYROIDES MARCHI *Spanish Algyroides*   Pl. 18

Range. Confined to S.E. Spain Map 59.

Identification. Adults usually less then 5 cm from snout to vent; tail about twice body-length. A rather small, flattened and lightly built lizard with large, weakly-keeled scales on back and small flank scales. Usually coffee-brown with dark flanks and, often, a dark vertebral streak. Underside whitish in females; breeding males have a yellow belly.

Habits. A shy but agile lizard which climbs well. Typically found in or near mature pine forest, often occurring along small fast-flowing streams. Clambers among boulders, tree-stumps, and fallen branches, hunting and hiding under loose bark, in cracks etc.

Variation. The throat of males is white in some populations, blue in others.

Similar Species. *Podarcis hispanica* (p. 142) has small scales on back. Unlike *A. marchi*, *Psammodromus* species (p. 120) have a weak collar, or none at all, flank scales about equal in size to back scales and different colouring.

Note. *Algyroides hidalgoi* Bosca, 1916 was described from the Sierra Guadarrama in central Spain, but has never been recorded since. Its existence was discounted until the discovery of *A. marchi* in 1958, by which time the original specimen had been lost. The description suggests that it may be most similar to *A. fitzingeri* (opposite). Although it is uncertain that *A. hidalgoi* really exists, it should be looked for in central Spain.

OPHISOPS ELEGANS *Snake-eyed Lizard*   Pl. 17

Range. Confined to small areas in S. Balkans: European Turkey, extreme N.E. Greece, small areas near Gulf of Corinth (?) and some N. Aegean islands (including Thasos). Outside Europe extends east to Iran and around Mediterranean to Libya; seven related species occur in dry steppe country of N. Africa, Middle East, and India   Map 60.

Identification. Usually under 5.5 cm from snout to vent; tail about twice body length. A small ground-dwelling lacertid easily identified in the hand by its eyes which lack obvious eyelids. Instead, the eye is

Snake-eyed Lizard

covered by a transparent 'spectacle' as in snakes, and cannot be closed (touch gently to check). Also distinguished from other Balkan lacertids by lack of collar. It has relatively large, keeled, overlapping body scales. Colour variable: often two pale, narrow stripes on each side, the upper one stronger and often bordered with black lines, spots or blotches. Flanks may be mottled, sometimes greenish; underside pale; tail often reddish. At close quarters has staring 'expression' produced by large eyes and over-hanging ridges above them.

Habits. A ground-dwelling lizard usually found on open arid plains, fields, and stony hillsides with sparse grass, crops, or low dense scrub. May occasionally occur on almost bare ground. Not fast but frequently dodges from plant to plant when pursued and may take refuge in dense vegetation or in crevices in the ground.

Variation. No obvious variation in Europe.

Similar Species. In S. Greece may possibly be confused with Greek Algyroides (*Algyroides moreoticus* p. 118), but *Ophisops* has distinctive eye and lacks collar.

PSAMMODROMUS ALGIRUS   *Large Psammodromus*   Pl. 17

Range. Iberia and a small adjoining area of Mediterranean France mainly west of the Rhône. Also N.W. Africa   Map 61.

Identification. Adults up to 7.5 cm, from snout to vent, rarely longer: tail two to three times body length. A moderately small, thick-necked lizard with a long thin, rather stiff, tail and no collar. Scales on back and flanks are large, flat and pointed with a prominent keel. They overlap strongly, as do the belly scales. Colour fairly constant: usually metallic brownish with two conspicuous white or yellowish stripes on each side, the upper ones bordered above by dark dorsolateral stripes. Flanks are often dark and there may be vague dark stripes on back. Some animals are almost uniform. Males often have one or more blue spots in the shoulder region. Underparts slightly iridescent – whitish or even tinged green. Breeding males have throat and sides of head orange, fading to yellow on chest. Babies are like adults, but tail is often orange.

Habits. Occurs from sea-level to over 1400 m in southern parts of range. A typical inhabitant of very dense bushy places, although it sometimes occurs in more open areas. Often found in degraded woodland, in under-growth in pine and *Eucalyptus* forest, and among very dense spiny shrubs, evergreen oak, heather, gorse, brambles and even prickly pear (*Opuntia*). Spends most of time around base of these plants hunting in leaf litter etc., but may climb in bushes and comes out regularly to bask, and sometimes makes excursions across more open areas. The most abundant lizard species in many parts of Iberia, but well-camouflaged and not always conspicuous. Squeaks when picked up. Tends to be replaced by *Acanthodactylus* and *P. hispanicus* in more open areas.

Variation. Some minor variation in pattern.

Similar Species. *P. hispanicus* (opposite), is much smaller, has weak collar and usually different colouring; also, scales on the sides of the neck are granular, not keeled. Spanish Algyroides (*Algyroides marchi*, p. 118), which is restricted to a small area of S.E. Spain, is smaller and flatter with no light stripes or reddish tail, large scales on back are blunt and scales on flanks are small.

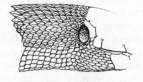 

Large
scales keeled

Spanish
scales granular

Psammodromus, scales on sides of necks

PSAMMODROMUS HISPANICUS *Spanish Psammodromus* Pl. 17
Range. Iberia, French Mediterranean coast and lower Rhône Valley. One or two closely related species occur in N.W. Africa Map 62.
Identification. Adults usually less than 5 cm, from snout to vent; tail 1½–2 times body length. A diminutive lizard with rather large, keeled and overlapping scales, and a weak collar. Colouring very variable: grey, metallic brown, olive or ochre above. Some animals quite uniform, others have pattern of white stripes that are often broken up into rows of short streaks with blackish bars or spots between the rows. Sometimes a pair of often faint stripes on each side and black, or black and white, spots on back. Belly whitish or reddish.
Habits. A lowland ground lizard found mainly in dry open situations, especially in areas with a patchy covering of low (often under 30 cm) dense, bushy plants. Here it is inconspicuous and usually glimpsed dodging from one clump to another. It also occurs in more barren habitats such as sand flats and gravel plains with very sparse vegetation, and in this environment often runs quite long distances at high speed. Takes refuge in the twiggy base of plants or buries itself among their roots, or sometimes under stones. Squeaks when picked up, and also more or less spontaneously in breeding season.
Variation. Individuals from E. Spain and France often have finer scaling than those from W. Iberia. In these animals the hind feet tend to be larger and the subocular scale is usually separated from the lip.
Similar Species. *Psammodromus algirus* (see opposite). Because *P. hispanicus* is so small, the large, overlapping scales are not always obvious and it is possible to mistake it for a young Small Lacerta. However, the weak collar of *P. hispanicus* (it is only well developed at the sides) will identify it, and if a lens is available, overlapping body-scales and keeling on underside of toes can be seen.

ACANTHODACTYLUS ERYTHRURUS *Spiny-footed Lizard* **Pl. 17**
Range. Iberia, except north. Also found in N.W. Africa. About 18 related
species occur across the arid and desert regions of N. Africa and the
Middle East to N.W. India; many of these have fringes of spiny scales on
the toes which act like snow shoes when the lizards cross loose sand. They
are not obvious in the European species   Map 63.
Identification. Adults up to 7.5 cm, from snout to vent; tail often twice as
long as body. A moderate-sized, ground dwelling lacertid with an alert,
upright stance. Head rather large, with pointed snout; tail very slender,
but strongly swollen at base in adult males. Adults very variable in

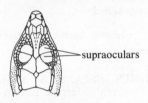

Spiny-footed Lizard

pattern, but usually grey, brown, or coppery with up to ten pale, often
weak, streaks, or rows of spots, separated by dark bars or blotches,
especially on flanks. Some animals almost uniform. Underparts white.
Juveniles very characteristic: black with white or yellowish stripes and
bright red tail and thighs. The red may persist in older animals. Easily
identified in the hand by lack of occipital scale, only two large supraoculars over each eye (Fig., above), and obvious groove on top of snout.
Habits. A ground-dwelling lizard often found in open sandy areas with
sparse, shrubby vegetation, or occasionally in completely bare places,
such as beaches or even rocky plains. Not particularly shy, but when
disturbed may run long distances in a series of straight bursts with the tail
raised in a gentle curve. Often skulks around base of open bushes but,
when really pressed, retreats into spiny vegetation or into a short burrow.
Has characteristic resting position with forequarters raised. Juveniles
often wave tail slowly when basking in the open.
Variation. Some variation in dorsal pattern, both within populations and
from place to place.
Similar Species. Unlikely to be confused with any other European lizard.

EREMIAS ARGUTA *Eremias*   **Pl. 17**
Range. E. Romania (Danube Delta area) and S.W. USSR   Map 64.
Identification. Up to about 7.5 cm snout to vent, tail as long or a little
longer. A quite plump lizard with a pointed snout and rather prominent
nostrils. Distinguished from all other east European lacertids by high

number of belly scales (14–20 across mid-belly), and by the subocular which does not reach the lip (Fig., p. 105). Usually grey or greyish brown, often with a pattern of ocelli or light, often broken stripes and irregular dark markings; sides may be darker than back.

Habits. Typically found in dry open places with some vegetation: steppe-type country, consolidated sand-dunes etc.

Variation. Considerable variation in pattern.

Similar Species. None in Europe.

Plate 19   GREEN LIZARDS 1: Sand Lizard

Lacerta agilis *Sand Lizard*   **134**
Not Greece, Italy, or most of Iberia. Medium-sized, robust
lizard with deep, rounded head, serrated collar and overlapping belly scales. *Scales on vertebral region usually narrowed, rarely green*. Colouring very variable. See **Pl. 22** for
juvenile.

a. Typical male: green flanks, brighter in breeding season.

b. Typical female.

c. Largely green male: frequent pattern in Romanian area.

d. Female with continuous, pale, vertebral streak: frequent
pattern in W. Balkans.

e. 'Red-backed' phase: not found in England.

19

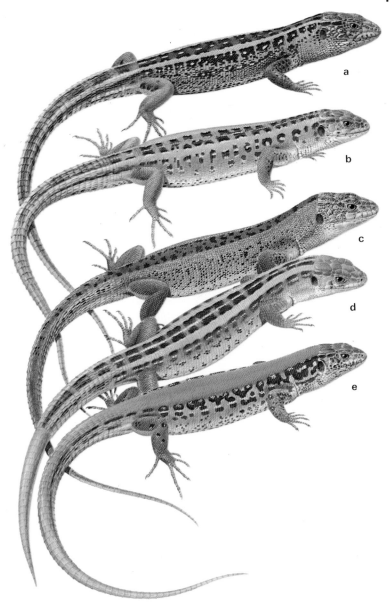

a

b

c

d

e

20

1

2a

2b

GREEN LIZARDS 2:   **Plate 20**

Ocellated and Schreiber's Green Lizard
(× ⅔)

Large, robust lizards with serrated collars. Confined to S.W. Europe. See **Pl. 22** for juveniles. Other Green Lizards in north of this area: *Lacerta agilis* (**Pl. 19**) and *L. viridis* (**Pl. 21**).

1. **Lacerta lepida**   *Ocellated Lizard*   **130**
   Iberia and S. France etc. Adults very large (up to 20 cm or more from snout to vent). Often blue spots on flanks. Occipital scale nearly always wider than hind edge of frontal scale (Fig., p. 127). Male (illustrated) has more massive head than female.

2. **Lacerta schreiberi**   *Schreiber's Green Lizard*   **131**
   Hilly areas of W. and central Iberia. Up to about 12 cm snout to vent. Occipital scale narrower than in *L. lepida*. In north of range often distinguishable from *L. viridis* by having eight (not usually six) rows of large, often dark-spotted scales across belly.

   2a. Male: usually green with black spots.
   2b. Female: often brownish with dark blotches.

Five of the seven species in this group occur in Europe, where they form a characteristic and spectacular part of the fauna. All are moderate to large lizards, mature animals being at least 7 cm from snout to vent and, in one species, sometimes over 20 cm. Adults, especially males, are often brilliant green above, or at least on the flanks, and frequently have a greenish or yellow belly (never strong red, orange or blue as in many Small Lacertas). Babies tend to be very characteristically patterned (see Pl. 22) with whitish bellies.

Green Lizards are all very robust with a deep, powerful head (usually much larger in males than females), the collar is deeply serrated and the belly scales overlap strongly and have angled sides (Fig., below). The small dorsal scales are strongly keeled (except in *L. lepida*), the supratemporal scales are quite deep and there are usually two postnasal scales (some exceptions, especially in *L. agilis*).

Green Lizards tend to live in and around dense vegetation, but also occasionally occur in other habitats. At any locality only one, two or very rarely three species are likely to be present. Like many Small Lacertas, Green Lizards tend to be highly variable but they are usually quite easily identified, except in parts of the Balkans.

collar ——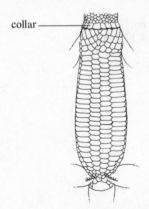

Green Lizard
(collar serrated; belly scales
overlapping, with angled sides)

Sharp-snouted Rock Lizard
(collar smooth-edged; belly scales
scarcely overlapping,
with straight sides)

Undersides of lacertid lizards, contrasting types

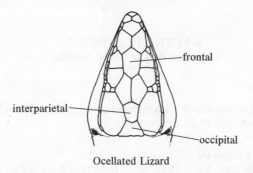

Ocellated Lizard

Key to Green Lizards (*Lacerta* part I)

1. Iberia, S. France, and N.W. Italy only. Occipital scale very big, nearly always wider than hind margin of frontal (Fig., above); dorsal body scales smooth or feebly keeled, belly scales in eight or ten rows. Often obvious blue spots on flanks of adults. Very large, may grow to over 20 cm from snout to vent

     Lacerta lepida, Ocellated Lizard (p. 130, Pl. 20 and 22)

   Occipital scale much narrower than frontal; dorsal body scales strongly keeled, belly scales in six or eight rows. Rarely much over 16 cm snout to vent, usually less   **2**

2. Usually under 9 cm (rarely to 10 cm) from snout to vent. A stocky lizard with relatively short legs and tail, and relatively stubby feet. If green pigment is present, it is usually confined to flanks and rarely extends to mid-line. Usually a band of distinctly narrow scales along centre of back. Rostral scale small, does not normally enter nostril; often only one post-nasal scale   *Lacerta agilis*, Sand Lizard (p. 134, Pl. 19 and 22)

   Adults over 9 cm from snout to vent, often considerably so. More elegant than *L. agilis*, usually with longer tail and longer, narrower toes. If green pigment present, then usually on back, and may cover whole body. Scales on centre of back not, or only slightly, narrowed. Rostral enters nostril in many cases; often two postnasal scales   **3**

3. W., N.W., and central Iberia only. Eight rows of belly scales; occipital scale often distinctly broader than inter-parietal (especially in adults). Belly spotted with black in males and some females; no obvious light spots on top of head. Never well-defined, narrow light stripes in

Plate 21   GREEN LIZARDS 3:
                Green and Balkan Green Lizards
                        (× ⅔)

Large, robust lizards with serrated collars. Absent from most
of Iberia. See **Pl. 22** for juveniles.

1. Lacerta trilineata *Balkan Green Lizard*   131
Balkans only. Up to 16 cm snout to vent or more. Often difficult to distinguish from *L. viridis* (see text) but frequently
bigger. Young and subadult animals may have characteristic
pattern of three or five narrow light stripes (**Pl. 22**).

   1a. Male: large head.
   1b. Nearly mature female.

2. Lacerta viridis *Green Lizard*   132
Usually under 13 cm snout to vent. Mostly green or brown.
Some animals, especially young, have *two* or *four* narrow
light stripes.

   2a. Male: large head.
   2b. Female.

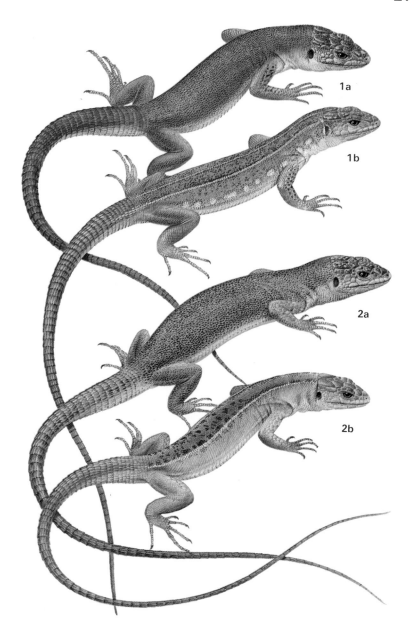

1a

1b

2a

2b

GREEN LIZARDS: Juveniles Plate 22

Young Green Lizards often have distinctive patterns. They can be distinguished from adult Small Lacertas by their typical juvenile shape (large rounded head, large eyes). As in adults, the collar is serrated and the belly scales overlap strongly.

1. **Lacerta lepida** *Ocellated Lizard* 130
   Iberia and S. France etc. Light, often dark-edged ocelli all over, or uniform. Occipital scale as wide as hind margin of frontal (Fig., p. 127).

2. **Lacerta schreiberi** *Schreiber's Green Lizard* 131
   W. and central Iberia. Light, dark-edged ocelli or bars on flanks only.

3. **Lacerta viridis** *Green Lizard* 131
   Not most of Iberia. Either fairly uniform, or with *two* or *four* narrow pale stripes.

4. **Lacerta trilineata** *Balkan Green Lizard* 132
   Often rather dark: fairly uniform, or with *three* or *five* narrow pale stripes, or with dark spots on midback.

5. **Lacerta agilis** *Sand Lizard* 134
   Often weaker version of adult pattern, but not green. Ocelli frequently present.

pattern. Babies have light, black-edged ocelli or bars on flanks

Lacerta schreiberi, Schreiber's Green Lizard (p. 131, Pl. 20 and 22)
Many areas, but only the north of Iberia. In N. Iberia, separated from *L. schreiberi* by following characters: usually six rows of belly-scales (rarely eight); occipital scale often narrower than interparietal; belly rarely spotted with black; light spots often present on top of head. Sometimes well defined narrow light stripes in pattern. Babies without black-edged ocelli or bars

Most areas: *Lacerta viridis*, Green Lizard (opposite, Pl. 21 and 22)
Balkans: *Lacerta viridis*, Green Lizard or
Lacerta trilineata, Balkan Green Lizard (p. 132, Pl. 21 and 22)

LACERTA LEPIDA   *Ocellated Lizard*   **Pls. 20 and 22**
Range. Iberia, S. France, extreme N.W. Italy. Also N.W. Africa   Map 65.
Identification. Up to 20 cm or more, from snout to vent; tail 1½ to over twice body length. Huge animals with total lengths of over 80 cm have been reported. The largest European lacertid, and size alone will identify most adults; males also have characteristic massive, broad head. Frequently, prominent blue spots present on flanks. Dorsal ground colour typically green, but sometimes grey or brownish, especially on head and tail. Ground colour usually overlaid with black stippling that may often form a bold pattern of interconnected rosettes. Belly and throat usually yellowish or greenish.

Subadults might be confused with adult *L. schreiberi* or *L. viridis*, but tend to be flatter-bodied with different patterning. Also the occipital scale is much wider (Fig., p. 127), dorsal scales are smaller (over 60 across mid-body) and not strongly keeled, and there are often ten rows of belly scales. Juveniles usually green with characteristic pattern of typically black-edged, white ocelli all over body; tail often reddish. Exceptional animals without ocelli can be recognised by scale characters.

Habits. Found in wide variety of arable and uncultivated habitats from sea-level up to 1000 m in Alps and Pyrenees, and 2100 m in S. Spain, although less common at higher altitudes. Prefers rather dry, bushy places such as open woodland and scrub, old olive groves and vineyards, road banks etc., but sometimes found on more open rocky or sandy areas. Often very noisy as it crashes through undergrowth. Usually takes refuge in bushes (often thorns), stone piles, dry-stone walls, rabbit burrows etc. Largely a ground lizard, but climbs well on rocks and even in trees. Feeds mainly on large insects, but also robs birds' nests in spring and occasionally takes other vertebrates (lizards and small mammals including even baby rabbits) and fruit.

Variation. Some animals from S.E. Spain are almost uniformly greyish

with weak blue spots on flanks, and whitish belly. Babies in this area may also be fairly uniform.
Similar Species. *L. schreiberi* (below); *L. viridis* (below).

LACERTA SCHREIBERI *Schreiber's Green Lizard* Pls. 20 and 22
Range. N.W., W., and central Iberia Map 66.
Identification. Usually less than 12 cm, from snout to vent; tail about twice body length. Typical Green Lizard shape. Males predominantly green with small black spots which tend to be larger on the back than flanks. Females more variable: usually brownish, although often with some green on back; may have white ocelli on flanks, and back and sides often marked with irregular, and usually large, black spots; these may be dense and arranged in three bands separated by unmarked areas. Belly heavily spotted with black in males; not or less so in many females. Throat blue in males and some females. Young strikingly marked on flanks with white or yellow, black-edged spots or bars; tail often orange or yellow.
Habits. Found mainly in comparatively moist, hilly areas and may reach altitudes of 1800 m, but not in north of range. Lives in typical Green Lizard habitats with lots of bushy vegetation such as overgrown roadside walls and banks, bramble patches etc. Where it occurs with *L. lepida* the latter is generally found in drier more open areas than *L. schreiberi*. In N.W. Spain, *L. viridis* sometimes replaces *L. schreiberi* at higher altitudes.
Variation. Females are rather variable. No subspecies are recognised.
Similar Species. *L. lepida* (opposite). *L. viridis* (below), from which *L. schreiberi* can be distinguished in N.W. Spain by following characters: distinctive range of patterns; never clearly defined, narrow, white stripes on back; males with no light spots on top of head; often dark-spotted belly; eight rows of belly scales; occipital scale often distinctly wider than interparietal.

LACERTA VIRIDIS *Green Lizard* Pls. 21 and 22
Range. Much of Europe: in north to Channel Islands, Rhine Valley (also isolated places in N. Germany and perhaps Poland), Czechoslovakia and S.W. Russia; extends south to N. Spain, Sicily, and Greece. Not known from many Mediterranean islands, but present on Euboa, Thasos, Samothrace, Corfu, and Elba Map 67.
Identification. Adults up to about 13 cm, from snout to vent; tail often twice body length or more. A large, elegant lizard with a rather short, deep head, especially in males. Males usually almost entirely green with a fine black stippling above and a darker, light-spotted head. Females very variable: sometimes uniform green or brown, or with blotches; frequently two or four narrow light stripes on body, which may be edged with black lines or spots. More rarely, both sexes have a bold irregular pattern

of interconnected black blotches. Belly yellowish, nearly always without black spots. Throat blue in mature males and some females. Young often beige, uniform or with a few light spots (without black edge) on flanks, or else with two or four narrow light lines.

Habits. Typically found in and around dense bushy vegetation with good exposure to sun, for instance in open woods, hedgerows, wood and field edges, bramble thickets, on overgrown embankments etc. In south of range, often confined to damp situations or to highland areas, where it may occur up to 1800 m. In north sometimes found in heath areas, provided bushes etc. are present. *L. viridis* hunts and climbs in dense vegetation but comes out to bask, especially in morning and evening. When pressed it takes refuge in bushes, rodent burrows, crevices etc. Food consists mainly of invertebrates, but fruit and eggs and young of small birds are also eaten at times.

Variation. Populations vary slightly in body size, colouring and minor details of scaling; a number of subspecies have been described. In Sicily and extreme S. Italy breeding males have blue on the sides of head. E. Balkan males are often uniform greeen, without black stippling, and in this region the hind legs and tail may often be uniform brownish. All-black specimens are known.

Similar Species. All other members of the Green Lizard group, but especially *L. trilineata* (below) and *L. schreiberi* (p. 131). Overlaps extensively with *L. agilis* (p. 134) but usually easily distinguished.

LACERTA TRILINEATA *Balkan Green Lizard*   **Pls. 21 and 22**
Range. S. and E. Balkans, E. Adriatic coast to Istria; Greek islands   Map 68.

Identification. Adults up to 16 cm or more, from snout to vent; tail twice body length or more. A large Green Lizard with the typical 'jizz' of the group. Like a big version of *L. viridis*. Adults fairly uniform bright green (more rarely yellow or brownish) generally with fine black stippling on back. Babies and subadults usually brown (babies frequently dark), often with three or five narrow light stripes or a few light spots on flanks, sometimes, or dark spots on midback. *L. trilineata* is closely related to *L. viridis* and the two can be very difficult to distinguish at times, especially as both are very variable. The table opposite, together with remarks under **Variation**, should identify most individuals.

In places where identification of adults is difficult, it helps to look out for striped babies or subadults; animals with three or five stripes (including one in the centre of back, which may be faint) are *L. trilineata*, those with two or four are *L. viridis*.

Habits. Similar to *L. viridis* but tends to be found in warmer, drier places and is largely confined to areas with a Mediterranean climate. Where the

	L. trilineata	*L. viridis*
Rows of belly scales	Usually eight	Usually six
Head of male	Snout typically narrow, but back of head broad. Top of head often with light vermiculations	Snout typically blunter and back of head not very wide. Top of head often with pattern of light spots

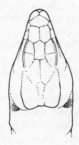 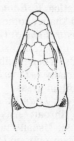

Supraciliary granules	Often a continuous line of granules	Often few, or even none
Temporal scales	Numerous (often over 20, sometimes less)	Fewer (usually less than 20, often less than 15)
Rostral scale reaches nostril	Yes	Often not
Throat in males	Often yellow	Often blue

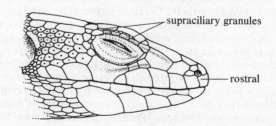

supraciliary granules

rostral

Green Lizards in S.E. Europe, features to check.
Temporal scales are dotted.

two species occur close together, *L. trilineata* is often replaced by *L. viridis* in moister habitats and at higher altitudes. But *L. trilineata* sometimes lives near water (e.g. in E. Romania and parts of S. Greece) and may even be seen swimming across shallow streams and ditches. Like *L. viridis* it is often found in bushy places, although the young may live in clumps of low herbage. Also occurs on overgrown sand-dunes, dry-stone walls, and in ruins on arable land.

Variation. *E. Romania and N.E. Bulgaria*: tends to have typical *L. viridis* head shape; some blue on side of neck in males.

Central and S. Greece: sometimes very like *L. viridis*; adults may have blue throat, and sometimes six rows of belly scales and rather few temporals. Young with three or five stripes should identify most populations, especially as *L. viridis,* if really present in south, is restricted to a few high mountain areas.

Greek Islands: rather variable; sometimes quite small, often with a blue throat; may be brownish (Milos) or yellowish (Andros and Tinos). Usually no identification problem as *L. viridis* is largely absent (present only on Corfu, Euboa, Thasos, and Samothrace).

It is probable that *L. trilineata* and *L. viridis* may occasionally hybridise. All black *L. trilineata* occur occasionally.

Similar Species. *Lacerta viridis* (p. 131).

LACERTA AGILIS *Sand Lizard*   **Pl. 19 and 22**
Range. Most of Europe north to S. and N.W. England and S. Scandinavia, but rare or absent from parts of W. and S. France, and from Italy, S. Balkans and most of Iberia. Also eastwards to central Asia   Map 69.
Identification. Most adults up to about 9 cm, from snout to vent, but usually smaller and rarely larger; tail about 1¼–1⅔ times body length. A short-legged, stocky lizard with a very short deep head (especially in males) and usually a distinct band of narrowed scales along the mid-back. Not very like other Green Lizards in build and, with experience, easily distinguished from them. Colouring extremely variable; usually a dark band or series of marks along centre of back that is often complex and may contain darker blotches, a light central streak (often broken up) and light spots. In most animals ocelli, dark spots, or mottlings are present on sides but these are separated from back band by an unmarked area. Males have green, yellow-green, or greenish flanks (very intense when breeding) and some may be almost entirely green, except for a dullish central band. Less commonly they have large ocelli all over the back. Females are grey or brown, rarely with green, and the dark central band tends to be broken up. Some specimens of both sexes have entire back brown or reddish (this colour variety is not found in England.) Underparts whitish, greenish or yellow, often with dark spots which are usually very numerous in males.

Young often have weaker version of adult markings (but no green) and frequently prominent ocelli as well, especially on flanks.

Habits. Occurs up to 2000m in south, but a lowland species in north of range. Largely a ground lizard and, in many areas, lives in a wide variety of fairly dry habitats such as field-edges, road embankments, grassland with occasional low bushes, rough grazing, hedgerows, and even in crops and gardens. In north, and in England, it is more restricted and is usually found on coastal sand-dunes with some plant cover and on sandy heaths (hence its English name). On heathland it tends to live in dense old heather stands, in which it clambers and is very inconspicuous. In southern regions, it is partly montane and occurs in dry upland pastures. Like other Green Lizards it is usually found in or near at least some dense vegetation, but this is usually lower and sometimes less extensive than that required by the other species.

Variation. Colouring very variable (see above and Pl. 19). All-black specimens are known and so are females with green flanks. A number of subspecies have been described mainly on the basis of pattern and minor details of scaling, especially that of the snout. W. Balkan specimens often have continuous white streak on midline. Males from Romania etc. may be almost entirely green.

Similar Species. Sometimes confused with *L. vivipara* (p. 137), *L. viridis* (see p. 127 and p. 131).

There are 24 species of lizard in Europe that are best called Small Lacertas. They were originally all placed in the genus *Lacerta* but really fall into two distinct groups: Wall Lizards (*Podarcis*) and the rest, i.e. Rock, Meadow and Viviparous Lizards (*Lacerta* part II). The two groups differ in many important internal features but are often almost impossible to tell apart when alive so it is easier to treat them as a single unit.

Small Lacertas are one of the most difficult groups to identify with certainty. Many of the species are closely related and very similar in appearance; at the same time they show great variation both within populations and from area to area. This makes it very difficult to produce a single key that will identify them all. Fortunately many of them have restricted ranges and usually not more than a few occur at any one locality. It is therefore easiest to deal with them by regions.

The regions used are as follows:

Area

1	North, western and central Europe	p. 137
2	Iberia and the Pyrenean region	p. 140
3	Balearic Islands	p. 146
4	Corsica and Sardinia	p. 151
5	Italy, Sicily and Malta	p. 153
6	East Adriatic coastal area	p. 159
7	South-eastern Europe	p. 166

Their boundaries are shown in the figure below.

Small Lacertas, areas used in this book for identification

Identification within these areas often depends on examining details of scaling, colour and pattern. The terms used for these features are shown in Figs., pp. 101, 102 and 103.

N.B. Most Small Lacertas may have conspicuous blue or black spots on the outer row of belly scales, or both. Because it is so widespread, this feature is not very helpful in identification and has usually been omitted from the species texts. In the descriptions, *streak* and *stripe* may include not only continuous marks but also rows of spots or blotches.

Small Lacertas are a group where 'jizz' is very helpful in identifying difficult animals, once sufficient experience is gained, but do not place too much reliance on it at first.

SMALL LACERTAS AREA 1: North, western and central Europe

Although this area includes the greater part of Europe, it contains only two native Small Lacertas: *Lacerta vivipara* and *Podarcis muralis*. These are the two most widespread members of the group and they are also likely to be encountered in other mainland areas (2, 5, 6 and 7). The only other native lacertids in area 1 are members of the Green Lizard group (p. 126) and two species of *Psammodromus* (p. 120) in a limited area of S. France.

N.B. *Podarcis sicula* (p. 155) has been introduced onto Ile d'If off the southern coast of France, and perhaps in Provence.

Key

Scarcely flattened, short-legged and small-headed. Collar distinctly serrated; scaling coarse (25–37 dorsal scales across mid-body). Granules between supraoculars and supraciliaries absent or at most four on each side; 5–15 femoral pores present   *Lacerta vivipara*, Viviparous Lizard (below, Pl. 23)

Rather flattened, legs fairly long and head quite large. Collar not usually distinctly serrated; scaling fine (42–75 dorsal scales across mid-body). Granules between supraoculars and supraciliaries extensive – usually at least five on each side; 13–27 femoral pores

     Podarcis muralis, Common Wall Lizard (p. 138, Pl. 23)

LACERTA VIVIPARA *Viviparous Lizard*   **Pl. 23**
Range. Most of Europe including Arctic Scandinavia, Britain and Ireland, but absent from the Mediterranean area: extends south to N. Spain, N. Italy and S. Yugoslavia and Bulgaria. Also through much of N. Asia to Pacific coast   Map 70.
Identification. Up to about 6.5 cm snout to vent; tail 1¼–2 times as long. A long-bodied, almost unflattened, short-legged lizard with a small, rather

rounded head and thick neck and tail. Collar distinctly serrated and back scales very coarse and usually keeled, only 25–37 across mid-back. (See key, p. 137, for other distinctive features.) Pattern very variable: most animals basically brown but may be grey or olive. Females usually have dark sides and vertebral stripe, often a number of light streaks (especially dorsolateral ones) and sometimes scattered light or dark spots or ocelli. Ocelli are frequently better developed in males, which often lack a continuous vertebral stripe. Underside with many dark spots in most males and in some females. Throat whitish or bluish; belly white, yellow, orange, or red. Young very dark, almost blackish-bronze.

Habits. Essentially a ground-dwelling lizard, although it may climb occasionally, especially in vegetation. Requires a fairly humid environment. Typically found among grass or other dense herbaceous plants. In the south of its range, where it is often montane (up to 3000m in Alps), it is largely confined to moist places: alpine meadows, moist ditches, marshes, edges of damp woods, rice fields etc. In the north, it is more widespread, being found in open woods, field-edges, heaths, bogs, grassland and sand-dunes, on sea-cliffs, hedge-banks and railway embankments and even in gardens. *L. vivipara* usually gives birth to fully formed young, although in the Pyrenees and Massif Centrale it sometimes lays eggs.

Variation. Great variation in pattern even within populations. Occasional individuals are yellow, greenish or black. Some animals are fairly uniform, others very heavily striped or ocellated.

Similar Species. *L. praticola* (p. 168). *P. muralis* (below) is flatter with (in each sex) a larger head and longer legs (see key, p. 137, for further differences). *L. agilis* (p. 134), even when young, is more robust with a larger, deeper head, usually a vertebral band of narrow scales, greater overlap of ventrals and a different range of patterns.

PODARCIS MURALIS *Common Wall Lizard*   Pl. 23

Range. Mainland Europe north to France, S. Belgium and S. Netherlands, Rhine Valley, Czechoslovakia and Romania, and south to central Spain, S. Italy and S. Balkans. Occurs on islands off Atlantic coast of Spain and France (including Channel islands) and islands in the Ligurian Sea. Also N.W. Asia Minor   Map 71.

Identification. Up to about 7.5cm snout to vent, but usually smaller, tail 1⅔–2¼ times as long. A small, often rather flattened Wall Lizard, usually with a smooth-edged collar and lightly keeled scales. Very variable in pattern and, for identification outside area I, see **Variation** and regional keys. Most individuals are brownish or grey (occasionally tinged green) often with conspicuous black and white bars on sides of tail. Females usually have dark flanks, sometimes pale dorsolateral streaks, which are best developed on the neck, and often a dark vertebral stripe or series of spots; this is nearly always better developed than the dark dorsolateral stripes, if any. The vertebral stripe may be replaced or accompanied by dark spots or the back may be unmarked. Males are sometimes similar but pattern is typically more complex: sides are often light spotted and back is more boldly marked. Reticulated animals may occur. Ground colour of belly may be whitish or pale buff, but often with at least some red, pink or orange, especially in males. Throat is usually whitish or cream with rusty markings and typically has a variable amount of black pigment which often extends on to belly as well and is best developed in males. Juveniles more or less like females but tail is sometimes light grey.

Habits. Widespread over most of its range, but restricted to sheltered sunny localities in the north, and often to mountainous areas in the southern part of its distribution, where it may occur at over 2000 m. Typically found in much drier, less grassy habitats than *L. vivipara*, but in south often encountered in rather humid, semi-shaded places. Typically a climbing species seen on field and garden walls, parapets, rock-faces, boulders and even on tree trunks. Southern populations often exist alongside more specialised climbing species (*P. hispanica* p. 142, various Rock Lizards) and here *P. muralis* climbs less high and on less precipitous surfaces, often occurring on overgrown screes, path sides, road banks, cliff bases, and sunny slopes in woods. In general, this species is very active, alert, and usually more adventurous and opportunistic than its relatives. More than any other Small Lacerta, it occurs near human habitations.

Variation. Considerable variation in pattern, even within populations; blackish or nearly uniform specimens occur occasionally, and belly can be yellowish. Tendency in several areas for increase in size and in amount of dark pigmentation, and for development of green on back: these colour changes may be largely confined to males, or affect both sexes. Principal regional variations are as follows:

Atlantic coast and islands off Spain and France. Tend to be large with bold markings (sometimes reticulated); some Spanish populations have green-backed males.

French Riviera. Some but not all populations have small, almost uniform individuals with few dark markings.

N. Italy and sporadic areas in N. Balkans. Again tend to be large and heavily marked; usually brown backed.

W. Italy, south to Naples. In north, variable but often very dark and males with bright green backs: further south both sexes and young extremely dark, with ground colour frequently reduced to yellow-green spots on back. More normal animals occur in mountains.

Ligurian islands. Generally like W. Italian animals. Back colour, degree of darkening and sexual differences vary from island to island. Dark back markings often form cross bands.

S. Italy. Somewhat *L. vivipara*-like with rounded head and tendency to serrated collar.

Similar Species. Females can look superficially like *L. vivipara* (p. 137).

More similar Small Lacertas exist in areas 2, 5, 6, and 7: see relevant keys and descriptions.

SMALL LACERTAS AREA 2: Iberia and the Pyrenean region

In this area there are six Small Lacertas of which three are endemic (*Lacerta monticola*, *Podarcis hispanica* and *P. bocagei*), one is introduced (*P. sicula*) and two are very widespread elsewhere in Europe (*Lacerta vivipara* and *Podarcis muralis*). The northern half of the area is one of the most difficult regions for positively identifying Small Lacertas, because it contains four very variable species that can often look alike. Other Lacertids found in Iberia comprise Green Lizards (p. 126), *Acanthodactylus* (p. 122), *Algyroides marchi* (p. 118), and two species of *Psammodromus* (p. 120).

Key

1. Northern mountains etc. Collar serrated, granules between supraoculars and supraciliaries few or absent, (0–4) dorsal scales coarse (25–37 across body) and usually keeled
   Lacerta vivipara, Viviparous Lizard (p. 137, Pl. 23)
   Collar not distinctly serrated, granules between supra-oculars and supraciliaries five or more, dorsal scales finer, usually more than 40 across body   **2**

2. Almeria area only. Fairly large; adults often 6 cm or more from snout to vent; often green backed; underside whitish or with greenish tinge, unspotted. Scales on back between hind legs usually distinctly keeled
   Podarcis sicula, Italian Wall Lizard (p. 155, Pl. 27)
   All parts of Iberia. In Almeria area, usually less than 6 cm from snout to vent, not green-backed, belly may be white, buff, pink or red, throat often with small black spots. Scales on back between hind legs not clearly keeled   **3**

3. N.B. Because of the great variation within species, the rest of the key will not identify all animals with certainty, so check species texts carefully.
   High mountains of N., W. and central Iberia (usually above 1100 m – Map 72). Underside frequently green or yellow-green
   Lacerta monticola, Iberian Rock Lizard (p. 141, Pl. 24)
   Mountains of N. and central Iberia etc. Atlantic coast and France (Map 71). Belly whitish, buff, pink or red; throat whitish with at least some dark *blotches* and rusty markings Fig., p. 146. If present, vertebral stripe is usually better developed than dark dorsolateral stripes or series of marks
   Podarcis muralis, Common Wall Lizard (p. 138, Pl. 23)

Widespread. Belly whitish, buff, pink, red, yellow or orange; throat often with *well-defined, small spots*, especially at sides Fig., p. 146. If present, vertebral stripe is usually weaker than dorsolateral stripes or series of marks (exceptions frequent in northeast and east)   **4**

4. Widespread. Belly whitish, buff, pink or red (occasionally yellow); back usually brown or grey. In N.W. Spain and N. Portugal, typically quite small and flattened
        Podarcis hispanica, Iberian Wall Lizard (p. 142, Pl. 24)
Extreme N.W. Spain and N. Portugal (Map 74). Belly usually whitish, yellow, salmon or orange; back may be green in males. More robust and less flattened than *P. hispanica* within range; throat and belly tends to be more heavily spotted   *Podarcis bocagei*, Bocage's Wall Lizard (p. 143, Pl. 24)

LACERTA MONTICOLA   *Iberian Rock Lizard*   **Pl. 24**
Range. Only in mountains of N., W. and central Iberia   Map 72.
Identification. Up to 7.5 cm snout to vent, tail about twice as long. A small to medium sized, rather robust Small Lacerta, often with a distinctive green underside. Pattern varies: sometimes a vertebral streak or double series of bold spots on midback. Males sometimes green above. Young have blue tail. A very variable species that is most likely to be confused with *Podarcis muralis*, but, if present, *green underside is diagnostic*. Some animals, especially young, have whitish bellies and are more difficult to identify with certainty. Considerable regional variation exists.
   Pyrenees. Following combination of features separates it from *P. muralis*: underside unspotted, sides dark but markings on back very weak or absent; rostral scale meets frontonasal (Fig., p. 142), supranasal contacts loreal (Fig., below).

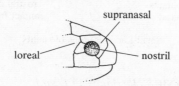

   Cantabrians (one of the most difficult areas). May look very like *P. muralis* but little or no spotting on underside, some males green above; rows of granules between supraoculars and supraciliaries frequently complete (often incomplete in *P. muralis*).
   Central Spain. Differs from *P. muralis* in usually unspotted underside, males sometimes green above; rostral usually contacts frontonasal scale.

Central Portugal. No *P. muralis* present. Rather like central Spanish populations but belly may have slight pink flush and heavy spotting; rostral often does not contact frontonasal scale.

Where they occur with *L. monticola, P. hispanica* and *P. bocagei* are smaller and more delicately built, lack green bellies and usually have dark dorsolateral stripes or series of spots better developed than vertebral stripe, if any.

Habits. Limited to a few mountainous areas and not usually seen below 1100 m (higher in south). Often found near or above tree-line in a variety of sometimes rather damp habitats: screes, large boulders, rocky hillsides with pine, heather and juniper scrub, in and around boulder-filled stream beds etc. A very cold-resistant lizard, restricted to areas where winters are long and summers often interrupted by rain, fog and even snow. Usually occurs at higher altitudes than *Podarcis* species, although may sometimes be found with *P. muralis*, in which case the latter usually climbs less than *L. monticola*.

Variation. See above.

Similar Species. *Podarcis muralis* (p. 138): as well as differences listed above, *L. monticola* usually has flatter, shinier back scales.

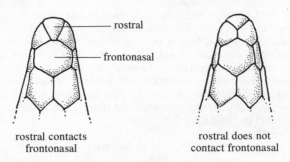

rostral contacts
frontonasal

rostral does not
contact frontonasal

Small Lacertas, tops of snouts

PODARCIS HISPANICA *Iberian Wall Lizard*   **Pl. 24**
Range. Iberia and the W. Mediterranean coastal area of France. Also N.W. Africa   Map 73.
Identification. Up to about 6.5 cm snout to vent but usually less, tail about twice as long. A rather small, delicately-built, often flat Wall Lizard; typically with a fairly pointed snout, brown or greyish ground colour and very variable pattern. Belly usually whitish, buff, pinkish or red (occasionally yellow) and throat pale often with small clearly-defined spots, especially at sides (Fig., p. 146).

Pattern often basically striped: in most areas dark vertebral streak absent or weaker than the dark dorsolateral streaks or series of marks (exceptions in northeast and east). Almost unmarked animals exist (mainly in east) and others have plain backs (particularly in south). Typically, females have strong regular stripes while males are more spotted and blotched. Males may be reticulated especially in northwest. Young may have blue tail.

The only Small Lacerta over most of the southern half of Iberia; *P. sicula* also occurs, but only near Almeria.

Habits. Found up to 1800 m in south of range. Usually a climbing species encountered on rocks, road-cuttings, walls, parapets, outcrops, and even occasionally on trees. Often replaced in less precipitous habitats by other lacertids (*Acanthodactylus*, *Psammodromus*, other *Podarcis* etc.). Where they are found together, *P. muralis* may climb less than *P. hispanica* and can be found on overgrown screes, road banks etc. Ecological separation of these two forms is often complex and other factors are involved: *P. muralis* tends to predominate at higher altitudes, in moister places and near human habitations.

Variation. Great variation in colouring and some in adult size and proportions.

Similar Species. *Podarcis muralis* (p. 138) sometimes has strong vertebral stripe (in most cases stronger than dark dorsolateral stripes or series of spots), usually blotched or heavily marked throat and often orange red belly; it is less delicately built than *P. hispanica*. *P. bocagei* (below); *L. monticola* (p. 141).

PODARCIS BOCAGEI *Bocage's Wall Lizard* **Pl. 24**
Range. Extreme N.W. Spain and N. Portugal, perhaps also neighbouring areas, especially to the south Map 74.
Identification. Up to 6.5 cm snout to vent, tail about twice as long. Very closely related to *P. hispanica* and only recently distinguished from it. Features in which *P. bocagei* differs from *P. hispanica* vary from locality to locality but it is usually possible to distinguish *P. bocagei* by 'jizz' where both species occur. Generally *P. bocagei* is more robust and less flattened than *P. hispanica*; back is often green in males; belly frequently yellow, salmon or orange (otherwise whitish) and flanks may be yellowish; spotting on underside often quite strong; females not as strongly striped as in *P. hispanica*.
Habits. Generally like *P. hispanica* but does not climb as much and is usually found in less precipitous habitats.
Variation. Very variable in colour and pattern. Some populations on islands off the coast of Spain have heavy spotting on underside. Dark dorsolateral streaks are sometimes close together.
Similar Species. *P. hispanica* (above).

Plate 23   SMALL LACERTAS 1:

Viviparous Lizard and Common Wall Lizard

The only two Small Lacertas native to N., W. and central
Europe; they also occur in many other continental areas.

1. **Lacerta vivipara**   *Viviparous Lizard*   137
   Small head and short legs. Serrated collar. Few supraciliary
   granules (see Fig., p. 102). Pattern very variable: often
   striped; no blue on flanks or belly scales.

   1a. Baby: very dark colouring.
   1b. Male.
   1c, 1d. Females: head and legs smaller than male.
   1e. Underside of breeding male: colour varies.

2. **Podarcis muralis**   *Common Wall Lizard*   138
   Head and limbs larger than in *L. vivipara* of the same sex.
   Collar more or less smooth. More supraciliary granules. Pat-
   tern very variable.

   2a. Male: widespread pattern.
   2b. Female: widespread pattern.
   2c. Male: more heavily marked animal.
   2d. Male: Rome area. Heavy markings and greenish
   ground colour. N.W. Italian and Ligurian island animals
   are rather similar but often have weaker dark markings and
   ground colour is not always green.
   2e. Breeding male: underside of weakly marked animal.
   2f. Breeding male: underside of W. Italian animal.

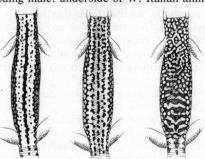

Common Wall Lizard, some variations
in back pattern.

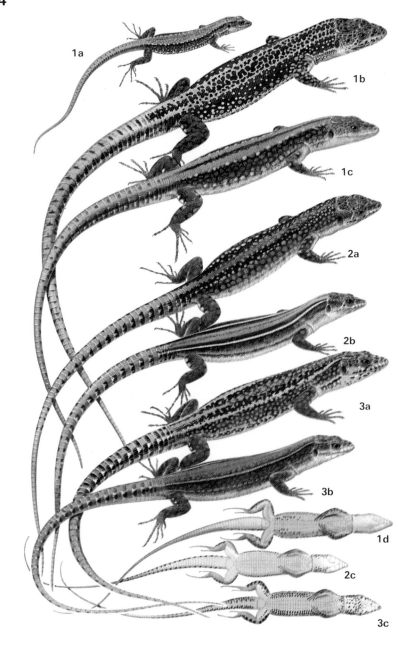

SMALL LACERTAS 2:   **Plate 24**
Iberia and Pyrenean region

See also *Lacerta vivipara* (**Pl. 23**, Pyrenees and Cantabrians etc.); *Podarcis muralis* (**Pl. 23**, France, N. and central Spain); *P. sicula* (**Pl. 27**, Almeria area only). Other Lacertids present: *L. agilis* (**Pl. 19**), *L. lepida*, *L. schreiberi* (**Pl. 20**); *L. viridis* (**Pl. 21**); *Acanthodactylus erythrurus*, *Psammodromus hispanicus*, *P. algirus* (**Pl. 17**); *Algyroides marchi* (**Pl. 18**).

N. Iberia, especially the north-west, is one of the most confusing areas for Small Lacertas because most species are highly variable, so check texts carefully.

1. **Lacerta monticola**   *Iberian Rock Lizard*   **141**
High mountains of N., W. and central Iberia only. Very variable but underside often green or yellow-green.

  1a. Young: blue tail (also found in some *P. hispanica*).
  1b. Male: back often bright green (not in Pyrenees).
  1c. Female: a common pattern in many areas (e.g. Cantabrians).
  1d. Underside of breeding male.

2. **Podarcis hispanica**   *Iberian Wall Lizard*   **142**
Iberia and west Mediterranean France. Often flattened and delicately built. Pattern highly variable. Unlike many *P. muralis*, dark dorsolateral stripe often stronger than vertebral one (if any). Throat pale, often with *small* spots.

  2a. Male.
  2b. Female.
  2c. Underside of breeding male.

3. **Podarcis bocagei**   *Bocage's Wall Lizard*   **143**
N.W. Spain and N. Portugal. Like *P. hispanica* but more robust. Back sometimes green in males; flanks may be yellowish and belly yellow, salmon or orange.

  3a. Male.
  3b. Female
  3c. Underside of breeding male.

Iberian Wall Lizard
often at least some well
defined spots

Common Wall Lizard
usually blotches or heavier
markings

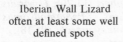

Wall Lizards, throat patterns

SMALL LACERTAS AREA 3: Balearic Islands

Small Lacertas of the Balearics are potentially confusing: the two endemic species (*Podarcis lilfordi* and *P. pityusensis*) have many often well differentiated island populations and over 45 subspecies have been recognised. The situation is further complicated by the presence of two introduced species (*P. sicula* and *Lacerta perspicillata*). However, distribution is very helpful in identification as most islands have only one or two species as follows:

Ibiza, Formentera and nearby small islands: *P. pityusensis* only
Majorca: *P. lilfordi* and *P. pityusensis*
Minorca: *P. lilfordi, P. sicula* and *L. perspicillata*
Small islands near Majorca and Minorca: *P. lilfordi* (*P. pityusensis* on Las Isoletas, near Majorca)

It is not impossible that some of these lizards may eventually be introduced to further islands. No other lacertids occur in the Balearics.

Key
Colour descriptions refer mainly to the larger islands and do not cover all variations.

1. Minorca only. Ten rows of scales across belly; lower eyelid with
large 'window'
Lacerta perspicillata, Moroccan Rock Lizard (opposite, Pl. 25)
Six (rarely eight) rows of scales across belly; lower eyelid without
large window   2

2. Minorca only. Back scales between hind limbs (and on upper
surface of lower hind leg) clearly keeled; scaling fairly fine
(60–75 across mid-back, rarely more). Underside whitish or

greenish without dark marks. Dorsal pattern variable; often boldly reticulated, or sides reticulated and back with an irregular vertebral streak; some individuals may be fairly uniform. Light dorsolateral streaks often not clear, or broken up   *Podarcis sicula*, Italian Wall Lizard (p. 155, Pl. 27)

Minorca, Majorca and nearby islands. Back scales between hind limbs (and on upper surface of lower hind leg) smooth; scaling often very fine (70–90 across mid-back, rarely fewer). Underside whitish, reddish, yellow, blue or black; throat often with dark markings. Dorsal pattern variable, not boldly reticulated; a pair of lightish dorsolateral stripes frequently distinct, often enclosing three dark streaks or rows of spots; some individuals may have very weak pattern. Some populations very dark

Podarcis lilfordi, Lilford's Wall Lizard (p. 150, Pl. 25)

Ibiza, Formentera, nearby islands and parts of Majorca. Back scales between hind limbs (and on upper surface of lower hind leg) often feebly keeled; scaling rather coarse (usually fewer than 70 scales across mid back, rarely more). Underside whitish or brightly coloured; throat sometimes with dark marks. Dorsal pattern variable; a pair of light dorsolateral streaks frequently distinct, often enclosing three dark streaks or rows of spots. Some populations dark

Podarcis pityusensis, Ibiza Wall Lizard (p. 150, Pl. 25)

LACERTA PERSPICILLATA *Moroccan Rock Lizard*   Pl. 25

Range. In Europe only Minorca (introduced). Occurs naturally in N.W. Africa: mainly in the mountains of Morocco but also on coast of Algeria   Map 75.

Identification. Adults only about 5 cm from snout to vent, tail up to about 1⅔ times body length. A small, rather flattened, Rock Lizard. May be more or less uniform olive with bronzy gloss, or green or blue-green, especially on the tail. Some individuals have small dark markings or even an extensive black reticulation; animals with two broad pale stripes exist. Underside bluish or whitish. Easily distinguished from other European Small Lacertas by combination of completely transparent 'window' in

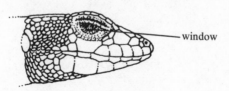

window

Moroccan Rock Lizard

Plate 25   **SMALL LACERTAS 3:**

Balearic Islands

Only other Lacertid present is *Podarcis sicula* (**Pl. 27**).

1. **Podarcis lilfordi**   *Lilford's Wall Lizard*   150
   Majorca, Minorca and nearby small islands. Highly variable
   in pattern. Scales very fine and smooth. Often dark spots on
   throat. *P. sicula* on Minorca has clearly keeled dorsal scales
   between hind legs and no dark spots on throat.

   1a. Melanistic animal.
   1b. Green-backed animal.

2. **Podarcis pityusensis**   *Ibiza Wall Lizard*   150
   Ibiza, Formentera and nearby islands, introduced into
   Majorca. Highly variable in pattern. Most easily separated
   from *P. lilfordi* by usually coarser scaling.

3. **Lacerta perspicillata**   *Moroccan Rock Lizard*   147
   Minorca only. Ten rows of scales across belly. 'Window' in
   lower eye-lid. Pattern often reticulated (3a), uniform (3b),
   or with two broad stripes.

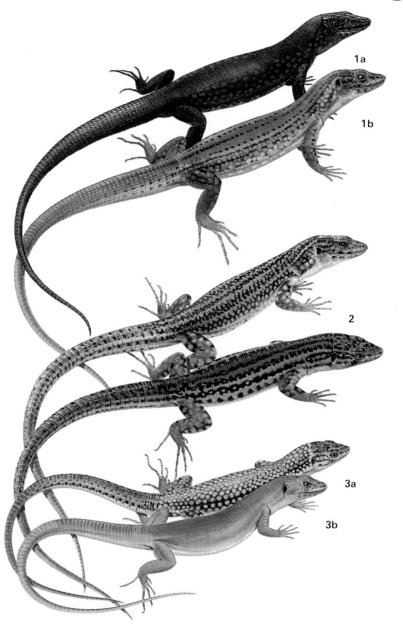

1a

1b

2

3a

3b

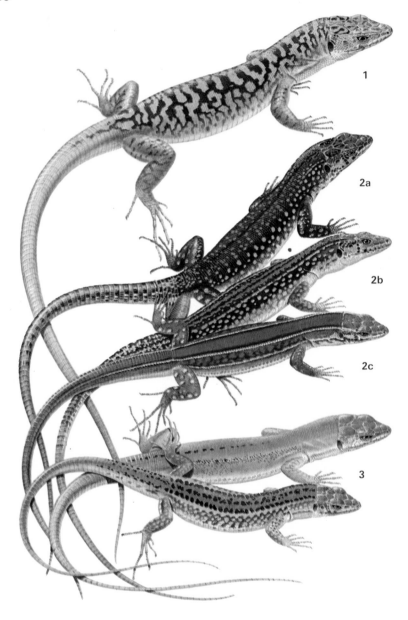

SMALL LACERTAS 4:   Plate 26
Corsica and Sardinia

Podarcis sicula (**Pl. 27**) also present; only other lacertid found
is *Algyroides fitzingeri* (**Pl. 18**). *P. sicula* differs from most
individuals of the other Small Lacertas in usually having
distinct keeling on the back scales between the hind legs and
no dark spots on throat (see key, p. 151, and texts for other
differences).

1. **Lacerta bedriagae**   *Bedriaga's Rock Lizard*   152
Body flattened. Usually reticulated.

2. **Podarcis tiliguerta**   *Tyrrhenian Wall Lizard*   153
Body not obviously flattened. Often striped, but highly variable.

    2a. Male: reticulated.
    2b. Male: striped.
    2c. Female.

SMALL LACERTAS 5:
Malta

3. **Podarcis filfolensis**   *Maltese Wall Lizard*   158
Malta and nearby islands. Only lacertid in the area; highly
variable.

lower eye-lid (Fig., p. 147) and ten (not six or eight) rows of large scales across belly.

Habits. An agile, climbing lizard, usually seen on and around rock-faces, walls, cliffs, large boulders etc., often near water. Frequently enters towns and may also be encountered on the boles of trees. Tail rather fragile and often regenerated.

Variation. Some variation in pattern (see above).

Similar Species. No really similar species within range.

PODARCIS LILFORDI *Lilford's Wall Lizard*   Pl. 25

Range. Balearics only: Majorca, Minorca and nearby rocks and islets   Map 76.

Identification. Up to 8 cm snout to vent (tail may be 1¾ times as long) but usually smaller. A rather robust Small Lacerta with very fine, smooth scaling (70–90 scales across mid-back, rarely fewer). In many populations, most animals are brownish or greenish above, often with lightish dorso-lateral streaks between which are three dark, often broken, stripes. Sides are sometimes reticulated. Some individuals have only a very faint pattern. Underside whitish, yellow or reddish, often with some dark marks, especially on throat. Tail of babies may be blue-green.

Habits. Mainly confined to small, rocky islets without much vegetation, but colonies do occur on the large islands as well. Usually ground dwelling, although does climb to some extent. A very tough lizard able to tolerate extremely hostile environments; it often eats a relatively high proportion of vegetable food.

Variation. Some island populations vary greatly in size, shape and colouring. Maximum snout to vent length ranges from under 6 cm to 8 cm. Members of some populations are fairly slender but most are stout with a rather pointed head, a thick (often 'turnip-shaped') tail and shortish legs. Melanistic populations are common, being black, bluish, or dark brown above and often largely blue or more rarely black beneath. Other variants in dorsal colouring occur: e.g. the back can be light brown or bright green and the tail of adults may be greenish.

Similar Species. Most likely to be confused with *P. pityusensis* (below) and perhaps *P. sicula* (p. 155 and Key, p. 146).

PODARCIS PITYUSENSIS *Ibiza Wall Lizard*   Pl. 25

Range. Balearics only: Ibiza, Formentera and nearby small islands. Also introduced to Majorca (e.g. Palma and some islets – Las Isoletas)   Map 77.

Identification. *Ibiza.* Up to 7 cm snout to vent but usually smaller (tail may be about twice length of body). A robust, rather short-headed, un-flattened Small Lacerta with relatively coarse, usually very slightly keeled scales (typically under 70 across mid-body, rarely up to 75). Most animals are green on back, although brown and grey ones occur. Lightish dorsolateral stripes usually well defined, and there are often three dark streaks or rows of spots between these. Underside whitish grey, yellow, orange or pink. Throat and sometimes belly may be spotted.

Formentera. Generally similar but up to 8cm snout to vent, green on back often brighter and more extensive and belly is greenish, often with some yellow or red towards tail.

Habits. A widespread, versatile Wall Lizard often found near human habitation on garden and field walls, ruins etc., but also in scrub areas and even in more barren country. Small-island populations may exist on almost bare rock with very little vegetation.

Variation. Small-island populations are extremely varied. Adult size ranges from slightly over 6cm snout to vent, to 9cm. Members of many populations are extremely robust but on some islands they are rather slender. Some are coloured more or less like large-island forms, others are light brown and a number tend to be melanistic with black, dark brown or bluish back and often a bluish belly. Dorsal pattern is frequently broken up so that dark stripes and light dorsolateral stripes are no longer clear. In some cases the flanks are brightly coloured (e.g. blue or orange).

Similar Species. Most likely to be confused with *P. lilfordi* (opposite).

SMALL LACERTAS   AREA 4: Corsica and Sardinia

The large Mediterranean islands of Corsica and Sardinia have only two endemic Small Lacertas: *Lacerta bedriagae* and *Podarcis tiliguerta*. A third, more widespread species, *P. sicula*, also occurs. The only other lacertid is *Algyroides fitzingeri* (p. 118) easily distinguished by its small size, coarse scales and usually sombre colouring.

Key

> Distinctly flattened; supratemporal scales not clearly turned down onto side of head. Back scales between hind legs unkeeled, more or less flat. Underside greyish, yellowish, green or red, often with dark markings especially on throat, or completely dark. Upperside rarely striped, usually boldly reticulated, sometimes spotted
>> *Lacerta bedriagae*, Bedriaga's Rock Lizard (p. 152, Pl. 26)
> Not distinctly flattened; supratemporal scales clearly turned down onto side of head in adults. Back scales between hind legs usually not or only lightly keeled, unflattened. Underside whitish, yellow, orange, salmon or red, typically with dark spots, especially on throat. Upperside often striped: light

dorsolateral streak or row of spots usually visible. Dark dorsolateral streak or series of spots is better developed than dark vertebral streak (if present)

Podarcis tiliguerta, Tyrrhenian Wall Lizard (opposite, Pl. 26)

Not distinctly flattened, supratemporal scales turned down onto side of head in adults. Back scales between hind legs usually distinctly keeled, unflattened. Underside pale without clear spots, although throat may be grey. If striped, dark dorsolateral streak or row of spots is less well developed than vertebral streak

Podarcis sicula, Italian Wall Lizard (p. 155, Pl. 27)

LACERTA BEDRIAGAE *Bedriaga's Rock Lizard* Pl. 26
Range. Corsica and Sardinia only Map 78.

Identification. Up to about 8 cm from snout to vent; tail about 1½ to twice this length. A medium-sized, distinctly flattened lizard with pointed snout and often bulging cheeks. Back scales flattish and unkeeled and supratemporal scales not clearly turned down onto side of head. Above usually greenish, yellow-green, brownish or greyish, with black or dark brown markings that often form a reticulation. This may be so extensive that the lizard is very dark with small light spots of ground colour, or so reduced that the lizard is almost unmarked. Neck, forepart of back and sides sometimes overlaid with brownish tinge. Very rarely, an animal may have some tendency to striping. Underparts greyish, yellowish, greenish, reddish or red; often with some dark marks especially on throat; in dark-backed individuals belly is also dark. Young are like adults but tail frequently a bright blue-green.

Habits. Largely a mountain lizard usually found from 600 m to over 2000 m but in N. Sardinia is known to occur on coast. *L. bedriagae* is essentially a climbing species most often seen on rocks and stony surfaces in a wide variety of habitats such as cliffs, screes, dry-stone walls rocky hillsides, boulders in scrub, light woods, heathland, edges of streams and even bare rock pavement.

Variation. Because it is restricted mainly to high ground, this species is broken up into a series of isolated populations. These tend to differ in colour and pattern and there is also considerable variation in these features within populations. Sardinian animals tend to be delicately built.

Similar Species. In Sardinia, most likely to be confused with the large often reticulated *Podarcis sicula* found there. However, this species is less flattened, usually has back scales between hind legs quite strongly keeled, nearly always a pale whitish or greenish underside without clear spots and the supratemporal scales are clearly turned down onto the side of the head in adults.

PODARCIS TILIGUERTA   *Tyrrhenian Wall Lizard*   **Pl. 26**
Range. Corsica, Sardinia and neighbouring small islands   Map 79.
Identification. Up to about 6.5 cm from snout to vent (rarely larger); tail up to about twice as long. A small unflattened Wall Lizard usually with convex, smooth or feebly keeled back scales, the supratemporal scales turned downwards onto the side of head (at least in adults), and usually a basically striped pattern which is very variable in form. Females tend to be some shade of brown above with pale dorsolateral streaks; these are each often bordered above by a dark dorsolateral stripe or series of spots that is usually better developed than the dark vertebral streak (if present). Males may also be brown but are often green on the back or sides or on both. Sides may be reticulated, sometimes with blue spotting. Dark marks on back may be more broken up and often more extensive than in females. In some cases, they form a general reticulation that covers the whole of the body, but light dorsolateral streak often still shows through as a series of spots. Occasionally, animals are almost unmarked and may have only a very faint light dorsolateral streak or series of spots. Underside may be whitish, yellow, orange, salmon or even red. Bright colour sometimes restricted to throat. Most animals have some dark spotting, especially on throat and lips.
Variation. Very variable in pattern. Animals on some small islands may be very dark.
Habits. Widely distributed from sea-level to over 1800 m but commonest at middle altitudes. Prefers dry stony places in scrub, open woods, field-edges, dry-stone walls, path and road-sides. Climbs to some extent but not so extensively as *L. bedriagae*. In lower areas, especially under 400 m, is partly replaced by *P. sicula* which predominates in richer grassy areas, in moist valleys, fields, and often in and near human settlements.
Similar Species. *P. sicula* (p. 155); *L. bedriagae* (opposite). *P. sicula* is often larger, usually has more strongly keeled scales, and is usually whitish or greenish beneath without spots on belly and throat. Corsican *P. sicula* often have a broad brown or dark vertebral stripe that is better developed than the dark dorsolateral stripe, if any. Sardinian animals are often boldly reticulated, or almost unmarked. *L. bedriagae* is flatter, usually reticulated, with flatter body scales and the supratemporal scales are not clearly turned down onto side of head.

SMALL LACERTAS   AREA 5: Italy, Sicily and Malta

There are five Small Lacertas in this area of which three appear to be endemic. These are *Podarcis filfolensis* of Malta, the Sicilian *P. wagleriana*, and *P. sicula* which is found in both Italy and Sicily and now occurs in areas 1, 2, 3, 4, 6 and 7 as well. Two much more widespread species are also present: *Lacerta vivipara* and *Podarcis muralis*. The only other Lacertid in the area is the Green Lizard (*Lacerta viridis*, p. 131).

Key

ITALY

1. Alps etc only. Short-legged and small-headed. Collar distinctly serrated. Scaling coarse (25–37 dorsal scales across mid-body). Granules between supraoculars and supraciliaries absent or at most four on each side. 5–15 femoral pores present *Lacerta vivipara*, Viviparous Lizard (p. 137, Pl. 23)

   All regions. Legs relatively long and head quite large. Collar not usually distinctly serrated, scaling fine (42–75 dorsal scales across mid-body). Granules between supraoculars and supraciliaries usually extensive – at least three on each side; 13–27 femoral pores   2

2. Underside usually with some dark markings, at least on throat. Belly may be red and throat may have some rusty markings
   Podarcis muralis, Common Wall Lizard (p. 138, Pl. 23)

   Underside nearly always without dark markings. Belly usually whitish or with greenish tinge (rarely red, especially on mainland; can be blue or blackish in some island populations).
   Podarcis sicula, Italian Wall Lizard (opposite, Pl. 27)

SICILY

   Usually well defined, light dorsolateral streaks. Markings on back may consist of simple vertebral streak (especially over loins) and similar simple dark dorsolateral streaks or rows of spots. Rarely uniform. Throat sometimes spotted; throat and belly often red, orange or pink in males; (for Egedi and Vulcano islands see text
   Podarcis wagleriana, Sicilian Wall Lizard (p. 158, Pl. 27)

   Light dorsolateral streaks usually absent or broken up. Sides and back often at least partly reticulated, or pattern weak and body more or less uniform. Throat not clearly spotted; belly whitish or greenish, occasionally grey.
   Podarcis sicula, Italian Wall Lizard (opposite, Pl. 27)

MALTA, GOZO and FILFOLA

   Only one highly variable species present.
   Podarcis filfolensis, Maltese Wall Lizard (p. 158, Pl. 26)

PODARCIS SICULA *Italian Wall Lizard* **Pl. 27**
Range. Italy, Sicily, Corsica, Sardinia, Minorca, Ile d'If (near Marseilles), S.E. Spain (Almeria area), E. Adriatic coast (south to Dubrovnik), European Turkey (Sea of Marmara area). Also Elba and many small islands in Tyrrhenian and Adriatic seas. Isolated colonies exist on coast of Libya and Tunis, in Philadelphia (USA) and possibly elsewhere in Europe, e.g. Provence Map 80.
Identification. Up to 9 cm but usually smaller. A highly variable Wall Lizard, usually with rather deep, often fairly long head and robust body. *Underside usually whitish, or with greenish tinge, nearly always without dark spots.* Typically green, yellowish, olive or light brown above. Females tend to be smaller, and smaller-headed, than males with a more obviously striped pattern. Main regional variations are given below.

Most of Italy, Elba, Corsica. Often under 7 cm in north. Usually basically streaked. Vertebral stripe may consist of a brownish area with darker markings; light dorsolateral streaks or series of spots often clear. Intergrade with more southern populations.

S. Italy and Sicily, European Turkey. Up to 8.5 cm or even bigger. Generally like N. Italian animals but often larger, more robust and bigger-headed. If present, vertebral streak is usually black and light dorsolateral streaks are not clear. Sides frequently reticulated or chequered and these markings may extend over back. Some animals have very faint pattern or are nearly uniform.

Sardinia and Minorca; also S. Corsica. Like S. Italian animals; often reticulated, or with very faint pattern, or uniform.

E. Adriatic coast. As N. Italian animals but rather large, dorsolateral streaks often not very clear; unpatterned animals occur occasionally.

Small island populations. Highly variable. In Tyrrhenian area, some populations dark, even black, or blue, or with a blue belly. Other belly colours occur and there are often large differences in back pattern.
Habits. Very variable. A vigorous, opportunistic lizard. In N. Italy, Corsica etc., typically found in grassy places, roadside verges, etc. In other areas, often also occurs in very open fields, flat derelict areas, sandy places, near sea, vineyards etc. and is capable of running long distances to shelter. Tends to climb less than some other Small Lacertas in range, but more than *P. taurica* (p. 170), *P. wagleriana* (p. 158) or *P. melisellenis* (p. 165) etc. Hunts on ground but may return to dry-stone walls, bushes etc. for shelter. In fact can climb quite efficiently and, in the absence of better adapted species, will occupy rock-faces with some vegetation, ruins etc. Tolerates close proximity to man better than many Wall Lizards. Sometimes eats a fairly high proportion of vegetable food. Often found in parks and gardens of towns.
Variation. Great variation in pattern, even within populations. In rare cases on mainland, and on a few small islands, belly may be red. Throat and sometimes belly occasionally grey.

Plate 27 SMALL LACERTAS 5: Italy and Sicily

Other small Lacertas present are *Lacerta vivipara* (extreme N. Italy only, **Pl. 23**) and *P. muralis* (not Sicily, **Pl. 23**). Only other lacertid is *L. viridis* (**Pl. 21**).

1. Podarcis sicula *Italian Wall Lizard*   **155**
(Also present in many areas outside Italy.) Highly variable but often green or olive-backed; underside usually whitish or greenish, unspotted. *P. muralis* typically has dark markings on throat and often on belly, which may be red.

  1a. Female: typical pattern in N. Italy.
  1b. Male: typical pattern in N. Italy.
  1c. Male: reticulate pattern (common in S. Italy, Sicily, Sardinia, Minorca etc.).
  1d. Male: uniform phase (often occurs with reticulated individuals).

2. Podarcis wagleriana *Sicilian Wall Lizard*   **158**
Sicily only. Differs from Sicilian *P. sicula* in better defined, pale, dorsolateral streaks, often simple row(s) of spots on back and red, orange or pink belly in breeding males.

  2a. Male.
  2b. Female.

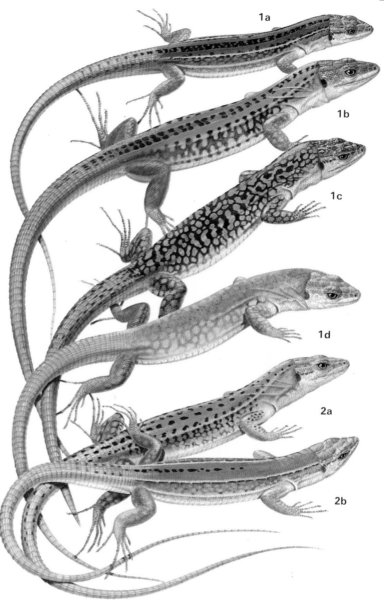

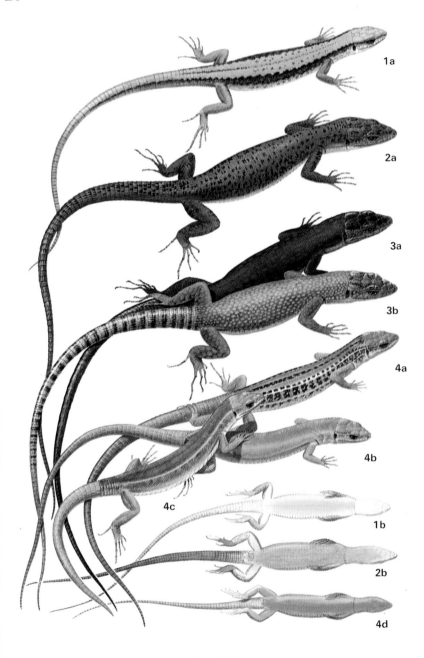

1a

2a

3a

3b

4a

4b

4c

1b

2b

4d

SMALL LACERTAS 6: Plate 28
East Adriatic Coastal area

For this area see also *Lacerta vivipara* and *Podarcis muralis*
(**Pl. 23**) *P. taurica* (**Pl. 29**) and *P. sicula* (**Pl. 27**). Other
lacertids present: *L. agilis* (**Pl. 19**); *L. viridis*, *L. trilineata*
(**Pl. 21**); *Algyroides nigropunctatus* (**Pl. 18**).

1. **Lacerta horvathi** *Horvath's Rock Lizard* 163
   Mountains of N.W. Yugoslavia and neighbouring areas. Flattened, head blunt. Throat white and unspotted; belly often
   yellow (1b). See text for separation from *P. muralis*.

2. **Lacerta mosorensis** *Mosor Rock Lizard* 163
   Mountains of S.W. Yugoslavia. Strongly flattened. Typically
   brownish above and yellow below (2b).

3. **Lacerta oxycephala** *Sharp-snouted Rock Lizard* 164
   S.W. Yugoslavia. Strongly flattened. Either dappled above
   (3b) or black (3a), especially at high altitudes and on some
   small islands; underside bluish.

4. **Podarcis melisellensis** *Dalmatian Wall Lizard* 165
   Not flattened. Often with light stripes or rather uniform;
   underside frequently orange-red in breeding males. For separation from *P. muralis, P. taurica* and *P. sicula* see key
   (p. **162**) and text (p. **165**).

   4a. Male: striped phase.
   4b. Female: uniform phase.
   4c. Female: lightly striped individual.
   4d. Breeding male: underside.

Similar Species. *Italy*: only species likely to be confused is *P. muralis* (p. 138) but this usually has dark markings on underside (at least on throat), and a different range of back patterns. *Sicily*: *P. wagleriana* (see below). *Tyrrhenian islands*: all other species have distinct black spotting on throat and often belly; this is visible even in most animals with dark undersides but is lacking in *P. sicula*. For other areas, see regional keys and descriptions.

PODARCIS WAGLERIANA   *Sicilian Wall Lizard*   Pl. 27

Range. Sicily (but not north-east); Egedi Islands (Flavignana, Levanzo and Marettimo) and Vulcano Island   Map 81.

Identification. Up to about 7.5 cm. A deep headed Wall Lizard with distinctive pattern; often green above but females especially sometimes olive or brown. Light dorsolateral streaks typically well-defined. There is frequently a simple dark vertebral streak or row of spots (often just over loins), or similar dark dorsolateral streaks or spots, or both. Sides dark-spotted or dappled in males, more uniformly dark in females. Underside may be white but often red, orange or pink in males; throat sometimes spotted. Animals without markings may occur: these are best distinguished from unmarked *P. sicula* by belly colour (if male) and less flattened body.

Habits. On Sicily, mainly a ground-dwelling lizard found in grassy places (rather like *P. taurica*, p. 170). Does not climb much on walls or on rocky slopes, in contrast to *P. sicula* in this area. Tends to be predominant species inland, while *P. sicula* is the commonest species on the coast.

Variation. Populations on small islands may have quite heavy spotting on throat and chest which distinguishes them from *P. sicula*. Vulcano animals are brownish and the light dorsolateral streaks are not clear.

Similar Species. Only likely to be confused with *Podarcis sicula* (p. 155).

PODARCIS FILFOLENSIS   *Maltese Wall Lizard*   Pl. 26

Range. Malta, Gozo and nearby islets; Filfola Rock. Also Linosa and Lampione islands   Map 82.

Identification. *Malta and Gozo*. Adults up to about 6.5 cm but often smaller, tail about twice as long. The only lacertid within its range. A small Wall Lizard with rather fine dorsal scaling (60–85 scales across mid-back). Colouring highly variable: ground colour grey, brown or green. Males may have dappled sides, light dorsolateral streaks and two or three dark stripes or rows of spots on back; sometimes heavily reticulated but may be only lightly marked. Females often lightly marked or plain. Underside white, yellow, orange or red, sometimes with spots especially on throat.

Habits. A typical Wall Lizard found in a wide range of rather dry habitats: gardens, dry-stone walls, stone-piles, road banks, rocky slopes etc. Also occurs on small, offshore rocks and islands.

Variation. Animals from populations on small islands tend to be bigger and more heavily marked than animals from the larger islands. On Filfola

Rock, grows to 8.5 cm and can be predominantly black with small greenish spots, or brown with heavy dark markings.
Similar Species. None within range.

<small>SMALL LACERTAS; AREA 6:</small> East Adriatic coastal area

The eastern side of the Adriatic sea from the Italian border region to N. Albania includes a total of eight Small Lacerta species. Of these, four are confined to the area, being found mainly near the coast and not extending inland more than 130km (usually less). They are *Lacerta oxycephala*, *L. horvathi*, *L. mosorensis* and *Podarcis melisellensis*. Of the more wide-ranging species, *P. sicula* is almost entirely restricted to the coast and islands in this area, while *P. muralis* is limited to rather cooler habitats and avoids the coast except in the north; *P. taurica* is found only in N. Albania. The final species, *Lacerta vivipara*, is confined to humid mountain regions.

The other lacertids in the area are *Algyroides nigropunctatus* (p. 115), distinguished by large scales and sombre colouring above, and some Green Lizards (p. 126).

Key

1. Mountain areas. Collar distinctly serrated, granules between supraoculars and supraciliaries few (0–4) or absent. Dorsal scales coarse (25–37 across body).
   Lacerta vivipara, Viviparous Lizard (p. 137, Pl. 23)
   Collar usually not very distinctly serrated, granules between supraoculars and supraciliaries often five or more. Scaling not very coarse (more than 40 scales across body)   2

2. Central pairs of scales on lower side of tail wide (largest at least twice as wide as adjoining scales, Fig., p. 164). Underside bluish. Dorsal scales smooth and flat. Head and body very flattened. Back buff-grey or greenish-grey with dappled pattern and tail banded blue-green and black; or entire animal blackish above
   Lacerta oxycephala, Sharp-snouted Rock Lizard (p. 164, Pl. 28)
   Central pairs of scales on lower side of tail not or only slightly wider than adjoining scales. Underside not usually bluish   3

3. Mountain areas only. First supratemporal scale large, often emarginates parietal scale (Fig., p. 162). Rostral scale usually contacts frontonasal (Fig., p. 142). Scales on back flattish, unkeeled. Belly usually white or yellow   4
   First supratemporal scale shallow, does not emarginate parietal scale. Rostral usually does not usually contact frontonasal

Plate 29   SMALL LACERTAS 7a:

South-eastern Europe

For this area see also *Lacerta vivipara*, *Podarcis muralis*
(**Pl. 23**); *P. erhardii* (south only, **Pl. 31**); *P. peloponnesiaca*,
L. graeca (S. Greece only, **Pl. 30**); *P. milensis* (S.W. Aegean,
Pl. 31); *P. sicula* (Turkey only, **Pl. 27**); *L. saxicola* (Crimea
only, p. 170). Other lacertids present: *L. agilis* (**Pl. 19**); *L.
viridis*, *L. trilineata* (**Pl. 21**), *Ophisops elegans*, *Eremias
arguta* (**Pl. 17**), *Algyroides moreoticus* and *A. nigropunctatus*
(**Pl. 18**).

1. **Lacerta praticola**   *Meadow Lizard*   168
   Limited range (Map 87). Small; coarse scales. Distinctive
   pattern. Belly often green or yellow (1b). Most likely to be
   confused with *L. vivipara*.

2. **Podarcis taurica**   *Balkan Wall Lizard*   170
   Collar serrated. Green or olive above, often with pale stripes;
   belly usually orange or red in males. Most likely to be
   confused with *P. sicula* (**Pl. 27**) in E. European Turkey
   and *P. melisellensis* (**Pl. 28**) in N. Albania; see text.

   2a. Male: typical pattern for north of range.
   2b. Male: frequent pattern in south of range.
   2c. Male: uniform phase in south of range.
   2d. Underside of breeding male.
   2e. Female.

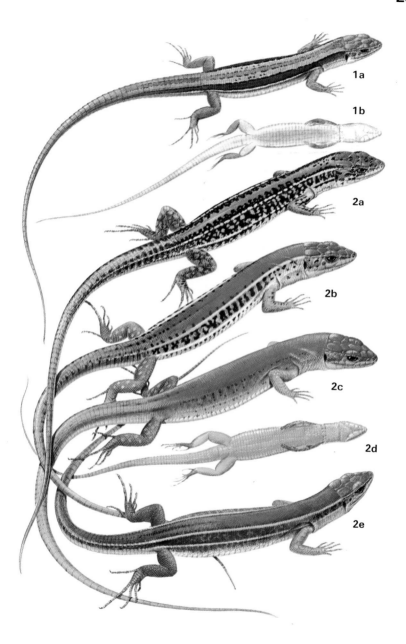

1a

1b

2a

2b

2c

2d

2e

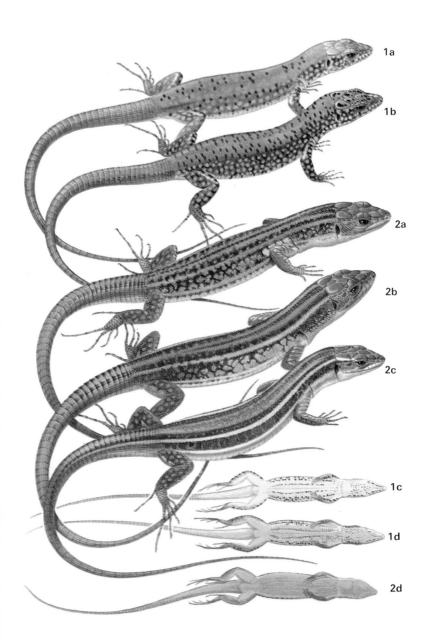

SMALL LACERTAS 7b: Plate 30
Southern Greece (Peloponnese)

For this area see also *Podarcis muralis* (mountains, **Pl. 23**); *P. taurica* (north, **Pl. 29**); *P. erhardii* (north-east, **Pl. 31**). Other lacertids present: *Lacerta trilineata*, possibly *L. viridis* (**Pl. 21**); *Algyroides moreoticus* (**Pl. 18**); possibly *Ophisops elegans* (**Pl. 17**).

1. **Lacerta graeca**   *Greek Rock Lizard*   **169**
   Rather flattened. Not striped. Belly often yellow or orange with dark spots. No large scales on cheek.

      1a. Female.
      1b. Male.
      1c, 1d. Underside.

2. **Podarcis peloponnesiaca**   *Peloponnese Wall Lizard*   **172**
   Often strongly striped, but variable in pattern. No dark spots on throat. Young may have blue tail. In north of range confusable with *P. erhardii* (**Pl. 31**) but fewer supraciliary granules (0–7 instead of 10–17; see Fig., p. 173). *P. taurica* has serrated collar.

      2a, 2b. Males: massive head; often blue on sides.
      2c. Female: strongly striped (young *Lacerta trilineata*, **Pl. 22** is stockier).
      2d. Breeding male: underside sometimes whitish.

(Fig., p. 142). Scales on back often convex and at least lightly keeled. Belly rarely yellow   **5**

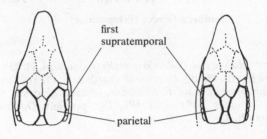

first supratemporal emarginates (cuts into) parietal

first supratemporal does not emarginate parietal

4. (North of about Šibenik). Usually one postnasal and five pairs of chin shields. Dorsal scales on lower hind leg smaller than back scales. Back rather pale, contrasting strongly with dark sides. Belly often yellow and throat white, in adults. Head blunt and short
    Lacerta horvathi, Horvath's Rock Lizard (opposite, Pl. 28)
  (South of about Šibenik). Often two postnasals and six pairs of chin shields. Dorsal scales on lower hind leg about as big as those on back. Back often mottled and may not contrast strongly with sides. Belly and throat usually both yellow or orange in adults. Head usually rather long   *Lacerta mosorensis*, Mosor Rock Lizard (opposite, Pl. 28)

5. Not on islands, or coast except in north. Underside usually with some dark marks, at least on throat; belly typically whitish, pink or red, throat whitish often with rusty pigment. Upperside brownish (almost never green) with darker markings. Iris often coppery. Tail may have conspicuous black and white spots on sides. Head sometimes rather flattened
    Podarcis muralis, Common Wall Lizard (p. 138, Pl. 23)
  Underside usually unspotted (or rarely more than a few spots at sides of neck), commonly greenish, white or orange-red. Back usually green or brownish. Some animals almost without other markings. Vertebral stripe if present may contain areas of lighter colour. Iris not coppery. Head usually rather deep.
Podarcis melisellensis, Dalmatian Wall Lizard (Pl. 28) ⎫
Podarcis sicula, Italian Wall Lizard (Pl. 27)   ⎬ (see p. 165)
Podarcis taurica, Balkan Wall Lizard (p. 170, Pl. 29)

LACERTA HORVATHI *Horvath's Rock Lizard* **Pl. 28**
Range. N.W. Yugoslavia and small part of adjoining Italy: Julian Alps, N.E. Istria, Velebit and Kapela Mountains, perhaps south to Šibenik Map 83.
Identification. Up to about 6.5 cm snout to vent, tail about 1½–2 times as long. A distinctly flattened Small Lacerta with a short blunt head. Usually pale grey-brown on back with sharply contrasting dark sides, often with a wavy upper edge; sometimes also a dark vertebral streak or irregular spotting on back. Underside unspotted, whitish or with yellow on belly. Iris pale beige. Young like adults, but tail often greenish-grey. See sections 3 and 4 of key (p. 159) for details of scaling.
Habits. Confined to rather moist mountainous areas, usually above 500 m. Often found in open beech or conifer forests or above tree-line. Strictly a rock lizard and occurs on cliffs, karst pavements, outcrops, road cuttings etc. Like other Yugoslav rock lizards, very agile, often leaping into air to catch prey, which it may ambush from crevices. Frequently occurs with *Podarcis muralis*, which tends to occupy less precipitous habitats.
Variation. Some minor differences in pattern and shape between populations. May possibly intergrade with *Lacerta mosorensis*.

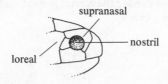

Similar Species. Similar to some *L. mosorensis* (below) but ranges almost entirely separate. Some *P. muralis* (p. 138) are also very like *L. horvathi*, but usually have dark markings on throat and often a reddish belly in males. Iris is often very coppery red. Also supratemporals are shallow and do not clearly emarginate parietal (e.g. Fig., opposite); rostral scale is usually separated from frontonasal (Fig., p. 142), and supranasal does not contact loreal as it does in most *L. horvathi* (Fig., above).

LACERTA MOSORENSIS *Mosor Rock Lizard* **Pl. 28**
Range. S.W. Yugoslavia (S. Dalmatia, Hercegovina, and Montenegro) Map 84.
Identification. Adults up to about 7 cm, from snout to vent; tail about 1¾–2¼ times as long. A distinctly flattened Small Lacerta with a long head and long slender tail. Brown, grey-brown or olive with an oily gloss and dark spotting or mottling. Flanks often rather darker than back. In some populations, unmarked animals occur and others are known with very dark sides and spots limited to centre of back. Underside unspotted,

sometimes white but usually deep yellow or even orange in adults. Young
similar to adults, but always with pale belly. For details of scaling, see
sections 3 and 4 of key (p. 159).
Habits. Largely confined to areas of high rainfall, at some altitude – usually
600–1500 m. Primarily a rock lizard, but does not climb as high as
L. oxycephala and is found in less sunny and more humid habitats than
this species, e.g. open deciduous woods, north-facing rocky slopes, open
shady holes on karst pavements, around springs etc.
Variation. Considerable variation in markings.
Similar Species. *L. oxycephala* (below) is only other lizard in area with
strongly flattened body. *Podarcis muralis* (p. 138) is less flattened, has a
shorter head, and is rarely yellow below; see key for further details.

LACERTA OXYCEPHALA   *Sharp-snouted Rock Lizard*   Pl. 28
Range. S.W. Yugoslavia (S. Dalmatia, Hercegovina, coastal Montenegro,
and some off-shore islands)   Map 85.
Identification. Adults usually up to about 6.5 cm, from snout to vent; tail
1½–2 times as long. A distinctly flattened, delicately built Small Lacerta
with a pointed snout, noticeably raised eyes, a rather short body, and a
slender tail. Hind toes relatively short and distinctively kinked. The only
species within range to have the central pairs of scales on underside of tail
very wide (see Fig., below).

Colour varies. Most lowland animals are light buffish grey above
(greenish in some lights) with a reticulated pattern, and the tail is conspicuously banded black and turquoise green (this pattern is lost on
regrown sections of the tail). Animals from highland areas and some
islands are much darker and may be entirely black above. Underparts
blue, more intense in males. Young are like lowland adults, but tail is more
brightly marked.
Habits. Occurs from sea level to about 1500 m, in a wide variety of
habitats, but most often found on *sunny* cliffs, boulders, rock-pavements,
stone piles, screes, walls, and buildings; occasionally seen on tree trunks.
Frequently enters towns and villages. Climbs higher and better than any
other European Small Lacerta; sometimes seen 20 or 30 m up cliffs

and walls, but normally much lower. Brightly coloured tail often waved nervously. Retreats into crevices or among stones when disturbed.
Variation. Some regional variation in colour – see above.
Similar Species. None very similar within range. Easily distinguished by colour and shape.

PODARCIS MELISELLENSIS *Dalmatian Wall Lizard* Pl. 28
Range. E. Adriatic coastal region and islands from Italian border area to N. Albania Map 86.
Identification. *Mainland.* Up to 6.5 cm snout to vent, but often smaller, tail about twice as long as body. A small, fairly stocky lizard with a rather deep, shortish head. Underside white or orange, or red, usually unspotted (if present, spots are few and, in most cases, confined to sides of neck region). Usually light-brownish above or with a green back. Pattern varies: some animals, especially on coast, almost without markings; others with prominent narrow, light dorsolateral streaks, and often a dark vertebral stripe, at least on hind-back, which may contain small areas of lighter pigment. Rest of pattern rather variable but females tend to be more regularly striped than males. Babies are never green.
Habits. Found in a variety of dry habitats: path and road banks, dry ditches, open woodland, scrub, dry stony pastures and their overgrown edges. Largely ground-dwelling but may climb on low walls and stonepiles. Certainly climbs far less than *P. muralis* and Rock Lizards. Tends to be replaced by *P. muralis* inland in moister, shadier places and at higher altitudes. On coast, occurs with *P. sicula* but this species tends to be confined to richer areas (often near human habitation), fields, vineyards, open road verges and even gardens in cities and villages; here *P. melisellensis* occupies more broken, often uncultivated country. Rarely, the two species may occur together on small islands, in which case *P. melisellensis* is sometimes predominant in coastal areas.
Variation. Considerable differences in pattern and size. Island populations very variable. Most extreme, on Brusnik Island grows to 7.5 cm snout to vent, and is black with large blue blotches on lower flanks. Animals from Vis tend to have sides heavily marbled.
Similar Species. *P. muralis* (p. 138 and key p. 162). *P. taurica* in N. Albania (p. 170). *P. sicula*: restricted to coast and islands; on mainland and large islands can usually be distinguished from *P. melisellensis* as follows: often larger, adults frequently over 6.5 cm (rarely over 6 cm in *P. melisellensis*); underside whitish (or tinged green) almost never brightly coloured; light dorsolateral streaks often broken up or faint; animals without any dark markings are uncommon; masseteric shield often not very big (large in most *P. melisellensis* and may contact supratemporals Fig., p. 166); body often more flattened, and head longer. Habitat can also be a useful clue. On small islands both species are much more variable and can sometimes be difficult to identify. Here 'jizz' is helpful, but previous experience on

mainland and large islands is important. On small islands normally one or other species occurs, rarely both.

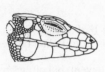

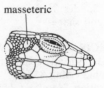

masseteric

Dalmatian   Italian

East Adriatic Wall Lizards, common arrangements of scales on cheek

SMALL LACERTAS   AREA 7: South-eastern Europe

S.E. Europe, as defined here (see Fig., p. 136), contains a wide variety of Small Lacertas, there being ten species in all. Two of these (*Lacerta vivipara* and *Podarcis muralis*) are widespread in the rest of Europe as well. Two others (*L. praticola* and *L. saxicola*) have additional populations in the Caucasus. One species (*P. sicula*) is probably an ancient introduction from the Italian region, while the remaining five are endemic to the area. Many of the species have restricted ranges and this is often helpful in identifying them. Other small lacertid lizards in S.E. Europe are *Algyroides* (p. 115), *Eremias* (p. 122), and *Ophisops* (p. 119), all of which are quite easily distinguished from the Small Lacertas. Three kinds of Green Lizard (p. 126) are also present.

Key

1. Collar usually distinctly serrated, throat scales fairly coarse, body scales usually well keeled   **2**

   Collar more or less smooth-edged, body scales often not very distinctly keeled, or smooth   **4**

2. Usually fairly dry places. Back often green; body scales small. 14–25 femoral pores on each thigh; typically 45–62 dorsal scales across back
   Podarcis taurica, Balkan Wall Lizard (p. 170, Pl. 29)
   (N.B. some Aegean island populations of *P. erhardii* may key out here – see text p. 172)

   Usually rather lush places. Brownish (rarely greenish), with coarse body scales. 5–15 femoral pores on each thigh; less than 44 dorsal scales across mid-back   **3**

3. Restricted range (Map 87). Pattern fairly characteristic and constant. Only one row of scales bordering pre-anal plate (Fig., p. 169). Scales on flanks rather smaller than those on back. A fairly long row of supraciliary granules (3–11)
   Lacerta praticola, Meadow Lizard (p. 168, Pl. 29)
   Much of northern Balkans, particularly mountains. Pattern variable. Usually scales bordering preanal plate irregular. Little variation in size of dorsal scales. Only a few supraciliary granules (0–4) *Lacerta vivipara,* Viviparous Lizard (p. 137, Pl. 23)

4. S. Greece only. Brownish, unstriped, flattened rock lizard; often with blue flank spots, at least over shoulder. Underside usually orange or yellow, typically with black spots, at least on throat. Head scaling characteristic: two scales behind nostril (postnasals); no large scales on cheek; first supratemporal usually larger than others and cutting into edge of parietal scale (Fig., p. 170)
   Lacerta graeca, Greek Rock Lizard (p. 169, Pl. 30)
   All areas. Not as above. Sometimes striped. Usually only one scale behind nostril and often one or more large cheek scales   5

5. Crimea only. A brownish or greenish, distinctly flattened Rock Lizard with no clear light stripes in body pattern.
   Lacerta saxicola, Caucasian Rock Lizard (p. 170)
   All other areas   6

6. Milos and nearby islands in S.W. Cyclades only. Males with very characteristic pattern: flanks, sides of head, and throat black usually with large light spots
   Podarcis milensis, Milos Wall Lizard (p. 173, Pl. 31)
   All other areas   7

7. Coastal areas and islands in Sea of Marmara only. Robust, often large Wall Lizard with a rather flattened body. Often greenish above with dark stripe on midline of back or reticulated; light narrow stripes or series of spots not usually very obvious. Belly whitish or tinged greenish.
   Podarcis sicula, Italian Wall Lizard (p. 155, Pl. 27)
   All other areas   8

8. Mainland only (but perhaps also Samothrace Island); mainly montane in south of range. At least slightly flattened. Usually brownish, often without clear light narrow dorsolateral stripes. Dark dorsolateral stripes, if present, are generally weaker than vertebral streak, if any. In males, underside usually dark spotted, belly often red, throat white with rusty marks. Females have at least some throat spots
   Podarcis muralis, Common Wall Lizard (p. 138, Pl. 23)

S. mainland and islands, except Milos group. Not very obviously
flattened, often with light dorsolateral stripes. Dark
dorsolateral stripes usually stronger than vertebral streak
if present. Throat may have spots, but belly unspotted;
belly often red or orange in males   9

9. Peloponnese only. Granules along edge of supraoculars few in
   in number (0–7); often a row of large scales under forearm
   Podarcis peloponnesiaca, Peloponnese Wall Lizard (p. 172, Pl. 30)
   Mainland south to N.E. Peloponnese, Aegean islands. In area of
   overlap with *P. peloponnesiaca* this species has more supra-
   ocular granules (10–17) and usually few large scales under
   forearm   *Podarcis erhardii*, Erhard's Wall Lizard (p. 171, Pl. 31)

LACERTA PRATICOLA *Meadow Lizard*   **Pl. 29**
Range. Confined to a few small, isolated areas in the Balkans (parts of
N.E. Yugoslavia, S. Romania, Bulgaria, and N.E. European Turkey).
Also Caucasus   Map 87.
Identification. Adults up to about 6 cm from snout to vent; tail 1½–2 times
as long. A small, fairly deep-headed lizard generally reminiscent of *L.
vivipara*, with short legs, usually a serrated collar and rather coarse keeled
scales. Upperparts greyish, brown, or olive-brown, with darker flanks; a
reddish brown band, often edged with dark spots, along centre of back.
Underside unspotted; throat whitish; belly greenish in males, yellowish in
females. Easily distinguished from *Lacerta vivipara* by characteristic
pattern; only one semi-circle of small scales around preanal plate (Fig.,
opposite); more supraciliary granules (3–11, compared with 0–4 in *L.
vivipara*); scales on flanks narrower than those on back. Other Small
Lacertas in range (*Podarcis muralis* and *P. taurica*) lack distinct band
along mid-back (although a dark streak may be present especially in *P.
muralis*), have more femoral pores on each thigh (13–27, instead of 9–13),
and finer scaling (over 41 scales across body, instead of 35–41, rarely 43).
If belly is brightly coloured in these species, it is usually reddish or orange.
Habits. A mainly ground-dwelling lizard. Usually found in rather moist
places with lush vegetation such as glades in woods, stream-banks,
marsh-edges, damp meadows in mountain areas etc. Also occasionally
on well-vegetated stony slopes. Often seen basking on old tree trunks,
isolated stones etc. Extends up to about 800 m.
Variation. Little obvious variation in Europe.
Similar Species. *L. vivipara* (p. 137), *Podarcis muralis* (p. 138), and possibly *P. taurica* (p. 170); see above for distinctions.

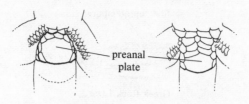

preanal plate

Meadow Lizard   Viviparous Lizard

Small Lacertas, vent regions

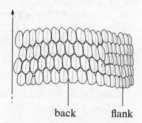

back   flank

Meadow Lizard, variation in size of dorsal scales

LACERTA GRAECA *Greek Rock Lizard*   Pl. 30

Range. S. Greece (Peloponnese) only   Map 88.

Identification. Adults up to about 8 cm from snout to vent; tail usually 2–2½ times as long. A moderate-sized, flattened lizard with a rather 'rangy' appearance, the head, legs, and tail being long. Usually appears glossy grey-brown (sometimes rather yellowish), but bronzy-brown in some lights. Males have dark flanks with well marked light spots and irregular dark spots or blotches on back. Females are smaller-headed with only poorly-defined light spots on sides and the darker markings are more scattered. Often one or two blue spots present above the shoulder (these may extend along flanks in males). Underside usually black-spotted (at least on throat) and deep orange or yellow, but may be paler. Shape and colouring are quite characteristic. Head scaling is also distinctive: two scales immediately behind nostril, no large scales on cheek, first supratemporal scale usually larger than others and emarginating parietal (see Fig., p. 162).

Habits. Largely confined to mountain areas and most common above 400 m. Often occurs fairly near water, or at least not in very dry situations. Climbs extensively and well on rocky outcrops, screes, walls, road-

first supratemporal

Greek Rock Lizard

parapets and cuttings, tree-boles etc. Avoids very hot sun, and can sometimes be found in light woods etc. Although mainly a climbing species,
sometimes hunts on ground near rocky outcrops etc.

Variation. Some variation in patterning.

Similar Species. Other Small Lacertas within range are less flattened, often
striped, and lack characteristic head scaling of *L. graeca*. These features
together with shorter head and often reddish or pinkish belly will distinguish *Podarcus muralis* (p. 138), superficially the most similar form.

LACERTA SAXICOLA   *Caucasian Rock Lizard*

Range. Crimea. Also Caucasus, Turkey, N. Iraq, N. Iran and S. Turk-
estan.

Identification. Up to about 8 cm, but usually smaller, tail about twice as
long. A distinctly flattened Rock Lizard with a smooth-edged collar, more
or less smooth or feebly keeled scales, a deep first supratemporal scale and
no clear, narrow, light stripes in pattern. Brownish or greenish above,
with dark markings that are strongest on sides and may form a reticulation;
yellow or greenish below.

Habits. Occurs in mountainous part of Crimea. A climbing lizard found
especially on rock faces, boulders, screes, etc.

Variation. Little in Crimea.

Similar Species. In Crimea, only likely to be confused with *Podarcis
taurica*, but this species is not flattened, has shallow supratemporals and
quite clearly keeled dorsal scales, usually narrow light stripes in pattern
and a typically bright orange or red belly in breeding males.

PODARCIS TAURICA   *Balkan Wall Lizard*   **Pl. 29**

Range. Balkans but not W. Yugoslavia etc. Extends north to Hungary,
S. and E. Romania and Crimea; also Corfu, Ionian islands, Thasopoulos
in N. Aegean, and one or two localities on coast of N.W. Asia Minor
Map 89.

Identification. Adults up to 8 cm from snout to vent (smaller in north of
range); tail sometimes twice body length. A rather robust, deep-headed,
Small Lacerta often reminiscent of a miniature Green Lizard. Usually

easily separated from other Wall and from Rock Lizards in its range by its distinctly serrated collar. Back of adults often bright grassy green in spring (more olive in summer). Rest of dorsal pattern varies geographically. Northern populations have a pair of narrow light dorsolateral stripes (or occasionally rows of spots) bordered towards centre of back by a brown area overlaid by black blotches. Southern populations tend to lack brown area, and the light stripes may be faint; some animals are almost uniform with a green back and some stippling on the flanks; a vertebral streak or row of spots may be present, especially over the hind quarters. Underside in all areas often unspotted whitish, but bright orange, red or yellow with greenish throat in breeding males. Young lack green on back and are frequently more strongly striped than adults.

Habits. Mainly a lowland species. Almost entirely ground-dwelling and usually climbs far less than other Wall Lizards in range. Typically found on flattish dry ground with at least some covering of grass or other vegetation; also on road-side banks, field-borders, among crops, etc. In south, can occur in more broken habitats, in brambles and sometimes by water. Very conspicuous when basking on stones, open ground etc., but colouring hides it well when hunting in vegetation. Takes refuge in holes in ground, under stones, in bushy plants, etc.

Variation. Considerable variation in size and colouring (see above). Collar serration occasionally rather weak (e.g. on Corfu).

Similar Species. *P. melisellensis* (p. 165) is similar to *P. taurica* and occurs close to it in N. Albanian region. However it is smaller, usually does not have such a distinctly notched collar and vertebral stripe, if present, often contains light areas. *P. sicula* (p. 155) is confined to Sea of Marmara area; it is larger, has a more or less smooth collar, somewhat flattened body, typically no clear narrow light stripes in pattern and nearly always a pale, often greenish tinged belly. Adult Green Lizards (*L. viridis*, *L. trilineata*, *L. agilis*) are bigger with deeper supratemporal scales; juveniles have much bigger heads and are stockier than equivalent sized *P. taurica*.

PODARCIS ERHARDII *Erhard's Wall Lizard* Pl. 31

Range. S. Balkans north to Albania, Macedonia and S. Bulgaria, and south to N.E. Peloponnese. Also many Aegean islands but not Milos group, Samothrace Thasos and Thasopoulos, and some other inshore islands. Mainland range rather broken up Map 90.

Identification. *Mainland.* Adults up to about 7cm snout to vent; tail about twice as long. A medium sized Wall Lizard often with a fairly deep head (which is also rather short in south of mainland range), smooth collar and more or less smooth body scales. Pattern variable but usually basically striped, especially in females. Light dorsolateral stripes are often present, and dark dorsolateral stripes or series of markings are nearly always better developed and broader than vertebral stripe, if any. Some males are largely reticulated. Ground colour greyish or brown; occasionally greenish. Belly and often throat white, yellow, orange or red, brightest in breeding males; dark spotting, if present, is typically confined to chin and sides of throat. Sometimes large blue spots on hind legs.

Habits. In dry, often stony or rocky places, usually with brambles or other low, dense, bushy vegetation. Climbs to some extent, but not as much as most Wall Lizards. On the mainland, tends to be replaced by *P. muralis* in more humid places or at higher altitudes and near human habitation. Island populations are often associated with dense growth of *Pistacea* bushes in which they hide, but can occur in more open places such as overgrown sand dunes. On some islands, inhabits the eyries of Eleonora's Falcon (*Falco eleonorae*).

Variation. *Island populations.* Considerable variation in size (up to 8 cm snout to vent), shape (robustness, length of limbs, tail-thickness) and colouring. Ground colour may be brown, grey, green, or very dark black-brown. Pattern varies: in extreme cases can be reticulated, or dark markings reduced, confined to front of body, or completely absent. Underside may be white, grey, yellow, red, greenish, bluish and sometimes hind parts more strongly coloured than rest. Skyros animals tend to look like *P. taurica* (collar serrated, scales keeled, back green with narrow pale dorsolateral stripes), but are usually considered to be *P. erhardii*. Locality is very useful in recognising island *P. erhardii*: it is the only Small Lacerta species on most N. Sporades and Cyclades islands but it is replaced by *P. milensis* in the Milos group.

Similar Species. *P. muralis* (p. 138) on mainland only. Usually flatter and often has different pattern: if dark streaks or rows of spots are present on back, the vertebral stripe or row is usually better developed than the dorsolateral ones; clear light dorsolateral stripes are uncommon. Belly may be pink or red but throat is usually whitish with rusty blotches and dark markings which are often heavy and may extend to belly. *P. peloponnesiaca* (below) in Peloponnese only. *P. milensis* (p. 173) has completely separate range.

PODARCIS PELOPONNESIACA *Peloponnese Wall Lizard* **Pl. 30**
Range. S. Greece (Peloponnese) only   Map 91.
Identification. Up to 8.5 cm snout to vent; tail about twice as long. Females smaller than males. A rather large, robust Wall Lizard with a massive head in adult males, only a few supraciliary granules present or none at all, a smooth collar and often a row of distinctly enlarged scales under the forearm. Pattern very variable but usually distinctly striped, females more strongly than males. Typically, light dorsolateral stripes are present, bordered above by dark streaks or rows of marks that are often broad and nearly always better developed than the vertebral stripe (if any). Back of males frequently greenish. Often one or more blue spots above shoulder

and blue may extend along flanks. Underside without dark spots, often uniform bright orange in males but may be white (as in females) or even spotted with red. Juveniles more or less like females, but tail may be blue.

Habits. The common Wall Lizard of the Peloponnese, occurring from sea-level to over 1500m. Found in a wide variety of dry, often broken habitats such as rocky, scrub-covered hillsides, olive groves, road-banks, ruins, stone-piles etc. Frequently seen perched on raised objects; low walls, stones, tree trunks etc., but also hunts on the ground. Often climbs extensively, although rather clumsily, even on sheer cliffs. Replaces *L. graeca* in dry places as the common climbing lizard of the area.

Variation. Considerable geographical variation in pattern, especially in extent of vertebral stripe, green on back and blue on sides; belly colour also varies. Pattern is sometimes faint.

Similar Species. Most similar to *P. erhardii* (p. 171) but only overlaps with this species in the N.E. Peloponnese. Here *P. erhardii* tends to be smaller and less boldly marked; it has a more complete row of supraciliary granules (typically 10–17 compared with usually 0–7 in *P. peloponnesiaca*) and few obviously enlarged scales under the forearm. Striped young of Balkan Green Lizard (*Lacerta trilineata*) could possibly be mistaken for female *P. peloponnesiaca*, but they have a notched collar.

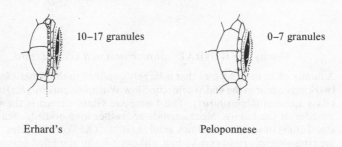

10–17 granules   0–7 granules

Erhard's   Peloponnese

Wall Lizards in Southern Greece, area above eye

PODARCIS MILENSIS *Milos Wall Lizard* **Pl. 31**

Range. Milos island group, S.W. Cyclades: Milos, Kimolos, Gerakunia (=Falconera), Eremomilos (=Antimilos), Velopoula (=Paropola)) Map 92 and Fig., p. 113).

Identification. Adults up to about 6.5cm, from snout to vent; tail about twice as long. A robust, deep-headed Wall Lizard with characteristic colour-pattern in the males. Back usually brown, often with a rather weak vertebral stripe; flanks, throat and sides of head black with prominent light green, blue, yellow or whitish spots. Belly also often marked heavily with black, but bright colour absent or limited to second rows of belly-scales from mid-line. Females more nondescript, often with light dorsolateral stripes and a few well-marked blotches on throat.

Habits. Most abundant in areas of cultivation, especially where dry-stone walls, banks and stone piles provide many refuges. Tends to sit and bask in large numbers on these, but hunts mainly on the ground, either in vegetation or in open areas. Also occurs at lower densities in a wide variety of habitats including scrub-covered hillsides, and even damp marshy land near sea. Often seen on walls with Kotschy's Gecko (*Cyrtodactylus kotschyi*).

Variation. Some of the smaller islands have populations that are rather dark, e.g. Gerakunia, Eremomilos. On the latter island the throat is often entirely black in males.

Similar Species. Balkan Green Lizard (*Lacerta trilineata*, p. 132) occurs within range, but is bigger and has distinctive pattern, even when young. *Podarcis erhardii* (p. 171) is found on nearby islands (e.g. Sifnos, Serifos, Folegandros, and Sikinos) but lacks characteristic male colouring of *P. milensis*.

Family **ANGUIDAE** *Slow Worm and Glass Lizard*

A family of 70 to 80 species that is largely confined to the Americas. Only two kinds occur in the Old World: the Slow Worm (*Anguis fragilis*) and the Glass Lizards (*Ophisaurus*). The European Glass Lizard is the largest member of the family. Most anguids are rather long bodied, with either small limbs or no obvious limbs at all, as in the Old World species. These are consequently rather snake-like, although easily identified as lizards by their closable eyelids and fragile tails. Unlike most snakes, their bodies are rather stiff. The smooth shiny scales include a bony layer that often persists long after death, and looks like a pale imitation of the living animal.

European anguids are secretive and are most usually encountered in the open after rain and at twilight. The Slow Worm takes a high proportion of small slugs, while the Glass Lizard feeds on larger invertebrates and occasionally animals up to the size of small lizards and mice.

Slow Worms are particularly long-lived, and have been known to survive 54 years in captivity. Male anguids fight fiercely in the breeding season. Glass Lizards lay eggs (about 8–10 in the European species), but Slow Worms usually give birth to live young (normally 6–12, but sometimes more).

ANGUIS FRAGILIS *Slow Worm* **Pl. 33**

Range. Found over almost whole mainland of Europe but not S. Iberia, Ireland or extreme north. Occurs in Britain. Also east to Urals, Caucasus and parts of S.W. Asia; N.W. Africa Map 93.

Identification. Adults up to about 50cm total length but usually smaller. Intact tail is rather longer than the body, but is frequently shorter in adults as it is often broken and scarcely regenerates. A very smooth-scaled, snake-like reptile. Usually brown or grey or even reddish or coppery above. Females frequently have a vertebral stripe and rather dark sides and belly; males are more uniform but may have occasional blue spots, especially in east of range. Young are strikingly coloured: gold or silvery above with very dark sides, belly, and vertebral stripe.

Habits. Prefers well vegetated habitats with extensive ground cover and is often found in rather damp situations. Occurs in pastures, glades in woods, in lush scrub-land, on heaths, hedge-banks, railway embankments etc. Usually slow-moving and secretive and most likely to be encountered abroad at evening or after rain. May occasionally bask openly in sun but normally gets heat by lying beneath sun-warmed objects (flat stones, sheets of old iron etc.) or beneath vegetation. Most commonly encountered when turning over stones, logs etc.

Variation. Some variation in proportions, number of scales round body etc. Animals from S. Greece (Peloponnese) have, on average, more scales around mid-body (up to 34 or even more, as against up to about 30 elsewhere). Some individuals here also have very dark flanks, usually with a wavy upper border on neck, and often only a short vertebral stripe just behind head.

Similar Species. Differs from snakes in having closable eyelids and easily breakable tail. Could be confused with Greek Legless Skink (*Ophiomorus*, p. 181).

OPHISAURUS APODUS *European Glass Lizard* **Pl. 33**

Range. Balkans as far north as Istria and N.E. Bulgaria. Also Crimea, Caucasus and parts of S.W. and central Asia Map 94.

Identification. Adults up to 120cm (unbroken tail is about 1½ times as long as body). Looks rather like a giant Slow Worm (*Anguis*, above). A heavy-bodied, snake-like animal, easily distinguished from other European reptiles that are more or less legless by a prominent groove on each side of the body. Adults may be as thick as a man's wrist and are usually uniform yellowish brown or warm brown, darkening with age although head may remain pale. Young have more strongly keeled scales than adults and distinctive colouring: greyish above with well-defined dark bars. Most individuals have minute vestiges of legs on either side of vent.

Habits. Usually found in fairly dry habitats, often frequenting rocky hill-

Plate 31   SMALL LACERTAS 7c:

South Balkans and Aegean Islands

See also **Pls. 29** and **30** for S. Balkan mainland etc.

1. **Podarcis milensis** *Milos Wall Lizard*   173
   Milos and nearby islands: the only small Lacerta in the area.
   Throat and sides of head largely black in males.

   1a. Male.
   1b. Female.
   1c. Underside of male.

2. **Podarcis erhardii** *Erhard's Wall Lizard*   171
   S. Balkans (not most of Peloponnese) and Aegean islands
   (not Milos group): on islands where it occurs, nearly always
   the only Small Lacerta present.

   On mainland, dark dorsolateral streaks if present nearly
   always better developed than vertebral one (cf. *P. muralis*).
   In N.W. Peloponnese, *P. peloponnesiaca* can be confused
   but has few supraciliary granules (0–7, not 10–17, see Fig.,
   p. 173).

   2a, 2c. Males.
   2b, 2d. Females.
   2e. Underside of breeding male (colour quite variable).

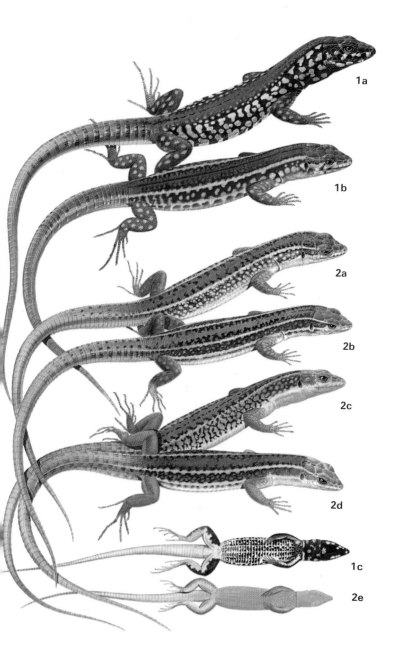

1a

1b

2a

2b

2c

2d

1c

2e

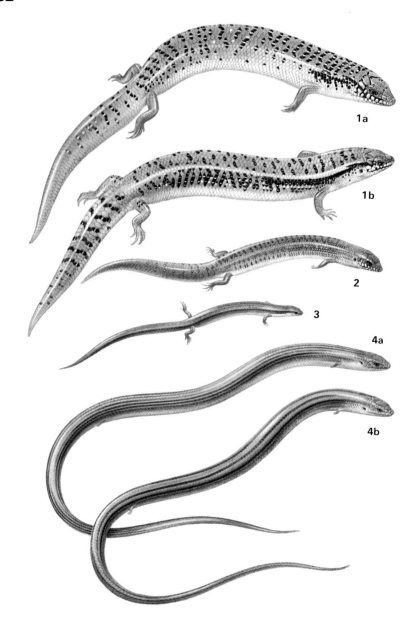

1a

1b

2

3

4a

4b

SKINKS   Plate 32
(× ½)

Small or medium-sized lizards with cylindrical bodies, thick necks, short legs and very smooth, shiny scales.

1. **Chalcides ocellatus**   *Ocellated Skink*   179
   Sardinia, Sicily, Malta, Naples area, Greece, Crete etc. Up to 30 cm. Pattern of dark-edged ocelli.

   1a. Typical form: Greece, Crete etc.
   1b. Striped form: other areas.

2. **Chalcides bedriagai**   *Bedriaga's Skink*   180
   Iberia only. Like small *C. ocellatus* (see also Fig., p. 179).

3. **Ablepharus kitaibelii**   *Snake-eyed Skink*   178
   Balkan area. Very small (usually under 13.5 cm total length). Eye lacks normal eye-lids and will not close when touched.

4. **Chalcides chalcides**   *Three-toed Skink*   180
   S.W. Europe, Italy, Sicily and Sardinia. Snake-like, with tiny limbs.

   4a. Typical French and Iberian pattern: numerous dark stripes.
   4b. Common Italian pattern: broad pale dorsolateral stripes.

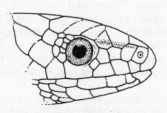

Snake-eyed Skink

sides with some cover, light woods, dry-stone walls and embankments, stone piles etc. May be found in cultivated areas, even near human habitations. Diurnal and crepuscular: often active after rain. Can move fairly fast when alarmed but lacks stamina. Tail does not break off very easily: when it does so, it regenerates only slowly.

Variation. Little variation.

Similar Species. Not likely to be confused with any other reptile.

Family SCINCIDAE *Skinks*

A large family of lizards widely distributed over the warmer parts of the world. About 700 species are recognised, of which only five certainly occur in Europe. A sixth species, *Chalcides moseri* Ahl, 1937 was recorded from the island of Santorin (Thera) in the Cyclades, but has never been seen since; the only specimen is lost, and the status of the form is uncertain. In Europe, skinks are small or medium-sized, ground-dwelling lizards with large, smooth, shiny scales. The head is small, the neck relatively thick and the body often elongate. The limbs are small or even absent and there are no femoral pores. Skinks are mainly diurnal, but often rather secretive. They feed largely on a wide variety of invertebrates. A fairly high proportion of species, including the European species of *Chalcides*, give birth to living young (about 3–10 in *C. ocellatus*, two or three in *C. bedriagai* and up to 23 in *C. chalcides*), but others, such as *Ablepharus kitaibelii*, lay eggs.

ABLEPHARUS KITAIBELII *Snake-eyed Skink* Pl. 32

Range. S. and E. Balkans, north to Hungary, S. Czechoslovakia and Romania; some Aegean islands (but not Crete). Also parts of S.W. Asia Map 95.

Identification. Up to about 13.5 cm total length (tail 1½–2 times length of body). A slim, diminutive, very glossy lizard with a relatively thick tail; legs very short and head small. At close quarters, easily separated from other skinks by eye which lacks obvious eyelids and does not close when touched. Bronze-brown to olive above with distinctly darker sides. Back may be plain or have small dark and light flecks (often in rows) or even stripes.

Habits. Mainly a lowland animal. Over much of range, often found in quite dry places: south facing slopes, meadows, and edges and clearings of open oak and chestnut woods, where it hides in fallen leaves, bush-bases etc. May also occur in places with a covering of grass or other low dense vegetation. This is especially so in the south of its range where it is sometimes encountered in quite moist habitats and tends to be active mainly in the spring and autumn and after rain. Often basks but sometimes active even in twilight. Not particularly agile, but can retreat effectively into its dense habitat.

Variation. Some regional variation in scaling, proportions and pattern. Southern animals tend to be smaller-headed than northern ones and, on the whole, are more uniform in colour. *Ablepharus* on small islands east of Crete have relatively large heads and relatively long limbs.

Similar Species. None really similar. Only other skink in range with legs, *Chalcides ocellatus* (below), is more robust, even when young, has different colouring and normal eye-lids.

CHALCIDES OCELLATUS   *Ocellated Skink*   Pl. 32

Range. Sardinia, Sicily, Malta, Pantellaria, and Portici near Naples; Greece (Attica region and Peloponnese), Euboa, Crete. Also N. and N.E. Africa and S.W. Asia   Map 96.

Identification. Up to 30 cm total length, of which tail may be about half, but is often much less. A fairly large, glossy, long-bodied skink with thick neck, small pointed head and short, five-toed limbs. Tail often considerably thinner than body. Loreal scale borders second and third labials (see Fig., below); 28–38 scales round mid-body. Often buff, pale brown or grey with a pattern of dark-edged ocelli, or short pale streaks bordered by dark pigment. The dark areas often join together to produce irregular cross-bars. In Europe, there are two fairly distinct forms. Greek and Cretan animals are relatively small (rarely much over 20 cm total length). Individuals from further west are usually larger, rather more flattened and have a pale dorsolateral stripe on each side, bordered by a dark streak on the flank.

Habits. Typically found in sandy places, often in lowlands and frequently near sea. Occurs in scrub areas behind beaches, in vineyards, field systems etc., where it often hides in crevices of dry-stone walls, in holes in the ground and under stones. May also burrow swiftly into loose sand or matted plant growth. Encountered in both dry and rather moist places. In Europe, largely diurnal, being most active early in morning, at evening and on warm but overcast days. May also be active at night during very

Ocellated Skink

Bedriaga's Skink

warm weather. Rather timid, retreating swiftly when approached. Tends to skulk close to cover. Very fast and agile.

Variation. See above. Considerable variation in pattern, particularly in amount of dark pigment.

Similar Species. None within range.

CHALCIDES BEDRIAGAI *Bedriaga's Skink*   Pl. 32

Range. Iberian peninsula only   Map 97.

Identification. Adults up to 16 cm total length, of which tail may be about half. Rather like a smaller version of *C. ocellatus*. An elongate, small-headed lizard with short, five-toed limbs. Loreal scale borders second upper labial only (Fig., p. 179); 24–28 scales round body. Usually buff, brown or grey with scattered black-edged ocelli; often a pale, dorsolateral band on either side. Some regional variation. Animals from S. Spain tend to be very short-legged with a roundish cross section and small ear openings (smaller than nasals); western individuals are longer legged with a squarish cross-section and larger ear openings; eastern animals are more or less intermediate in these features and tend to be more strongly marked.

Habits. Rather variable. In many areas, especially in south of range, lives in sandy places either with sparse vegetation or with a good cover of low plants. If ground cover extensive, may be quite abundant but secretive; often keeps out of sight and is most usually encountered when plants are uprooted and stones and logs turned over. Can burrow very quickly in loose sand. May also occur in hilly areas where it tends to be less secretive than elsewhere and may be found in grassy places and in leaf litter.

Variation. Considerable variation in proportions (see above) and in colour; also some minor differences in scaling.

Similar Species. None within range.

CHALCIDES CHALCIDES *Three-toed Skink*   Pl. 32

Range. Iberia, S. France, Italy, Sicily, Elba and Sardinia. Also N.W. Africa   Map 98.

Identification. Up to about 40 cm but usually smaller; unbroken tail about half of total length. A very elongate, snake-like skink, with tiny, three-toed limbs and 22–24 scales round mid-body. Typically olive, grey, brown, bronze or even sand-coloured, often with a metallic gloss. Considerable variation in pattern. French and Iberian animals usually have 9–13 narrow dark stripes on back and are only occasionally unmarked. Elsewhere, animals may have two pale, often dark-edged streaks, while others are more or less uniform (proportion of unmarked animals varies from place to place: they are absent from Sardinia).

Habits. Usually found in damp places with a low but dense herbaceous plant-growth: grassy slopes, water meadows, fields near streams etc. Rare in mountain areas. Diurnal. Very swift and agile: when it travels over the surface of vegetation, its body bends from side to side so fast that it can scarcely be seen. Takes refuge in holes and dense herbage. Very sensitive to cold, emerges late from hibernation and avoids wind. Occasionally encountered in dry situations.

Variation. Considerable variation in colour (see above); also some in relative length of legs and toes (second hind toe tends to be longer than third in east of range, often equal to third in west).

Similar Species. None really similar; easily separated from snakes and legless lizards by its tiny limbs.

OPHIOMORUS PUNCTATISSIMUS *Greek Legless Skink*   **Pl. 33**
Range. S. Greece and Kythera island (perhaps also N. Greece). Also S.W. Asia Minor   Map 99.

Identification. Up to 20 cm total length, of which tail (if unbroken) is about half. A small, shiny, snake-like, legless lizard with (viewed from above) a pointed snout. 18 (occasionally 20) rows of scales round mid-body. Typically cream, buff, or brown above, paler and greyer elsewhere. Usually there is a pattern of fine dark lines or rows of flecks which is best developed on the tail and weakest on the back. These markings are more obvious in young animals.

Habits. Often occurs in spring on loamy slopes with grass or some other low vegetation and scattered stones, under which it is usually found. Prefers stones that are naturally half submerged. Appears to go deeper into ground in dry weather. Burrows swiftly in loose soil. When disturbed, often moves conspicuously striped tail more than head.

Variation. Some in colouring.

Similar Species. Slow Worm (*Anguis fragilis*, p. 175) is larger with a different pattern, blunter snout and usually 23 or more rows of scales round body. Worm Snake (*Typhlops vermicularis*, p. 188) might also be confused with *Ophiomorus*.

Family **AMPHISBAENIDAE** *Amphisbaenians*
(Worm 'Lizards')

The members of this and one other related family have usually been known as Worm Lizards; however, they have many anatomical peculiarities and it is now believed that they are not lizards but constitute a separate group that is quite distinct from lizards and snakes although related to both. For this reason it seems better to call these animals Amphisbaenians.

Amphisbaenians are very specialised reptiles adapted to an almost exclusively subterranean existence and are rarely encountered on the surface. Most species feed on invertebrates, especially ants and termites: the majority including the one European species appear to lay eggs.

BLANUS CINEREUS *Amphisbaenian*   **Pl. 33**

Range. Iberian Peninsula. Also Morocco and Algeria   Map 100.

Identification. Up to about 30cm total length but usually smaller. At first sight, looks like a rather plump earthworm. Head small and pointed with tiny eyes, tail short, body with a series of grooves that separate rings of small squarish scales. Colour variable: may be yellowish, brown or grey, often heavily tinged with pink or violet; underside paler than back.

Habits. Rarely seen on surface of ground although may come up occasionally, particularly in heavy rain, at evening or at night. Otherwise entirely subterranean and usually found when turning stones and logs, when ground is being dug or ploughed, and when plants are uprooted. Often occurs in moist places, both in soils with a lot of humus and in ones that are predominantly sandy. Frequently found in pine woods and in cultivated areas.

Variation. Some variation in colour.

Similar Species. None.

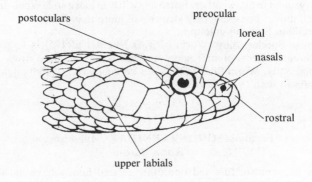

HEAD SCALES OF SNAKES

Snakes – Ophidia

Some 2700 species of snakes exist, of which only 27 occur in Europe. All are obviously scaly and legless (or at most with tiny vestiges of hind legs), and have eyes that cannot be closed. Legless lizards may be superficially similar to snakes and so may amphisbaenians, but in Europe legless lizards have closable eyes and, unlike most snakes (except the Worm Snake, *Typhlops*), their belly scales are not enlarged. Amphisbaenians are easily distinguished from snakes because their bodies have circular grooves along their length, like earthworms.

Identification. Many scale features useful in identifying snakes are illustrated in the key and texts. Head scaling is shown in Fig., below and opposite. Other helpful characteristics are body-proportions (stout or slender), head-shape, colour and pattern.

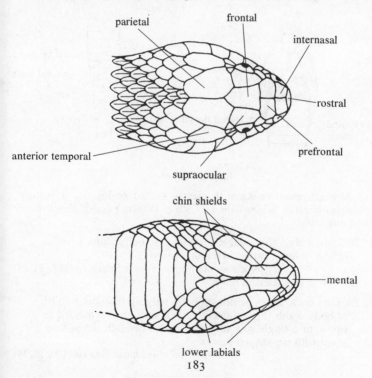

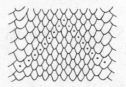

Counting dorsal scales. It is sometimes necessary to make a count of the longitudinal rows of small scales on the upper surface of the body. This is done across the body, half-way between the head and vent. Starting at one side of a belly scale, count diagonally forwards to the middle of the back and then diagonally backwards to the other side of the belly scale. See Fig., above.

Counting ventral scales. In a few cases it may be helpful to count the belly scales. The first belly scale counted is that bordered by the lowest dorsal scale row on each side. It is found by following these dorsal scale rows forwards along the neck until they break away from the belly scales. A count finishes on the scale in front of the preanal scale (Fig., below).

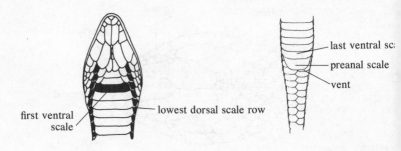

first ventral scale

lowest dorsal scale row

last ventral sc:

preanal scale

vent

Key to Snakes

N.B. Any European snake with clearly keeled scales *and* a vertical, slit-shaped pupil in bright light is a Viper (*Vipera*) and is dangerously venomous.

1. Balkans only. No enlarged scales on belly; adults small (35 cm or less); rather like a dry worm
   Typhlops vermicularis, Worm Snake (p. 188, Pl. 34)
   Row of large scales on belly   **2**

2. Balkans only. Large scales on belly only up to about a third of body width (Fig., opposite). Tail very short, rounded at tip, with a single row of broad scales beneath. Eyes very small with slit-shaped pupils
   Eryx jaculus, Sand Boa (p. 189, Pl. 34)

Broad scales on belly more than a half of body width (Fig., below); undamaged tail not very short and not rounded at tip, a double row of broad scales beneath. Eyes not very small **3**

Sand Boa

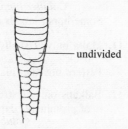

most other snakes

Snake bellies

3. Dorsal scales clearly and strongly keeled (Fig., below) **4**
Dorsal scales unkeeled or, if lightly keeled, pupil is round and 23–27 rows of dorsal scales are present. Scales may be grooved in one species **7**

keeled

unkeeled

Dorsal scales of snakes

4. Pupil round, preanal scale usually divided (Fig., below) **5**
Pupil slit-shaped in good light, preanal scale usually undivided (Fig., below)
Vipera, Vipers (see separate key on p. 214)

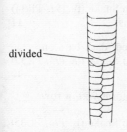

divided

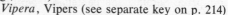

undivided

Snake preanal scales

5. Nostrils not clearly directed upwards; internasals broad and rectangular (Fig., p. 202); often a pale collar behind head *Natrix natrix*, Grass Snake (p. 201, Pl. 37)
Nostrils directed upwards; internasals narrow towards front (Fig., p. 202); no obvious pale collar behind head **6**

6. E. and central Europe. Usually eight upper labials; fourth and sometimes fifth in contact with eye; three or four (or even more) postoculars (Fig. 202); usually 19 rows of dorsal scales at mid-body *Natrix tessellata*, Dice Snake (p. 204, Pl. 37)
W. and S.W. Europe. Usually seven upper labials, third and fourth in contact with eye; two (rarely three) postoculars (Fig., p. 202); usually 21 rows of dorsal scales at mid-body
Natrix maura, Viperine Snake (p. 203, Pl. 37)

7. Frontal scale very narrow and deep set (Fig., p. 191); a distinct brow ridge over eyes extending forwards onto snout, which gives snake characteristic expression
Malpolon monspessulanus, Montpellier Snake (p. 190, Pl. 34)
Frontal not very narrow; no very prominent brow ridge **8**

8. S.E. Europe and Malta only. Pupil vertically slit-shaped in bright light *Telescopus fallax*, Cat Snake (p. 207, Pl. 38)
Most areas. Pupil always round in S.E. Europe and Malta **9**

9. Iberia and Balearics only. Rostral low, anterior temporal usually single, largest upper labial reaches or approaches parietal (Figs., p. 207); pupil may be vertically oval in bright light
Macroprotodon cucullatus, False Smooth Snake (p. 206, Pl. 38)
Most areas. Rostral narrower and higher, anterior temporal often double, largest upper labial usually well separated from parietal; pupil round **10**

10. Iberia, Sardinia and Pantellaria. No upper labials reach eye; characteristic pattern
Coluber hippocrepis, Horseshoe Whip Snake (p. 191, Pl. 34)
Some upper labials reach eye (rare exceptions) **11**

11. Malta only. Usually a series of well-separated, dark bars on back *Coluber algirus*, Algerian Whip Snake (p. 194, Pl. 35)
Pattern not like this **12**

12. Balkans only. Extremely slender. Fairly uniform with a row of prominent, dark spots on sides of neck
Coluber najadum, Dahl's Whip Snake (p. 194, Pl. 35)
Not extremely slender; pattern different **13**

13. Balkans, S. Italy, Sicily and Malta. Pattern of red or brown, black-edged spots or stripes
   Elaphe situla, Leopard Snake (p. 197, Pl. 36)
   Pattern not like this **14**

14. Balkans, Italy and Sicily. Back scales lightly but distinctly keeled in adults, 23–27 rows of dorsal scales at mid-body, two preoculars present (Fig., p. 199). Usually with prominent stripes or with blotches
   Elaphe quatuorlineata, Four-lined Snake (p. 198, Pl. 36)
   Back scales unkeeled; often one preocular **15**

15. Usually 23 or more rows of dorsal scales at mid-body; if 21 then no well-defined dark streak from eye to neck **16**
   19 or 21 (rarely 23) rows of dorsal scales at mid-body **17**

16. 23 (rarely 21) rows of dorsals at mid-body; rostral scale not clearly pointed behind
   Elaphe longissima, Aesculapian Snake (p. 199, Pl. 36)
   S.W. Europe. 27 (rarely 25 or 29) rows of dorsals at mid-body; rostral scale pointed behind
   Elaphe scalaris, Ladder Snake (p. 200, Pl. 36)

17. Usually a dark streak from eye to neck; 19 or 21 (rarely 23) rows of scales at mid-body **18**
   No dark streak from eye to neck; usually 19 rows of dorsal scales at mid-body
   Coluber viridiflavus, Western Whip Snake (p. 195, Pl. 35)
   Coluber gemonensis, Balkan Whip Snake (p. 196, Pl. 35)
   Coluber jugularis, Large Whip Snake (p. 196, Pl. 35)

18. Belly more or less uniform; usually a dark stripe from nostril to eye; often third and fourth upper labials reach eye (Fig. p. 206); usually 19 rows of dorsal scales at mid-body
   Coronella austriaca, Smooth Snake (p. 204, Pl. 38)
   Belly with bold, contrasting pattern; usually no dark stripe from nostril to eye, fourth and fifth upper labials reach eye (Fig., p. 206); usually 21 rows of dorsal scales at mid-body
   Coronella girondica, Southern Smooth Snake (p. 205, Pl. 38)

NOTE. The **Dwarf Snake** (*Eirenis modestus*) of S.W. Asia has been recorded from European Turkey on two occasions and may be established in the area, but this is unconfirmed. A combination of 17 rows of dorsal scales at mid-body and a dark collar just behind the head distinguish it from other snakes in E. Europe.

Family **TYPHLOPIDAE** *Worm Snakes*

There are about 200 species of Worm Snakes, all very similar in appearance, which occur throughout the warmer parts of the world. Typically they are small (usually under 30 cm but sometimes to over 70 cm), slender with an inconspicuous head, and reduced eyes; there are no enlarged ventral shields and the body is completely covered with small, shiny scales. Worm Snakes are usually secretive burrowers. The single European species lays four to eight elongate eggs.

TYPHLOPS VERMICULARIS *Worm Snake*   **Pl. 34**
Range. S. Balkans north to Albania, S. Yugoslavia and S. Bulgaria; a few Greek islands (e.g. Corfu, Skyros and some Cyclades). Also S.W. Asia, Caucasus and N.E. Egypt   Map 101.
Identification. Adults occasionally up to 35 cm, including tail, but usually smaller. Quite different from other European snakes and more like a dry shiny worm. Very slender and cylindrical and slightly thicker towards tail. Head inconspicuous, rather flattened with rounded snout, not distinct from body. Eyes on top of head, but underneath scales and appear as two tiny black spots. Tail rounded, very short (as wide as long) with a distinct spine at tip. Scales smooth, 21–24 rows around body. Differs from all other European snakes in not having large ventral scales. Colour usually brownish, often tinged yellow, pinkish, or purple. Belly slightly paler than upper surface.
Habits. Mainly subterranean in fairly dry, open habitats without a dense covering of high vegetation. Grassy fields and slopes with scattered stones are often favoured, but Worm Snakes are sometimes encountered in more barren areas, and even fairly close to sea. In spring, can often be found by turning half sunken stones, but in summer retreats deeper into ground. Occupies narrow burrows (like those of worms) down which it retreats very quickly when disturbed. Occasionally seen on the surface, especially at twilight or in wet weather, and more rarely during the day. Pointed tail is used to gain purchase when travelling over the ground. Feeds mainly on small invertebrates, especially ants and their larvae.
Variation. Little variation in Europe.
Similar Species. Unlikely to be confused with any other European snake. In Greece etc., sometimes found in same habitats as the Greek Legless Skink, *Ophiomorus punctatissimus,* p. 181, which can appear superficially similar. But the skink is relatively thicker, has a much longer tail, a pointed head with eyes on side, and usually a pattern of stripes or rows of spots that increase in intensity towards the tail-tip.

Family **BOIDAE** *Sand Boas*

Boid snakes constitute a rather primitive family of about 80 species. Most of these are confined to the tropics although a few are found in more temperate areas. The family contains the largest known snakes (Pythons and Anacondas), but many species are quite small. This is true of the European Sand Boa, one of a group of ten species adapted to dry, or even desert conditions and found mainly in central and S.W. Asia and N. Africa. Like many other boids, Sand Boas give birth to living young (6–18 in the European species, sometimes more).

ERYX JACULUS *Sand Boa*   **Pl. 34**
Range. S. Balkans north to S. Albania and Yugoslavia, S. Bulgaria, and S.E. Romania (where may be extinct); occurs on some Greek islands. Also S.W. Asia and N. Africa   Map 102.
Identification. Adults up to 80 cm, including tail, rarely more and usually less. A very stout snake with short, blunt tail (usually less than one-tenth of total length) and poorly defined, rather pointed head; snout chisel-shaped and overhanging; eyes very small with slit-shaped pupils (in good light). Belly scales extremely narrow – about a third of body width or less. Dorsal scales, including those of most of head, small, rather glossy, and not obviously keeled; 40–50, or more, rows at mid-body. Colouring very variable. Usually pale greyish, buffish, brownish, or even reddish with darker bars and blotches that often join forming an irregular network enclosing isolated areas of ground colour. Frequently a dark ∧-shaped mark on back of head, and dark streak from eye to corner of mouth. Belly pale yellowish or whitish.
Habits. Found principally in dry habitats, usually with good covering of light soil or sand, such as arable land, dry beaches, or even sandy soil at the bottom of rocky hollows etc. Spends much of time in rodent galleries but may burrow actively in loose soil. Usually encountered during day only when dug or ploughed up, or when stones, logs, etc. are turned over. May come to surface, especially at night or twilight, when it is fairly swift (animals uncovered during day tend to move slowly). Feeds largely on small rodents, but lizards, nestling birds, and even slugs may be eaten occasionally. Large animals are constricted before swallowing. Apparently hunts mainly in mammal burrows, but sometimes lies beneath surface of soft soil and catches passing prey. Produces live young.
Variation. Considerable variation in colour and pattern.
Similar Species. None within European range. Adults have general build of large viper, but head is narrower, and even undamaged tail has blunt, rounded tip.

Family COLUBRIDAE   *Typical snakes*

This very large family, which may not be a natural one, is extremely widely distributed, being absent only from much of Australia, from very cold areas and from some islands (e.g. Ireland and New Zealand). It contains the majority of European snake species. All European colubrids have the head covered by large scales. Most are essentially diurnal and have round pupils, the only exceptions being the crepuscular Southern Smooth Snake (*Coronella girondica*), False Smooth Snake (*Macroprotodon cucullatus*) and Cat Snake (*Telescopus fallax*); in these, the pupils are round, often oval and slit-shaped respectively. The two latter species and the Montpellier Snake (*Malpolon monspessulanus*) are the only European colubrids with fangs, which are at the back of the upper jaw. Most species lay eggs, but the Smooth Snake (*Coronella austriaca*) produces from 2–15 living young. The number of eggs laid by the other species is rather variable: *Coluber hippocrepis* 5–10; *C. jugularis* 6–16; *C. najadum* 3–6; *C. viridiflavus* 5–15; *Coronella girondica* about 7; *Elaphe longissima* 5–15; *E. quatuorlineata* 3–18; *E. situla* 2–7; *E. scalaris* 6–12; *Macroprotodon cucullatus* 5–7; *Malpolon monspessulanus* 4–20; *Natrix maura* 4–20; *N. natrix* 11–50; *N. tesselata* 5–25; *Telescopus fallax* 7–8.

Within a species, clutch size may correlate roughly with the size of the mother.

MALPOLON MONSPESSULANUS   *Montpellier Snake*   Pl. 34

Range. Iberia, Mediterranean coast of France, Italy (Liguria and Trentino only), E. Adriatic coast, S. Balkans, and a few Greek islands (Corfu, Cephalonia, Zante, Thasos, Samothrace, Skopelos, Euboa). Also N. Africa, W. Caspian area and S.W. Asia   Map 103.

Identification. Adults up to 200 cm, including tail, but usually less. A large, formidable, often uniform snake with rather stiff, slender body and narrow characteristically shaped head: eyes very large and 'eye-brows' raised and overhanging, extending forwards onto snout as two strong ridges with a hollow between them. Snout overhangs lower jaw and the frontal scale is very narrow. The combination of large eyes and strong 'brows' give this snake a very penetrating expression. Dorsal scales smooth or grooved (but not keeled), in 17 or 19 rows at mid body. Pattern very variable; ground colour grey, reddish-brown, olive, greenish, or blackish. Many adults are more or less uniform, but may have scattered light or dark spots, or both. Some have flanks darker than back and others retain a weak version of juvenile colouring. Belly is often yellowish, mottled or suffused with dark pigment. Some hatchlings are fairly uniform, others have a series of vague dark blotches on back and rows of small darker spots on sides. Irregular, light spots may also be present and the head and throat often bear regular, well-defined light and dark markings.

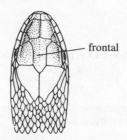

frontal

Montpellier Snake

Habits. An active and terrestrial snake occurring up to 2000 m in southern part of its range. Most usually found in warm, dry habitats, nearly always with some plant cover in which it often hides. Prefers open rocky or sandy country with bushy vegetation, but is also encountered on arable land, in open woods and even in salt-marsh and sand-dune vegetation near sea. May sometimes occur on edge of moist woods (e.g. in Italy) and on river banks, and sometimes even swims. When threatened, hisses loudly and for long periods; may also flatten body and spread neck. Temperament varies but provoked animals often try to bite. Food includes large proportion of lizards (adults even take full grown Ocellated Lizards, *Lacerta lepida*); other snakes and small mammals (up to size of small rabbits) are also eaten, as well as occasional birds (especially the young of ground-dwelling species) and, in the case of juveniles, invertebrates. Prey is hunted largely by sight.

Venom. Prey animals are killed within minutes by action of venom. Fangs are at back of upper jaw, so the snake must take a very secure grip before they can function. Because of this they are only liable to be used effectively on human beings if the snake is actually picked up (a severe bite from a free snake is unlikely). In man, prolonged bites to the hand produce numbing and stiffness in the arm, as well as swelling and even fever. This usually passes in a few hours.

Variation. Considerable variation in colouring. Western animals usually have 19 rows of dorsal scales at mid-body, eastern ones tend to have 17.

Similar Species. *Malpolon* is unmistakable if the head can be seen.

COLUBER HIPPOCREPIS *Horseshoe Whip Snake*   **Pl. 34**
Range. Iberian Peninsula (particularly south, west and east), S. Sardinia, Pantellaria. Also N.W. Africa   Map 104.
Identification. Adults up to 150 cm, but usually smaller. A fairly slender snake with a characteristic pattern. The only European snake with broad belly scales (apart from vipers) that regularly has a row of small scales below eye. Head well defined, eyes fairly large (with round pupil) and scales smooth. A series of large, closely spaced spots on back which are

Plate 33
LEGLESS LIZARDS and AMPHISBAENIAN
(*1* × ½; *2-4* × ⅔)

European legless lizards have closable eye-lids, breakable tails and unenlarged belly scales.

1. **Ophisaurus apodus** *European Glass Lizard* 175
S.E. Europe. Very large (up to 120 cm). Prominent groove on flank.

    1a. Adult: colour uniform.
    1b. Young: pale with dark bars.

2. **Anguis fragilis** *Slow Worm* 175
Very smooth scales. Blunt head.

    2a. Male: often rather uniform; may have blue spots.
    2b. Female: often with dark flanks.
    2c. Young: gold or silvery usually with very dark vertebral stripe, flanks and belly.

3. **Ophiomorus punctatissimus** *Greek Legless Skink* 181
Greece only. Small (up to 20 cm). Pattern strongest on tail. Head (viewed from above) pointed.

4. **Blanus cinereus** *Amphisbaenian* 182
Iberia. Blunt, short tail. Ring-like grooves on body.

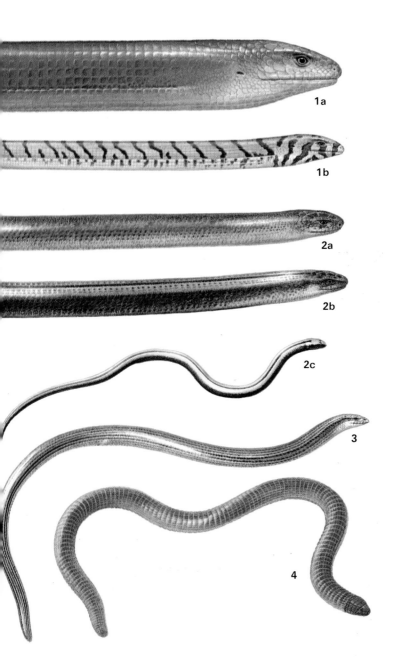

1a

1b

2a

2b

2c

3

4

1

2a

2b

3a

3b

4

Plate 34
WORM SNAKE, SAND BOA, MONTPELLIER
SNAKE and HORSESHOE WHIP SNAKE
(*3* and *4* × ⅔)

1. **Typhlops vermicularis** *Worm Snake* **188**
   S. Balkans. Like small, dry, shiny worm. Eyes small. Tail
   thicker than small head.

2. **Eryx jaculus** *Sand Boa* **189**
   S. Balkans. Tail blunt. Eyes small with vertical pupil. Belly
   scales narrow (Fig., p. 185).

   2a. Head and neck.
   2b. Tail.

3. **Malpolon monspessulanus** *Montpellier Snake* **190**
   Brow-ridges give penetrating expression. Frontal scale
   narrow.

   3a. Adult: often fairly uniform.
   3b. Young: may be uniform or spotted.

4. **Coluber hippocrepis** *Horseshoe Whip Snake* **191**
   S., W. and E. Iberia. Pantellaria, S. Sardinia. Bold pattern
   of dark-edged blotches. Row of small scales under eye.
   Adults often generally dark; juveniles brighter.

often blackish or dark brown with a black edge; flanks also have one or more rows of smaller dark spots. Ground colour olive, yellowish or reddish but frequently largely hidden by dark pigment so that snake appears mainly blackish. Often a ∧ or ∩-shaped mark on back of head (may be joined to first spot on neck). Belly yellow, orange, or red, usually with dark spots, especially at sides. Young generally like adults but more contrasting: ground colour not overlaid by dark pigment and spots on back are yellowish, grey or greenish. Dorsal scales in 25–29 rows at mid-body; 220–258 ventral scales.

Habits. A fast, diurnal snake found in dry, often rocky places, scrub covered hillsides etc. Also occurs in and around human habitations and buildings. Largely ground-dwelling but can climb well in bushes, on shelving rock faces and stone walls. Food of adults consists of mainly small mammals and birds: the young take lizards.

Variation. Some variation in colouring.

Similar Species. None within range. Young may look rather like juvenile *Elaphe situla* but the two species do not occur in the same area and *E. situla* lacks a row of small scales below the eye. See also *Coluber algirus* (below).

COLUBER ALGIRUS *Algerian Whip Snake* **Pl. 35**

Range. In Europe, confined to Malta. Also N.W. Africa   Map 105.

Identification. Adults up to about 100 cm, including tail, usually smaller. A slender snake with a well-defined, rather narrow head, and prominent eye (roundish pupil). Scales smooth. Adult usually greyish or brown, with dark head or collar and usually series of well separated dark bars on back. Two rows of dark spots on each flank; upper row out of phase with bars on back, lower row reaches edge of ventrals. Pattern may fade with age. Belly whitish. Young similar to adults, but pattern bolder and ground colour may have yellowish or pinkish tinge. Dorsal scales in 25 rows at mid-body; 210–225 ventrals.

Habits. Apparently often lives in dry stony places and sometimes in ruins, rockpiles etc. Not common on Malta. Has been found in large dry ditches and on dry roadside banks. Probably an introduction from N.W. Africa.

Variation. Not much in Europe. May occasionally have a complete row of small scales below the eye.

Similar Species. None on Malta. See also *Coluber hippocrepis* (above).

COLUBER NAJADUM *Dahl's Whip Snake* **Pl. 35**

Range. S. Balkans: from Greece (including some off-shore islands) north to S. Bulgaria and S. Yugoslavia, and the E. Adriatic coastal region north to Istria. Also Caucasus and S.W. Asia   Map 106.

Identification. Adults usually less than 100 cm, including tail, but may reach about 135 cm. Easily identified by build and pattern. A very slender snake with narrow well-defined head, large eyes (with round pupil), smooth scales, and very long tail (often up to about a third of total length). Foreparts usually grey-green to olive-brown often becoming browner (or reddish-brown) towards tail. A row of large black to olive spots on sides of neck, each of which may be surrounded by concentric dark and light rings; front pair may join to form a collar behind head, especially in east of range. These spots are usually more prominent and extend further along body in young animals. Belly yellow or whitish and unspotted. 19 rows of dorsal scales at mid-body; 205–235 ventrals.

Habits. Diurnal and mainly terrestrial in dry, often stony habitats, usually with bushes and some dense, grassy vegetation in which it climbs. Found in open areas in woods, by overgrown walls, stony banks, path edges, etc. Very fast moving. Bites when handled. Feeds mainly on small lizards and grasshoppers; small mammals may also be taken occasionally.

Variation. Some variation in colour, and extent of neck markings.

Similar Species. None. Differs from other *Coluber* species within range in build and pattern, and in having a keel on each side of ventrals.

COLUBER VIRIDIFLAVUS *Western Whip Snake* Pl.35

Range. Extreme N.E. Spain, France (except north), S. Switzerland, and N.W. Yugoslavia, and south to Sicily and Malta. Occurs on Corsica, Sardinia, and various small islands (e.g. Krk and Pelagosa in Adriatic; Elba, Montecristo and Pontini islands in Tyrrhenian Sea). Sporadic in north of range   Map 107.

Identification. Adults up to about 150 cm, including tail, but may occasionally grow to almost 200 cm. A rather slender snake with a smallish but fairly well-defined head, smooth scales, fairly prominent eye, and round pupil. Over most of range has greenish-yellow ground colour, largely obscured by black or dark green pigment that forms indistinct crossbars on foreparts and reduces ground colour on rest of body to yellowish streaks or rows of spots. These characteristic markings on tail are often visible as snake retreats into cover. Belly yellowish or greyish, sometimes with small, dark spots. Most adults from northeast of range, S. Italy, Sicily, and some islands are almost entirely black. Young are pale grey or olive with bold head pattern (strong light markings); there may also be dark marks on foreparts. Full adult colouring is developed in about fourth year. Dorsal scales usually in 19 rows at mid-body; 180–230 ventral scales.

Habits. Largely diurnal and terrestrial, although can climb well among rocks and in bushes. Found in wide variety of mainly dry, well vegetated habitats, such as sunny, rocky hillsides, wood-edges, maccia and scrub, open woods, bushy areas, ruins and gardens. Occasionally also in damp meadows. Occurs up to 1500 m. Frequently very abundant; individuals often stay within a limited area. Very fast and agile, and hunts by sight. Extremely aggressive when captured and bites hard and persistently. Food of adults includes many lizards and a varying proportion of mam-

mals; also some nestling birds, other snakes (even vipers), and frogs. Juveniles take mainly small lizards and large grasshoppers.
Variation. Some variation in colouring (see above).
Similar Species. Most likely to be confused with *C. gemonensis* (below) and *C. jugularis* (below). *C. algirus*, *C. hippocrepis* and *Elaphe* species have characteristic patterns and higher numbers of dorsal scale rows. *Malpolon* (p. 190) has characteristic head-shape.

COLUBER GEMONENSIS   *Balkan Whip Snake*   Pl. 35
Range. E. Adriatic coast (including many islands), and Greece. Gioura island in Cyclades   Map 108.
Identification. Adults normally under 100 cm, including tail, occasionally longer. A rather slender snake with a fairly well-defined head, smooth scales, fairly prominent eye and round pupil. Olive-grey, grey-brown, or yellowish-brown with dark spots on foreparts that are often divided by light streaks and may form very irregular bars. Rest of body tends to have regular narrow light and dark stripes. Small white spots frequently present on edges of some dorsal scales. Underside yellowish or whitish; dark spots typically present on ventral scales, at least on sides of neck. Young very similar to those of *C. viridiflavus*. Dorsal scales usually in 19 rows at mid-body; ventrals usually 162–186.
Habits. Very similar to *C. viridiflavus* and occurs in similar places: scrub areas, vineyards, overgrown ruins, open woods, road banks etc. Diurnal and terrestrial although sometimes climbs in bushes etc. Bites fiercely when handled. Feeds mainly on lizards but may take large grasshoppers, small mammals and nestling birds.
Variation. Some minor variation in boldness and extent of dark markings. Animals from Gioura are black when adult and have high number of ventral scales (196–203).
Similar Species. Overlaps with the similar, and closely related, *C. viridiflavus* in north of range. *C. viridiflavus* has larger adult size, different adult colouring (often black in overlap areas, no small white spots on scales), and higher number of ventral scales than *C. gemonensis* in this area (188 or more). This last character will usually distinguish juveniles. *C. jugularis* (below) is also similar. *Elaphe* species have different patterns and more dorsal scale rows. Montpellier Snake (*Malpolon*, p. 190) has characteristic head shape.

COLUBER JUGULARIS   *Large Whip Snake*   Pl. 35
Range. Mainly S. and E. Balkans, north to S.W. U.S.S.R., Romania, Hungary and Yugoslavia (not west). Many Aegean islands (not Gioura). Also S.W. Asia   Map 109.
Identification. Adults often up to about 200 cm, including tail; sometimes 300 cm (250 cm in Europe). One of our longest snakes, with a fairly well-defined but smallish head, smooth scales, fairly prominent eye and

round pupil. When seen clearly, only likely to be confused with *C. gemonensis* (opposite). Body colour yellow-brown, olive-brown, or reddish above, with a pattern of (often rather weak) narrow stripes that extend all over body; no obvious dark blotches. Belly light yellow, orange, or orange-red, without dark spots even at sides of neck. Young greyish or brownish, usually with well spaced, short bars on back and no bold light markings on head; dark streak often present on midline of crown, belly may have a few dark spots at sides. Usually 19 rows of dorsal scales at mid-body; 189–215 ventral scales.

Habits. Generally like *C. viridiflavus* and *C. gemonensis*. A diurnal, very swift and largely terrestrial species living in dry, open habitats usually with some vegetation: rocky hillsides, embankments, vineyards, gardens, scrub, dry-stone walls etc. Often not very inclined to retreat and bites readily when handled. Adults eat mainly small mammals. Young take a high proportion of lizards and grasshoppers etc. In Aegean, does not usually occur on same islands as Four-lined Snake (*Elaphe quatuorlineata*, p. 198).

Variation. Some variation in colouring, but fairly uniform in Europe.

Similar Species. *C. gemonensis* (opposite) is rather similar, but is smaller with dark blotches and often small light spots and streaks on forepart of body, paler belly, with some dark spots, fewer ventral scales (162–186), and different markings in young. *Elaphe* species occurring in range have different patterns and more rows of dorsal scales. Montpellier Snake (*Malpolon*, p. 190) has characteristic head.

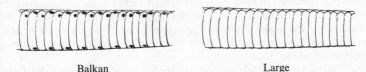

Balkan   Large

Whip snakes, undersides of necks

ELAPHE SITULA *Leopard Snake*   Pl. 36

Range. S. and W. Balkans, some Aegean islands, S. Italy, E. Sicily, Malta, S. Crimea. Also Asia Minor and Caucasus   Map 110.

Identification. Up to about 100 cm but usually smaller. A medium-sized fairly slender snake with characteristic pattern. Head rather narrow but well-defined, pupil round and scales smooth. Unlike most other *Elaphe*, adults retain juvenile pattern, often consisting of a row of black-edged brown to red spots on back and a row of smaller spots on each flank. Sometimes back spots are dumb-bell shaped or divided in two, or replaced by two dark-edged stripes. Ground colour is yellowish, greyish or buff. Underside is yellowish-white near head but becomes heavily marked towards tail so that mid and hind belly is often largely black. Head is boldly marked (see Plate). Eye is brown-red. Dorsal scales in 27 (occasionally 25) rows at mid-body; 220–260 ventral scales.

Habits. Usually found below 500 m. A largely ground-dwelling snake, active by day but also sometimes seen at dusk. Usually in sunny habitats, especially those including numerous rocks and stones: field-edges, road banks, stone-piles, screes, dry-stone walls; also sometimes marshes and stream edges. May be encountered in gardens and around barns and houses which it sometimes enters. Climbs quite well on stone-piles, walls and bushes. Sometimes vibrates tip of tail rapidly. Prey may be constricted. Food of adults consists almost entirely of small mammals, especially rodents. Young eat lizards.

Variation. Considerable variation in pattern.

Similar Species Young *Coluber hippocrepis* (p. 191) may have similar markings, but do not occur in same areas, *Elaphe situla* is not likely to be confused with species within its range, although Smooth Snakes (*Coronella sp.*, p. 204) may be vaguely similar as may young *Elaphe quatuorlineata*. The latter usually have very dark spots on back and two preoculars are present (Fig., opposite).

ELAPHE QUATUORLINEATA *Four-lined Snake* **Pl. 36**

Range. S.E. Europe north to Istria and S.W. USSR; many Aegean islands; central and S. Italy and Sicily; also parts of S.W. Asia Map 111.

Identification. Adults up to about 250 cm, including tail, but most animals under 150 cm. A large, moderately built snake that is more robust than other big colubrids within its range. Head rather long and somewhat pointed, pupil round and back scales lightly but distinctly keeled in adults giving the snake a rather rough appearance. Two preocular scales present (see Fig., opposite). Dorsal scales in 25 (rarely 23 or 27) rows, ventrals 195–234.

Colouring varies. *Western areas* (Italy, Sicily, W. Balkans, S.W. Bulgaria, Greece and Cyclades): adults yellowish, pale brown or grey with four dark stripes along the back and a dark streak on the side of the head. Underside usually yellowish often with some darker markings, especially on tail. Young have a row of dark, often black-edged, broad spots or bars on back and one or two series of smaller spots on each flank; head boldly marked; belly with dark markings that may form two streaks. Adult pattern is developed after about three years. *Eastern areas* (N.E. Greece, European Turkey, Bulgaria and Romania): young as in western populations. Adults lack stripes and tend to retain the juvenile markings, although they often become more uniform through darkening of the ground colour.

Habits. A rather phlegmatic, slow-moving snake that occurs to over 1200 m in south of range. Often found along wood-edges, hedges, open woods, rocky overgrown hillsides etc. Prefers some shade and likes a warm, rather humid environment; may be encountered in marshy areas and near pools and streams. Often hunts in warm, cloudy conditions and at dusk. Climbs and swims well. Food consists mainly of small mammals (up to the size of rats and young rabbits), but birds, especially nestlings, eggs and occasionally lizards may be eaten. Sometimes raids poultry yards. The young take a relatively high proportion of lizards. Like other *Elaphe* species, constricts larger prey. In Aegean, does not usually occur on same islands as Large Whip Snake (*Coluber jugularis*, p. 196).

Variation. Considerable variation in adult colouring (see above). Animals from some of the Cyclades do not grow large and develop striped patterning when quite small. Individuals from Amorgos (which were once regarded as a separate species, *E. rechingeri*) seem to be rather variable, and can be dark with poorly developed stripes; the young here may sometimes be rather pale.

Similar Species. *E. longissima* (below) is much more slender, lacks keels on dorsal scales at all ages and has only one preocular scale.

preoculars

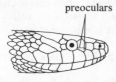

Four-lined Snake

Aesculapian Snake

ELAPHE LONGISSIMA *Aesculapian Snake* **Pl. 36**
Range. Central France, S. Switzerland, S. Austria, Czechoslovakia, S. Poland, and S.W. USSR; south to extreme N.E. Spain, Sicily and S. Greece. Also W. Sardinia, a few isolated localities in Germany and one in N.W. Spain. Outside Europe, occurs in Turkey and N. Iran Map 112.
Identification. Adults up to 200cm including tail but usually under 140cm. A large, slender snake with a rather narrow, well defined head, round pupil and smooth flat scales. Ventrals with a slight keel on each side. Adults usually more or less uniform grey-buff to olive-brown, often with small white spots on the scale edges. In some animals, there is also a vague pattern of dark or light stripes along the body (especially in Italy and Sicily). Usually a dark streak on temple and a vague yellow patch behind this. Underside pale yellowish or whitish. Young with 4–7 rows of small dark spots on body and a boldly marked head: often a dark ∧ or ∩-shaped mark on neck, a bar across snout in front of eyes and another on temple which is followed by brightish yellow blotch. Scales in 23 (rarely 21) rows, 210–248 ventrals.
Habits. Found up to about 1800m in some areas. Usually encountered in

Aesculapian Snake, belly showing keeled ventrals

dry habitats such as dry sunny woods, shrubby vegetation etc. but also on old walls, ruins and even hay stacks. In north of range confined to favourable localities such as sheltered, south facing slopes on light soils. Enjoys sun but retreats from excessive heat. A very adept climber, even ascending vertical tree trunks. Sometimes holds ground when approached and makes chewing movements with jaws. Food consists of mainly small mammals (especially mice and voles) which are constricted. Birds, especially nestlings also taken. Young often eat lizards.

Variation. Some variation in pattern (see p. 199). Black or very dark animals occur occasionally.

Similar Species. *E. scalaris* (S.W. Europe only, below), *E. quatuorlineata* (Italy and Balkans, p. 198). Whip Snakes (*Coluber spp.*, p. 191) and Montpellier Snake (*Malpolon*, p. 190) differ in general appearance and lower number of dorsal scale rows. Young may look rather like Grass Snake (*Natrix natrix* opposite).

ELAPHE SCALARIS *Ladder Snake*   Pl. 36

Range. Iberia, Mediterranean littoral of France, Iles d'Hyères, Minorca Map 113.

Identification. Adults up to about 160 cm, including tail, but most individuals less than 120 cm. A large, moderately built snake with a pointed, over-hanging snout and short tail. Pupil round, scales smooth; roştral shield very pointed behind. Adults fairly uniform in colour: yellow-grey to mid-brown with a pair of dark brown stripes on back; belly unmarked or with a few dark spots, eye dark brown. Young boldly marked with 'H'-shaped blotches on back which may join to form 'ladder'; irregular spots, streaks or bars on sides. Belly yellowish or whitish, marked with black that sometimes covers whole surface. Dorsal scales in 27 (rarely 25 or 29) rows at mid-body; 201–220 ventral scales.

Habits. Largely diurnal. Usually found in sunny, often stony habitats, typically with some bushy vegetation: hedges, vineyards, field-edges, scrub, open woods, overgrown dry-stone walls etc. Occurs mainly on ground, but also climbs well in bushes and even on trees or rock piles. Aggressive when captured. Adults eat warm-blooded prey, especially mammals (rodents, small rabbits etc.) but also birds (mainly nestlings). Very young animals seem to take grasshoppers and similar sized prey. Large prey is constricted.

Variation. Considerable variation in pattern with age but otherwise fairly constant.

Similar Species. In north-east of range poorly marked adults could be confused with *Elaphe longissima*, p. 199) but latter is more slender, has more rounded snout (with rostral shield less pointed behind), a 'keel' on each side of the ventrals, and only 23 rows of dorsals at mid body. Montpellier Snake (*Malpolon*, p. 190) lacks stripes on back, has more rounded snout, narrow frontal, and only 17 or 19 rows of dorsal scales at mid-body. Young animals may look superficially like Southern Smooth Snake (*Coronella girondica*, p. 205), but their pattern is rather different and they have more rows of dorsal scales.

NATRIX NATRIX   *Grass Snake*   Pl. 37

Range. Nearly all Europe; north to about 67°N in Scandinavia, to S. Finland, and USSR; absent from some islands, e.g. Ireland, Balearics, Malta, Crete, and some Cyclades. Also occurs in N.W. Africa and Asia east to Lake Baikal   Map 114.

Identification. Usually up to 120 cm, including tail, often less but occasionally up to 200 cm. Females grow larger than males. An often rather large snake (usually quite thick-bodied as an adult), with fairly well-defined, rounded head, round pupil, and keeled dorsal scales, usually in 19 rows at mid-body. Colour very variable, but many specimens have characteristic yellow (or, less commonly, white, orange or red), black bordered collar just behind the head. Body usually olive-grey, greenish, olive-brown or even steel-grey with various dark blotches and sometimes light stripes. Commonest patterns tend to vary from region to region as follows:

Britain, France, Switzerland and *central Italy*. Collar rather pale and sometimes absent in adults; usually dark bars on flanks, sometimes small spots on back.

S. Italy and *Sicily*. Often bars on back as well as sides.

Iberia. Adults often very uniform, without a clear collar.

N. and *N.E. Europe*. Collar well developed, yellow or even orange; body usually with dark spots.

S.E. Europe and *N. Italy*. Collar well developed, body often spotted and flanks often barred. Many animals have two light stripes running length of body.

Cyclades. Collar sometimes not obvious. Body often with three rows of dark blotches. Many specimens are almost entirely black, others flecked light yellow.

Corsica and *Sardinia*. Collar usually weak, body often with dark bars on each side that meet or almost meet at the mid-line.

Habits. Largely diurnal. Over most of its range it is a snake of damp places and in the south (where it may reach altitudes of 2400 m) usually occurs near water. In N. Europe, *N. natrix* is more of a lowland animal, but is less restricted in habitats and may sometimes be found in quite dry woods, hedgrows, and meadows. Swims well and may hunt in water at times, but is less aquatic than both *N. maura* and *N. tessellata*. When disturbed may hiss and strike with mouth closed, but rarely bites. Often voids evil-smelling contents of anal gland when handled, and may feign death, lying on back with mouth open and tongue hanging out. Food consists predominantly of frogs and toads, but newts, tadpoles and fish are also occasionally taken and even small mammals and nestling birds.

Variation. Apart from the variations in colour listed above, black specimens occur widely but are very rare in Britain.

Similar Species. Young Aesculapian Snakes (*Elaphe longissima*, p. 199) may look similar. Most likely to be confused with *N. maura* or *N. tessellata*. Pattern is often useful in identification. Apart from this, the following characters are helpful (see also Fig., below).

i   Lateral nostrils (not directed upwards).
ii   Broad rectangular internasals.
iii Typically 7 upper labials with 3rd and 4th entering eye.
iv   Usually 19 rows of dorsal scales.
v   Usually a single preocular.
vi   Two to four postoculars.
vii Keeling of dorsal scales is not especially strong and
     does not always extend onto tail.

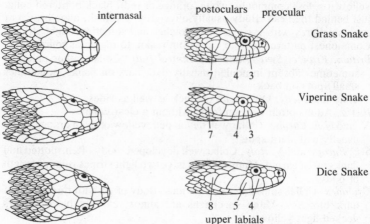

Grass Snake

Viperine Snake

Dice Snake

upper labials

NATRIX MAURA *Viperine Snake* **Pl. 37**
Range. Iberia, France (except north), S.W. Switzerland, N.W. Italy, Balearic islands, Iles d'Hyères, and Sardinia; perhaps Sicily. Also N.W. Africa Map 115.
Identification. Adults occasionally up to about 100 cm, including tail, but most animals less than 70 cm. Females grow larger than males. A medium-sized snake with well defined, fairly broad head, and rather thickset body in adults. Pupil round and dorsal scales strongly keeled in 21 rows (rarely 19 or 23). Colour varies: usually brown or greyish but may be tinged with yellow, red or olive. Typically two rows of staggered dark blotches down mid-back, which may merge to produce bars or a well-defined zig-zag stripe. Flanks have dark blotches, or more usually large light-centred ocelli. Some specimens have two narrow, light yellow or reddish stripes running along back. Head is typically boldly marked: often one or two ∧-shaped marks on crown and neck that may be joined by a central blotch; light upper lip scales have conspicuous dark borders. Belly whitish, yellow, red, or brown chequered with black or dark brown.
Habits. Diurnal. Usually found in or near water, both still and flowing. Prefers weedy ponds and rivers, but also found in brackish conditions and by mountain streams, etc., up to more than 1400 m in the south of its range. Also occurs in very damp woods and meadows. Often seen when swimming and diving, or when basking on water's edge where it may rest on low bushes, rocks etc. When disturbed often retreats into water and dives, but if cornered hisses fiercely and flattens body and head and strikes repeatedly (usually with mouth closed). This behaviour, especially in animals with zig-zag pattern on back, produces a very viper-like impression. When picked up, *N. maura* often voids smelly contents of anal gland. Feeds mainly on frogs, toads, newts, tadpoles, and a varying proportion of fish. Earthworms are also eaten occasionally.
Variation. No subspecies recognised, but varies considerably in colour and pattern. A few animals from Upper Rhône have some characters typical of *N. tessellata* (e.g. 19 rows of dorsal scales at mid-body, eight upper labials etc.) but they resemble *N. maura* in other respects.
Similar Species. Animals with zig-zag stripe on back can look like vipers (p. 210); this impression is enhanced by behaviour (see above). True vipers have vertical pupils and smaller head scales. Most likely to be confused with other *Natrix*. For distinction from *N. natrix*, see this species. *N. maura* can be separated from *N. tessellata* in the small area where their ranges meet, by the following characters (see also Fig., opposite).

i   Usually 7 upper labial scales, 3rd and 4th often entering eye
     (typically 8, 4th and often 5th entering eye in *N. tessellata*).
ii   2, rarely 3, postoculars (3 or 4, even 5 or 6 in
     N. tessellata).

iii   Usually 21 rows of dorsal scales at midbody (19 in most
       N. tessellata).
iv   About 147–164 ventral scales (160–190 in *N. tessellata*).
v   Head broader and snout more rounded in most *N. maura*
       and body often thicker.
vi   Pattern usually bolder in *N. maura* and ocelli often present
       on flanks.

NATRIX TESSELLATA *Dice Snake*   Pl. 37
Range. Most of Balkans, Italy (except extreme south), north to S. Switzerland, E. Austria, Czechoslovakia, and S. USSR. Isolated colonies exist in
W. Austria (Vorarlberg), N.E. Switzerland (Vierwaldstattersee), on mid-
Rhine and Elbe, the islands of Crete and Kithera. Also eastwards to S.W.
and central Asia   Map 116.
Identification. Adults up to 100 cm or more, including tail, but usually less
than 75 cm. Females grow larger than males. A medium-sized snake
usually with a rather small, narrow, pointed head, round pupil, and very
strongly keeled dorsal scales, usually in 19 rows at mid-body. Colouring
variable: most frequently greyish or brownish but sometimes yellowish or
greenish; often with pattern of regular dark spots evenly dispersed over
body. These spots may be large, small, or sometimes completely absent,
or they may fuse to form dark bars on back and flanks. Those on flanks
often alternate with narrower light bars. Sometimes a ∧-shaped mark on
nape, but head markings often obscure. Underside whitish, yellow, pink,
or red, chequered or with one or two irregular dark stripes, or almost
entirely black.
Habits. Generally very like *Natrix maura*, but even more aquatic, spending much of its time in water and often remaining beneath surface for
considerable periods. Diet consists almost entirely of fish, but amphibians
are also taken occasionally.
Variation. Varies greatly in pattern. Animals are known that have red and
black flanks, or broken stripes or are completely black. Black animals
occur on Serpilor (= Snake) Island, off the Danube Delta, and here tend to
have 21 rows of dorsal scales and 4–6 postoculars.
Similar Species. Only likely to be confused with other *Natrix* species. See
N. natrix (p. 201) and *N. maura* (p. 203) for separation.

CORONELLA AUSTRIACA *Smooth Snake*   Pl. 38
Range. S. England, France, N. Iberia, east to S. Scandinavia and USSR,
and south to Italy, Sicily, and Greece. Also N. Asia Minor to N.
Iran   Map 117.
Identification. Adults usually up to about 60 cm, including tail, occasionally over 80 cm. A moderately small snake with a cylindrical body, poorly
defined neck, and rather small head with fairly pointed snout. Eyes small
with round pupil; scales smooth. Colouring variable: usually greyish,

brownish, pinkish, or even reddish, sometimes more intense on each side of mid-line giving the effect of two often vague streaks. Usually small dark spots or blotches present on back; these are clearest on neck (where there are often two short dark stripes) and often form irregular transverse bars or are arranged in two lines. Nearly always a dark stripe from side of neck through eye to nostril and sometimes a vague 'bridle' on snout as well. Belly usually darkish: red, orange, grey, or blackish, generally with some mottling or fine spotting. Usually 19 rows of dorsal scales at mid-body. For head scaling see Fig., p. 206.

Habits. Occurs from sea level to over 1800 m in south of range, where it tends to be montane. A diurnal, although rather secretive, snake found in a variety of dry sunny habitats. In England largely confined to sandy heathland but elsewhere occurs in hedgerows, wood-edges, open woods, bushy slopes, embankments etc. In south is found in more open places, often with only sparse vegetation, such as screes, stone piles and even cliffs and rock-cuttings, where it lives in crevices. Also encountered in moist habitats on rare occasions.

Rather slow moving but bites readily when handled and voids smelly contents of anal glands. Said to be intelligent (for a snake). Food consists largely of lizards (often 70 per cent of diet), especially lacertids up to the size of a halfgrown Green Lizard (*L. viridis*), also Slow Worms (*Anguis*). Rest of diet made up of small snakes (even young vipers), small mammals and their young and even insects. Holds larger prey in coils of body. Produces 2–15 fully formed young, which mature in about fourth year.

Variation. Considerable variation in pattern. S. Italian and Sicilian animals are often almost uniform above.

Similar Species. *Coronella girondica* (see below); has been confused with vipers, but lacks keeled scales and vertical pupil.

CORONELLA GIRONDICA *Southern Smooth Snake* Pl. 38

Range. Iberia, S. France, Italy, Sicily. Also N.W. Africa Map 118.

Identification. Adults usually up to about 50 cm, including tail, rarely to over 80 cm. Very similar to *C. austriaca* but tends to be more slender with a more rounded snout. Colour above brownish, greyish, ochre, or pinkish, with irregular darker bars that are usually bolder than in *C. austriaca*. Easily distinguished from *C. austriaca* by a number of characters. Belly often yellow, orange or red overlaid with black in a bold diced pattern, sometimes forming two lines – but not more or less uniform as in *C. austriaca*. *C. girondica* typically lacks dark stripe from nostril to eye, but in most cases has a clear 'bridle' over snout. There are usually eight (not seven) upper labials (see Fig., p. 206), the fourth and fifth reaching the eye (not third and fourth as in many *C. austriaca*). The rostral scale is not large and does not extend between supranasals (see Fig., p. 206). There are usually 21 rows of dorsal scales at mid-body (not 19 as in most *C. austriaca*).

Habits. Generally a more lowland species than *C. austriaca* but does occur in mountain regions, occasionally even up to 1500 m, although usually lower. In contrast to *C. austriaca*, is not very active by day and comes out to hunt in evening. Found in a wide variety of dry habitats, especially hedgerows, open woods etc. Often seen around piles of old vegetation, but also sometimes frequents rocky places, stone piles, dry-stone walls etc. Much more docile than *C. austriaca* and rarely bites. Feeds mainly on lizards, including nocturnal geckoes when these are available, also small snakes and even some insects.

Variation. Some variation in pattern but no obvious geographical trends.

Similar Species. *Coronella austriaca* (p. 204); False Smooth Snake (*Macroprotodon cucullatus* below). Young Ladder Snakes (*Elaphe scalaris*, p. 200) are more boldly marked with finer scaling (25–29 scales across mid-body). Vipers have vertical pupils and keeled scales.

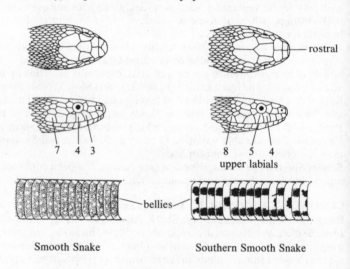

rostral

7   4   3

8   5   4

upper labials

bellies

Smooth Snake   Southern Smooth Snake

MACROPROTODON CUCULLATUS *False Smooth Snake*   **Pl. 38**
Range. S. Iberia, Balearic Islands. Also N. Africa eastwards to Israel   Map 119.
Identification. Adults up to 65 cm, including tail, but more usually under 45 cm. A small snake with a fairly well defined head that is distinctively flattened, especially the snout. Eyes small, with often oval pupil, and fairly near front of head. Scales smooth; usually from 19 to 23 rows at mid-body. Upperparts rather pallid grey or brown with small dark markings that often form vague bars or even streaks. In most cases a blackish

collar on neck that may extend on to top of head. A dark streak usually present from nostril, through eye, to lower cheek. Belly yellow, pink, or red, with weak dark markings or a bold black 'diced' pattern, which may consist of a central band or two stripes. At close quarters can be recognised by often oval pupil (N.B. tends to be round in poor light), flat snout, low rostral scale which is scarcely visible from above, usually single anterior temporal and parietal scale usually in contact with, or almost reaching, sixth, upper labial (Figs., below).

Habits. Mainly a lowland species; not usually active by day, but hunts at dusk and at night. Found in a variety of warm, dry habitats including sandy, open wood and scrub areas. Encountered most often in stony places, rock piles, old walls, and ruins where it is found during the day either under stones, in burrows of other animals or buried in soil. Generally slow moving but reasonably swift when disturbed and bites when handled. When alarmed may throw head back to expose underside of neck. Food is mainly small lizards (most often Small Lacertas and geckoes), some of which are caught when resting in their hiding places.

Venom. Venom apparatus similar to that of following species; small size of this snake prevents effective use on human beings.

Variation. Colouring rather variable, but no geographical trends noted.

Similar Species. At first sight may be very like a Smooth Snake (*Coronella* spp., p. 204).

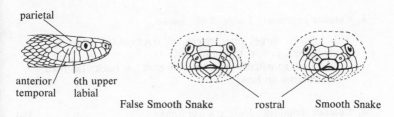

parietal

anterior temporal / 6th upper labial

False Smooth Snake   rostral   Smooth Snake

TELESCOPUS FALLAX *Cat Snake*   Pl. 38

Range. E. Adriatic coast and islands, S. Balkans, Greek islands, and Malta. Also Caucasus and S.W. Asia Map 120.

Identification. Adults usually up to about 75 cm, including tail, but sometimes over 100 cm. A slender snake with a broad, flat head. Body often deeper than wide; snout tapering but blunt, eyes small with vertical cat-like pupil (almost round in poor light). Head scales large, dorsal scales smooth in 17 to 23 rows at mid-body. Usually grey, beige, or brownish with a conspicuous dark spot or collar just behind head, and series of dark transverse bars or blotches on back. These are often oblique, especially on neck where they are also best developed. Weaker bars present on

Plate 35   **WHIP SNAKES**
                                 (× ⅔; 4 ×½)

Active, slender diurnal snakes. The first three species on this
plate have fine striping on hind parts (1d) and are easily
confused, so check range and texts carefully.

1. Coluber viridiflavus *Western Whip Snake*   195
Absent from most E. Europe (overlaps with *C. gemonensis* in
N.W. Yugoslavia). Adults with heavily marked fore parts (1a)
or entirely black above (1b). Young with bold head pattern
(1c).

2. Coluber gemonensis *Balkan Whip Snake*   196
W. and S. Balkans. Usually under 100cm. Fore parts of adults
with dark blotches and usually small white spots on some
scales. Belly pale yellowish or whitish, frequently with some
dark spots. Young similar to those of *C. viridiflavus* in pattern.

3. Coluber jugularis *Large Whip Snake*   196

   3a. Adult: large; fine stripes all over body; underside
   unspotted, yellow to orange-red.
   3b. Young: usually well spaced bars on back; no bold
   light marks on head.

4. Coluber najadum *Dahl's Whip Snake*   194
Very slender. Distinctive neck pattern.

5. Coluber algirus *Algerian Whip Snake*   194
Malta only. Widely separated bars on back. Ground
colour may be brown or tinged yellow or pink.

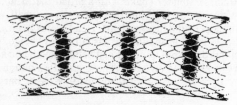

Algerian Whip Snake, alternative pattern

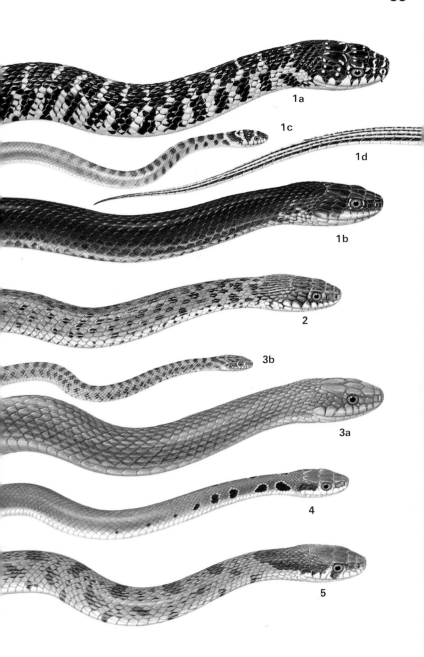

1a

1c

1d

1b

2

3b

3a

4

5

RAT SNAKES

Plate 36

(× ½; *3* × ⅔)

Medium-sized to large snakes. Young often have distinctive patterns. Adults eat small mammals and often climb.

1. Elaphe scalaris *Ladder Snake*   200

Iberia and Mediterranean France only. Young usually with bold 'ladder' pattern which is reduced to two simple stripes in adults. Rostral scale pointed behind.

2. Elaphe longissima *Aesculapian Snake*   199

Not most of Iberia. Slender. Juveniles spotted, with yellow blotch on side of head (rather like Grass Snake, *Natrix natrix*, **Pl. 37**, but scales not keeled). Adults uniform or with faint stripes (see Fig. below), often with small white flecks.

3. Elaphe situla *Leopard Snake*   197

Balkans, S. Italy, Sicily and Malta. Variable pattern of brown to red, dark-edged markings, consisting of spots or stripes. Juveniles have similar markings to adults.

4. Elaphe quatuorlineata *Four-lined Snake*   198

Balkans and Italy. Back scales lightly keeled in adults, giving rather rough appearance. In some areas adults typically with four dark stripes, in other places they are darker with blotches (see Fig. below). Young usually boldly spotted, but pattern variable.

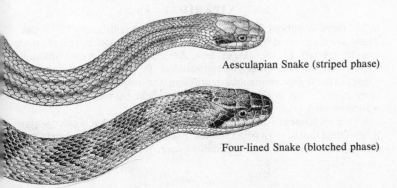

Aesculapian Snake (striped phase)

Four-lined Snake (blotched phase)

flanks and often a dark stripe from each eye to angle of mouth. Belly pale yellowish, whitish, or even pinkish, sometimes heavily suffused with grey or brown, which may form irregular streaks or spots.

Habits. Mainly a lowland snake, but can occur in mountains in south of range. Usually found in stony places, rocky degraded woodland, old walls, rock piles, ruins, etc., but also occasionally in heaps of old vegetation and sandy areas with bushy plant cover. Mainly hunts at twilight, but sometimes active at night in summer, and by day in cooler part of year. Feeds almost entirely on lizards; large *Telescopus* take prey up to size of sub-adult Balkan Green Lizard (*Lacerta trilineata*). May drag victims from their refuge, but also stalks them in open – moving forwards cautiously from behind cover (probably origin of name 'Cat Snake'). Once caught, lizards are held in jaws while venom takes effect. *Telescopus* varies in temperament – some animals bite when handled.

Venom. Has grooved fangs at back of upper jaw; these inject venom into prey, causing death of small lizards in two or three minutes. Unlikely to be dangerous to man, as mouth too small to allow fangs to be used effectively.

Variation. Markings vary in intensity. Some populations (Crete and nearby islands) tend to be fairly uniform, either pallid or with very weak markings above, or finely and evenly spotted with dark brown.

Similar Species. Only other snakes in range with vertical pupil are Sand Boa (*Eryx* p. 189, which has blunt tail, plump body, small head scales) and Vipers (which have plump body, more head scales and keeled body scales).

round   oval   vertical, cat-like

Pupil shapes in snakes

Family **VIPERIDAE** *Vipers*

In all, there are about 43 species of True Vipers (subfamily Viperinae). These are distributed throughout Europe, Asia, and Africa, and are quite closely related to the Asian and American Pit Vipers (subfamily Crotalinae), which include the rattlesnakes. Pit Vipers differ from True Vipers in having a conspicuous depression (the 'pit' of their name) in front of each eye. This is a heat sensitive organ and enables them to locate warm-blooded prey, even in the dark.

All vipers possess a characteristic venom apparatus that is more sophisticated than that of most other snakes. Each of the two venom glands leads directly into the base of a long, hollow fang. When the snake strikes, the fangs are embedded in the prey and venom is expelled from the fang tip, which means that it is very efficiently transmitted deep into the tissues of the victim. The fangs are also mobile; when in use they project nearly at right angles to the upper jaw, but at other times the fangs are rotated backwards so that they lie against the roof of the mouth, enclosed in a sheath of soft tissue.

All seven European vipers belong to one genus, *Vipera*. They are the only dangerously venomous snakes in the area covered by this book. In most parts of the European mainland, at least one species is present and sometimes two, or even three, are found close together. They are absent from many, but not all, islands including quite large ones such as Corsica, Sardinia, Crete, Balearics, and Ireland.

European vipers are fairly heavy-bodied snakes with short tails and well defined, frequently triangular, heads. The dorsal body scales are strongly keeled and the shields on top of the head often nearly all fragmented. The eye is rather small and the pupil vertical. Unlike most other European snakes, vipers have an undivided anal scale. They vary considerably in head profile and some species have a soft, scaly 'nose-horn' on the tip of the snout.

Vipers are mainly ground dwelling, although some species will occasionally climb on stone piles and on bushes, and they may also swim sometimes. All species are often active by day, but most of them become at least partly nocturnal wherever the night temperature is high enough. European vipers feed on small mammals (mice, voles, shrews etc), but some also take birds or lizards, and one, *V. ursinii*, often eats a high proportion of large insects.

All European vipers are relatively slow moving unless disturbed and frequently hunt from cover, striking mammalian prey as it passes and then tracking it by scent after the venom has taken effect. In contrast, birds, lizards and insects are usually held, and swallowed as soon as they stop moving. Vipers will also hunt in the burrows of mammals for prey.

Most species give birth to live young (up to 20 in some cases); but *V. lebetina*, lays eggs in Europe. Before mating, rival males may take part in a combat 'dance' in which they rear up and press against each other, the weaker animal eventually retiring from the contest. In Britain, *V. berus* matures at about three years old and females appear to breed every other year.

In areas where the climate makes it necessary, vipers hibernate, often communally. Some species (at least *V. berus*, *V. aspis* and perhaps *V. ammodytes*) may migrate from their winter refuges and breeding grounds to other areas for feeding; the distances involved are not large – usually a few hundred metres.

Vipers are not aggressive, unless disturbed or molested, when most species will bite fiercely.

Identification. Some species of vipers have very distinctive features and

Plate 37   WATER SNAKES
(× ⅔)

Medium to large snakes with clearly keeled body scales,
large scales on head and round pupils. Belly pattern often
chequered. Typically found in fairly moist places, or in water.

1. **Natrix tessellata** *Dice Snake*   204
   Not W. Europe. Pattern variable but often spotted. Nostrils
   directed upwards, snout rather pointed. Usually 19 rows of
   scales at mid-body.

2. **Natrix maura** *Viperine Snake*   203
   W. and S.W. Europe. Pattern variable; often ocelli on sides.
   Nostrils directed upwards. Usually 21 rows of scales at mid-
   body.
   Two animals, showing variation in pattern.

3. **Natrix natrix** *Grass Snake*   201
   Usually a white, yellow or orange collar with dark edge. Often
   no keeling on tail scales. Nostrils not turned upwards. Colouring very variable.

   3a. Typical W. European pattern.
   3b. Widespread pattern in N. and N.E. Europe.
   3c. Striped morph found in S.E. Europe and N. Italy.
   3d. Uniform colouring typical of Iberian snakes.

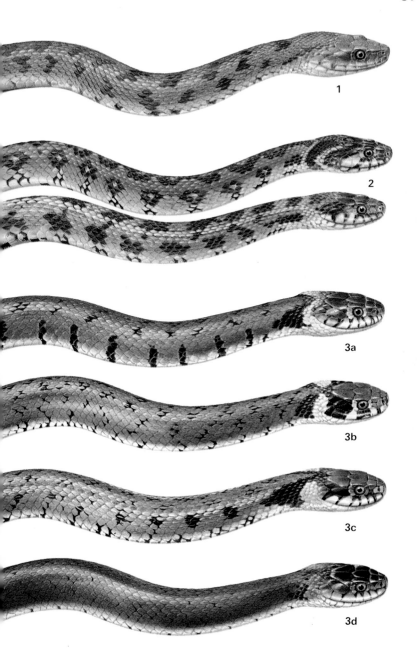

1

2

3a

3b

3c

3d

1

2

3

4a

4b

Plate 38
SMOOTH SNAKES, FALSE SMOOTH SNAKE
and CAT SNAKE

1. **Coronella austriaca**   *Smooth Snake*   204
Stripe from neck to eye and usually to nostril. Third and
fourth labials often border eye. Belly rather uniform (Fig.,
below). Two animals, showing pattern variants.

2. **Coronella girondica**   *Southern Smooth Snake*   205
Stripe from neck to eye, rarely to nostril. 'Bridle' on snout.
Fourth and fifth labials border eye. Belly chequered or
striped (Fig., below).

3. **Macroprotodon cucullatus**   *False Smooth Snake*   206
S. Iberia and Balearic Islands only. Pupil often oval in bright
light. Often a dark collar or hood. Rostral scale low; largest
upper labial scale usually touches or comes close to parietal
scale (see Figs., p. 207).

4. **Telescopus fallax**   *Cat Snake*   207
S.E. Europe and Malta only. Vertical pupil. Body scales
smooth (cf. vipers).

    4a. Typical pattern.
    4b. Pale individual.

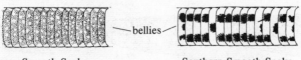

—bellies—

Smooth Snake   Southern Smooth Snake

are easily identified. Others are extremely variable and can cause difficulties, especially as it is inadvisable to handle them. However, in virtually all areas, there are no more than two or at the most three species to be considered. Principal features to look for are general appearance, snout profile (flat, turned up, or with a nose-horn), pattern, and, if possible, size of scales on top of head and other minor features of head scaling (see key). If the snake is not disturbed, many of these features can often be seen with binoculars.

Key to Vipers

Because some European Vipers are variable, it is very difficult to produce a simple, yet entirely effective key for them. All identifications must, therefore, be checked with the relevant species texts.

1. W. Cyclades only. No large scales on top of head, even over
   eyes　　　　　　　　*V. lebetina*, Blunt-nosed Viper (p. 224, Pl. 40)
   All other areas. Some large scales on top of head – at least
   over eyes　　　　　　　　　　　　　　　　　　　　　　　　　　　2

2. European Turkey only. Large scales over eyes, but rest of
   head scales small. Snout rounded with no nose-horn.
   Characteristic bold pattern on head
   　　　　　　　　　　V. xanthina, Ottoman Viper (p. 223, Pl. 40)
   Not like above　　　　　　　　　　　　　　　　　　　　　　　3

3. A very distinct nose-horn present (Fig. *a*, below). Central head
   scales small　　　　　　　　　　　　　　　　　　　　　　　　4
   No distinct nose-horn present, but snout-tip upturned in profile (Fig. *b*, below). Central head scales often small　　　　5
   No distinct nose-horn and snout not upturned in profile
   (Fig. *c* below). Central head scales usually large (frontal
   and parietals well developed)　　　　　　　　　　　　　　　6

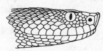

a	*b*	*c*
Nose-horned Viper	Asp Viper	Adder
(*V. ammodytes*)	(*V. aspis*)	(*V. berus*)

4. E. Europe only. Rostral scale does not clearly extend onto
   front of nose-horn, which is covered with 9–20 small scales
   　　　　　　　　　V. ammodytes, Nose-horned Viper (p. 222, Pl. 40)

Iberia only. Rostral scale clearly extends onto front of nose-
horn, which is usually covered by less than nine scales
V. *latasti*, Lataste's Viper (p. 219, Pl. 40)

5. N.E. Spain, France (except north), Italy, Sicily, Elba,
Switzerland and S.W. Germany. Snout nearly always clearly
upturned in profile (raised section covered behind by 2–3
scales). Typically has two rows of scales beneath eye.
Pattern variable   V. *aspis*, Asp Viper (p. 218, Pls. 39 and 40)
N.W. Iberia. Snout may be weakly turned up. But usually
only one row of scales beneath eye
V. *berus*, Adder (p. 217, Pl. 39)
Iberia, except extreme north. Snout always distinctly upturned; raised section usually covered behind by 4 or more
scales
a few V. *latasti*, Lataste's Viper (p. 219, Pl. 40)

6. N.B. Rare individuals of V. *aspis* which lack a clearly upturned
snout may key out here. See V. *aspis* texts for eliminating
such animals, p. 218.

Widespread (see Map 122). Snout rather blunt (viewed
from above). Nostril large and in centre of nasal scale.
Two apical scales in contact with rostral. Scales on top
of snout numerous (more than 13). Upper preocular normally not in contact with nasal scale. (See Fig., p. 216
for details of head scaling.) Typically has simple dark
zig-zag stripe on back   V. *berus*, Adder (p. 217, Pl. 39)
Restricted range (see Map 121). Small, usually under 50cm.
Scaling often appears rougher than V. *berus*; head narrower
and snout more tapering. Nostril small and towards lower
edge of nasal scale. One apical scale in contact with
rostral. Normally less than 12 scales on top of snout.
Upper preocular normally in contact with nasal scale (see
Fig., p. 216 for details of head scaling). Zig-zag stripe
tends to have clear, dark edge
V. *ursinii*, Orsini's Viper (below, Pl. 39)

VIPERA URSINII   *Orsini's Viper*   Pl. 39
Range. Discontinuous. In Europe occurs in isolated, often quite small
populations in S.E. France, central Italy, E. Austria, Hungary, Romania,
W. Yugoslavia, Albania, and Bulgaria. Extends eastwards to Central Asia
and also occurs in Asia Minor and N. Iran   Map 121.
Identification. Adults usually less than 50cm, including tail; rarely over
60cm, females tend to be larger than males. The smallest European viper.
A small, thick-bodied, narrow headed viper that often has a rough appear-

ance. Only likely to be confused with *V. aspis* or *V. berus*. Differs from *V. aspis* in lacking an obvious upturned snout and always having several large scales on top of head (frontal and parietal scales well developed) and a low number of dorsal scales (nearly always 19 rows across midbody but see **Variation** below). Differs from *V. berus* in smaller adult size, in having a narrower head with more tapering snout, and in several features of head scaling: only a single apical scale in contact with rostral, fewer scales on top of snout (12 or fewer), nostril small and near bottom of nasal scale, upper preocular scale nearly always in contact with nasal scale (see Fig., below for details of scaling). *V. ursinii* tends to have fewer scales across mid-body than *V. berus* (19 instead of usually 21). The scales of *V. ursinii* are often wavy in cross-section, have a more pronounced keel, and may be rather short so that the dark skin between them sometimes shows through; these features produce the rough 'texture' of *V. ursinii*.

Pattern is not very variable: tends to be greyish, pale brown, or yellowish with a dark zig-zag dorsal stripe that is usually edged with black and may be occasionally broken into spots. Flanks often rather dark, underside may be blackish, whitish, or dark grey, or even rosy, with or without spots. Underside of tail tip sometimes dark or with yellow markings. Almost completely black individuals may occur, especially in Yugoslavia.

Habits. Over much of its range in Europe, this species is montane, sometimes being found over 2000 m. Here it lives on well drained hillsides with some vegetation, or more commonly on high, often dry, meadows. But in Austria, Hungary, Romania, and nearby areas it is mainly a lowland form, occurring in both dry and moist meadows, and even occasionally in marshy conditions. Food varies: some populations prey mainly on lizards, others mainly on grasshoppers: small rodents are also sometimes eaten. Unlike other vipers, *V. ursinii* is usually quite docile and almost never bites. It only rarely occurs at the same localities as *V. berus* and in such cases *V. berus* tends to occupy the damper situations.

Venom. The venom is weaker than that of the other *Vipera* species. This together with its placid disposition, makes *V. ursinii* the least dangerous of

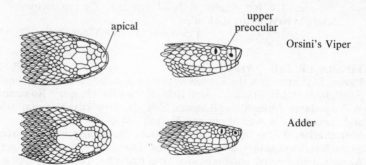

apical

upper
preocular

Orsini's Viper

Adder

European vipers. It should still be treated with respect, especially as misidentification is possible.

Variation. There is some variation in snout shape, eye size, and colouring (especially in darkness of flanks, continuity of vertebral stripe, and ventral pigmentation). On the basis of these differences several subspecies have been described. East Romanian and Russian animals usually have 21 rows of dorsal scales across the mid-body. These, and some central European populations, often have the canthi raised so that the snout is slightly concave above.

Similar Species. *Vipera berus* and *V. aspis* (see above).

VIPERA BERUS *Adder or Common Viper* **Pl. 39**

Range. Occurs over much of Europe extending north to beyond the Arctic Circle and south to N.W. Spain, N. Italy, and much of the N. Balkans. Rather sporadic in central Europe and southern parts of range. Also extends across USSR to Pacific coast Map 122.

Identification. Adults usually up to 65 cm, including tail, exceptionally almost 90 cm; females tend to be larger than males. (N.B. North-western Spanish and south-east European populations are discussed separately under **Variation**). A thick-bodied viper with a flat (not upturned) snout, nearly always several large scales (including frontal and parietals) on top of head, a single row of small scales (suboculars) beneath eye, and usually 21 dorsal scale rows at mid-body.

Most likely to be confused with *V. ursinii* (see opposite for distinction) or *V. aspis*. Latter usually distinguishable from *V. berus* by its clearly upturned snout; in rare cases where this is poorly developed *V. aspis* tends to have other characters which are uncommon in *V. berus* (e.g. one of the characteristic *V. aspis* colour patterns, fragmented head scales, two rows of small scales beneath eye).

Most *V. berus* have clearly marked dark, zig-zag vertebral stripe. This is usually without a very distinct paler, central band (as in some *V. aspis*). In rare cases, vertebral stripe is straight-edged, broken up, faint, or even absent. Colouring varies according to sex: many males are very contrasting, often being whitish or pale grey with intense black markings; females are frequently brownish or reddish with dark brown markings. Other colour combinations exist and entirely black specimens are not rare. Belly is grey, grey-brown, or black, sometimes with white spots; tail tip yellow, orange, or even red beneath.

Habits. Occurs in wide variety of habitats particularly in north of range. Here it is found on moors, heaths and dunes, and in bogs, open woods, field-edges, hedgerows, marshy meadows, and even saltmarshes. In south, becomes more restricted, and is usually encountered in mountain areas; where it occurs in lowlands (e.g. parts of N. Italy), it occupies moist habitats. Occurs up to about 3000 m in Alps. Largely diurnal, especially in north, and feeds mainly on small mammals; lizards are also taken.

V. berus swims well, and more often than other European vipers.

Venom. Quite potent, though bites are probably not as dangerous as those of *V. aspis* and certainly those of S. European species. However human fatalities have occurred.

Variation. *Balkan area*. In south-east of its range, *V. berus* is very variable and more extreme animals may look like *V. aspis*, with a pattern of cross bars on back, and sometimes two rows of scales beneath eye. However such animals should not be confused with *V. aspis* as they occur outside its range, also the snout is not clearly upturned and the central head scales are not normally fragmented.

N.W. Iberia. Here, again, *V. berus* may look rather like *V. aspis* and is sometimes regarded as a separate species, *V. seoanei*. The central head scales are often fragmented, snout may sometimes be lightly upturned, and colouring may be like *V. aspis* from S.W. France (i.e. a straight, wavy, or zig-zag vertebral stripe with a paler centre that may reduce the dark areas to a series of spots on each side of it). Other animals are coloured like typical *V. berus*, or even entirely black. Confusion is likely only in small area of overlap (see Maps 122 and 123). In this area, Spanish *V. berus* can usually be separated from *V. aspis* by lack of strongly upturned snout, nearly always single row of scales beneath eye, and usually a lower ventral scale-count (in most cases under 143 in Spanish *V. berus* and over 140 in Spanish *V. aspis* with extremes of 147 and 137 respectively).

Similar Species. *V. ursinii* (p. 215); *V. aspis* (below); Viperine Snake (*Natrix maura*, p. 203).

VIPERA ASPIS   *Asp Viper*   Pls. 39 and 40

Range. W. and central Europe from N.E. Spain through France (except north), east to S.W. Germany (Schwarzwald), Switzerland and Italy, and south to Sicily; occurs on Elba and Montecristo. Balkan records exist but most appear to result from misidentified *V. berus*; others may be based on rare *V. berus–V. ammodytes* hybrids.   Map 123

Identification. Adults usually up to 60cm, including tail, occasionally 75cm. Males tend to grow larger than females. A widespread and extremely variable viper that can usually be identified by characteristic head profile: snout is distinctly upturned, but lacks nose-horn (Fig., p. 214). Problems arise with rare individuals that have poorly developed snout, and in parts of N. Spain where *V. berus* may sometimes have the snout-tip slightly raised (see above). In such cases other features must be checked.

V. aspis has typical viper appearance with broad triangular head, but body is rather slender. Very variable in colour beneath. Underside of tail tends to be yellow or red. *V. aspis* usually has 21 or 23 rows of dorsal scales at mid-body.

Principal goegraphical variants are described below; they gradually merge into each other.

France (except south-west), Alpine region, N. and central Italy. Typically, animals from this area have characteristic pattern of dark transverse bars on back; these are often staggered on each side of the body and may be joined by a narrow vertebral streak. Completely black specimens are fairly common especially in highland areas. Apart from upturned snout, these populations nearly always have fragmented scales on top of head (except supraoculars and sometimes frontal), and two rows of scales beneath eye.

S. Italy, Sicily, Montecristo. Scaling as above, but pattern consists of broad, wavy, dorsal stripe that is often rich brown and has darker edge; it may be broken up into series of oval blotches.

S.W. France and central Pyrenees. Dark vertebral stripe may be wavy, zig-zag or almost straight, its centre distinctly pale, often greyish (such a pale centre is rare in *V. berus*). In some cases, really dark pigment on back may be limited to a row of blackish spots on each side of paler central band. Scaling more variable than elsewhere, in some populations there are often several large scales on top of head, and sometimes only a single scale-row beneath eye.

N.E. Spain. Usually have barred pattern, but sometimes rather like S.W. French animals.

Habits. Generally like other vipers: diurnal, but also partly nocturnal where climate allows. Often found in dry habitats, especially dry open hillsides, but extends into high wet mountainous regions (2500m in Pyrenees, 3000m in Alps). Feeds mainly on small mammals and, more rarely, lizards etc. Where it overlaps with *V. berus*, *V. aspis* tends to be limited to warmer areas, and in hilly country generally occurs at lower altitudes.

Venom. This is said to be rather more potent than that of *V. berus*. Human deaths have occurred.

Variation. A very variable species (see above), that has been divided into a number of subspecies. Hybrids with *V. berus* are believed to occur but only very rarely.

Similar Species. *V. berus* (see above and p. 217). *V. latasti* (below) and *V. ammodytes* (p. 222) both have a nose-horn, and only overlap with *V. aspis* in very restricted areas (N.E. Spain and N.E. Italy respectively). *V. ursinii* (p. 215). Viperine Snake (*Natrix maura*, p. 203).

VIPERA LATASTI *Lataste's Viper*   **Pl. 40**

Range. Iberian Peninsula, except extreme north. Also N.W. Africa   Map 124.

Identification. Adults usually under 60cm, including tail, occasionally up to 75cm; males larger than females. The only viper in Iberia that usually has a distinct nose-horn. Occasionally the snout-tip is just turned upwards as in *V. aspis*; in such cases range is useful in identification as the two species overlap only slightly. Also dorsal pattern tends to differ, and

Plate 39 VIPERS 1

Usually thick-set snakes, with very well-defined heads, vertical pupils and keeled body scales. Often a zig-zag stripe on back. All are venomous.

1. Vipera ursinii *Orsini's Viper* 215
Limited range (Map 121). Rather narrow head. Rough skin texture. Nostril low down in nasal scale. Vertebral stripe often black-edged.

2. Vipera berus *Adder* 217
Not extreme S. Europe. Rather variable. Nostril in centre of nasal scale. Vertebral stripe usually not dark-edged. Males tend to be greyer and brighter than females.

  2a. Male.
  2b. Female.
  2c. N. Iberia: common pattern in area.

3. Vipera aspis *Asp Viper* (see also **Pl. 40**) 218
Mainly Switzerland, France, Italy and neighbouring areas. Highly variable in pattern. Usually has turned-up snout and often two rows of small scales under eye.

  3a. S.W. France etc.: typical pattern.
  3b. N. and E. France, N. Italy, Switzerland: barred pattern frequent; bars often narrower and completely separated.

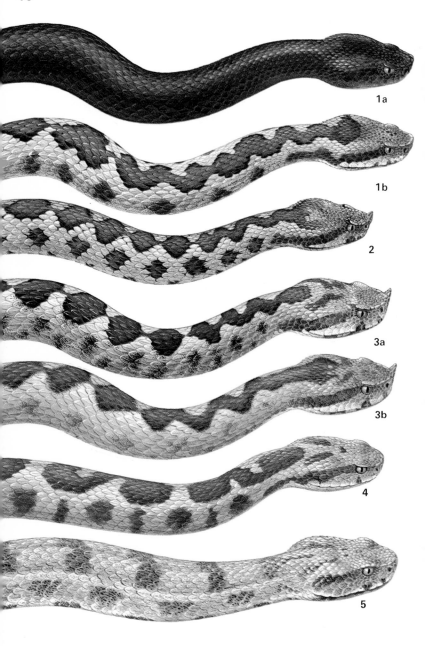

1a

1b

2

3a

3b

4

5

VIPERS 2   **Plate 40**

1. Vipera aspis   *Asp Viper* (see also **Pl. 39**)   218

     1a. Black phase, especially common in Switzerland and N. and central Italy. N.B. black specimens of other vipers also occur, particularly of *V. berus*.

     1b. S. Italy, Sicily and Montecristo. Typical pattern: broad, wavy, brownish stripe or series of blotches.

2. Vipera latasti   *Lataste's Viper*   219
Iberia except north. Usually a distinct horn or nose.

3. Vipera ammodytes   *Nose-horned Viper*   222
Balkans and neighbouring regions. Horn on nose.

     3a. Male.
     3b. Female.

4. Vipera xanthina   *Ottoman Viper*   223
Only E. European Turkey. Bold head pattern. Large scale over each eye.

5. Vipera lebetina   *Blunt-nosed Viper*   224
W. Cyclades only. No large scales on top of head, even over eyes.

V. latasti has narrower rostral scale (1½–2 times as deep as wide, compared with 1½ times or less in *V. aspis*; the raised portion of the snout
tends to have more scales than in *V. aspis* – usually 4 or more for *V. latasti*,
2 or 3 for *V. aspis*). Body relatively stout with broad, triangular head
covered by small scales, except for large supraoculars and sometimes
frontal. Usually two rows of scales between eye and supralabials. Normally 21 rows of dorsal scales at mid-body. Ground colour usually
greyish, brownish, or more rarely reddish. Pattern fairly constant; typically a wavy or zig-zag dorsal stripe with darker edge. Belly generally
greyish or blackish, usually with lighter or darker spots. Often some
yellow on underside of tail.

Habits. Generally like other Vipers; diurnal, but nocturnal as well in warm
conditions. Said to prefer dry, hilly regions but is found only up to about
1300 m in Europe. Occurs in rocky areas, open forests, and occasionally
on sandy ground. Preys mainly on small mammals, also young birds and,
at least when juvenile, lizards and invertebrates.

Venom. Quite irascible, but bite is not considered very serious.

Variation. Does not show much variation.

Similar Species. Only likely to be confused with *V. aspis* (see p. 218)
or *V. berus* (p. 217). *V. ammodytes* is similar but does not overlap.

VIPER AMMODYTES *Nose-horned Viper*   **Pl. 40**

Range. Mainly Balkans; north to N.E. Italy, S. Austria, and S.W. and S.E.
Romania; extends south to the Peloponnese and Cyclades. Also S.W.
Asia   Map 125.

Identification. Adults usually under 65 cm, including tail, but occasionally
up to 90 cm. The only eastern European snake with a distinct nose-horn.
Body fairly stout with well-defined triangular head which is covered with
small scales, except for a single large scale over each eye. Two rows of
small scales separate eye from upper labials. Rostral scale does not extend
upwards on to nose-horn, which is covered by about 9–20 small scales.
Usually 21 or 23 rows of dorsal scales at mid-body. Colour and pattern
fairly constant. Males often light grey and females greyish, brownish, or
red-brown (rarely yellowish or pinkish). Nearly always a clearly defined,
dark-edged vertebral stripe which may form zig-zag or consist of a series
of connected lozenges (occasionally these may not be joined). Very rarely
vertebral stripe is a continuous straight-edged band or is very faint.
Underside greyish, or pinkish with darker spots or mottling. Underside of
tail may be red, yellowish, or greenish. Melanism is rare.

Habits. Found in a wide variety of habitats, but most favoured ones are on
dry rocky slopes, with some vegetation and good exposure to sun. Also
occurs in light woods, screes, rock-piles, and dry-stone walls in cultivated
areas. Occasionally climbs in bushes, and also on rock faces where it may
be seen working its way along crevices looking for lizards. Occurs from
sea level up to about 2500 m in south of its range. Usually encountered by
day, but said to be sometimes nocturnal in warmer parts of range. A slow

rather phlegmatic snake, not very irascible. When disturbed hisses loudly.
Feeds mainly on small mammals, birds, and lizards.
Venom. Highly venomous. Its bite is potentially more dangerous than that
of any other widespread European Viper.
Variation. Three subspecies have been recognised in Europe, but the
distinctions between them are not clear-cut. Populations vary in average
body size, colour of the tail tip, details of scaling on snout, and angle of
nose-horn. Largest specimens occur in north-west, where tail-tip tends to
be red (less commonly yellow). The number of scales on nose-horn is
greatest in the south, and the rostral scale is highest in the east.

Similar species. None within range.

VIPERA XANTHINA *Ottoman Viper*   **Pl. 40**
Range. In Europe confined to area around Istanbul (European Turkey).
Also found in Asia Minor, neighbouring USSR and Lebanon. Occurs on
some E. Aegean islands not included in this guide   Map 126.
Identification. Adults up to 120cm, including tail, but usually smaller. A
large, thick-bodied viper, easily separated from other species within its
European range by its lack of nose-horn and characteristic, often vivid,
head pattern. Scales on top of head small, but supraoculars relatively
large; usually two or three scale rows between eye and upper labials.
23–25 scale rows at mid-body.

Usually a stripe running from eye to angle of mouth and often a blotch
across the mouth below the eye. Also, two converging stripes on top of
head; these may extend between eyes or, if not, there may be two clear
small spots in front of them. All these head markings are usually very bold.
Body grey, yellowish, olive, or brownish. Dark vertebral stripe often
darker edged, wavy or made up of connected lozenges or sometimes
broken into a series of blotches. Flanks often darker than back with dark
spots or bars. Underside often greyish; underside of tail tip frequently
yellow or orange. In general, males are more contrastingly coloured than
females.
Habits. Occurs in wide variety of habitats including open woods, rocky
hillsides, pastures, and even swamps. Also found in cultivated areas
where it is attracted by water. Often active at night in hotter parts of year,

Ottoman Viper

but also diurnal. Fairly sluggish but strikes quickly. Feeds on mammals and birds when adult, lizards when young. In Asia Minor occurs from sea-level to over 2000 metres.

Venom. A dangerous snake: its bite may be fatal to man and domestic animals if not treated.

Variation. No geographical variation in Europe, but considerable individual variation in colour.

Similar Species. None within European range. See *V. lebetina* (below).

VIPERA LEBETINA *Blunt-nosed Viper*   Pl. 40

Range. In Europe, confined to W. Cyclades: Milos, Kimolos, Polyagos, Siphnos and perhaps Kithnos and Antimilos. Also S.W. Asia and N.W. Africa   Fig., p. 113.

Identification. Adults up to 150 cm, including tail, but rarely much above 80 cm in Europe. Easily identified as it is the only viper species in its Aegean range. Head fairly rounded, with no large scales on its upper surface (not even over the eyes), two or three rows of small scales between the eyes and the upper labials. Usually 23 scale rows at mid-body.

Very variable in colouring but pattern usually not very vivid. Females usually dark brownish, males greyer and lighter (but both sexes brighter in spring – frequently straw-yellow and light grey respectively). Often four rows of blotches on body, the two central ones joining on the mid-line. Some specimens are a uniform brick red. Juveniles are typically blue-grey with four series of dark olive markings – the two central ones not usually meeting on back. Underside pale, speckled with dark pigment; underside of tail-tip sometimes yellow. In general, males are more contrastingly coloured than females.

Habits. Found in a wide variety of habitats on the islands including dry sunny hillsides and cultivated land. Said to prefer sheltered sunny places along water courses; also occurs in marshes etc. May climb in bushes. Largely nocturnal in hotter part of year, but diurnal at other times. During day is rather sluggish. Feeds mainly on mammals and birds and even other snakes, but also takes lizards, especially when young. In Europe lays eggs.

Venom. Over most of its range considered to be very dangerous. European individuals are relatively small and probably rather less toxic than elsewhere, but they must still be treated with extreme caution.

Variation. Considerable variation in colour in Europe.

Similar Species. None within its known European range. Lack of large supraoculars and of strongly contrasting head markings differentiate it from *V. xanthina*, its nearest relative.

Identification of Amphibian Eggs

In nearly all cases, the eggs of European amphibians are laid in water. This usually takes place in the spring, but may be earlier in the South, and some species lay again later in the year (e.g. discoglossids, p. 60, Parsley Frog, p. 71, Natterjack, p. 73). Eggs are usually enclosed in a gelatinous capsule. In some species this is very small when the eggs are laid but rapidly swells in the next day or two.

Important recognition features are size of eggs and capsules, shape of capsule (round or elongated), colour of eggs, and whether they are laid separately, in small groups, or in large clumps, strings or bands. In some species eggs are simply broadcast but in others they are carefully attached to plants or stones. The place used for depositing eggs varies: for instance, some forms choose cold mountain streams, while others prefer turbid,

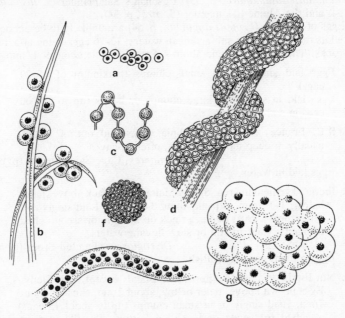

Eggs of frogs and toads (not to same scale)

a.	Painted Frogs	e.	Typical Toads
b.	Fire-bellied Toads	f.	Tree Frogs
c.	Midwife Toads	g.	Typical Frogs
d.	Spadefoots		

225

lowland pools. Species distribution is a very useful means of checking identifications. Another clue is the presence of adult animals in the vicinity.

Eggs can be most easily examined if placed with water in a transparent plastic bag. A lens is also very helpful. If at all possible, do not separate attached eggs from their moorings, or keep them too long in plastic bags. After examination, they should be carefully returned to the place where they were found.

Key to Amphibian Eggs

Some salamanders habitually give birth to fully developed young or to larvae and consequently have no free eggs. These are the Fire Salamander (*Salamandra salamandra*, p. 33), Luschan's Salamander (*S. luschani*, p. 34) and the Alpine Salamander (*S. atra*, p. 34).

Eggs of the Olm (*Proteus anguinus*, p. 54) are unlikely to be encountered as they are laid in subterranean waters, 12–70 eggs being attached to rocks. They are white and about 4–5 mm, capsule about 9–12 mm.

1. Eggs laid singly or in small clumps (maximum of 15–20 eggs)   2

   Eggs laid in strings or large clumps or bands (up to 10,000 eggs in some cases)   6

2. S.E. France, N. Italy, Sardinia. Eggs laid out of water, usually in deep moist crevices, often in caves
                              Hydromantes, Cave Salamanders (p. 53)
   Eggs laid in water   3

3. Iberia, Tyrrhenian area, Sicily, Malta. Eggs black above, paler below, 1–1.5 mm, capsule about 3 or 4 mm. Laid singly and often form a layer one egg thick on bottom, or are attached to plants. Laid in still or slow flowing water
                              Discoglossus, Painted Frogs (p. 62)
   Eggs brown, grey or whitish   4

4. Not Iberia or most Mediterranean islands except N.E. Sicily. Eggs brown above, paler below, about 2 mm, capsule about 7 mm. Laid singly or in small clumps (up to about 15 eggs) attached to weeds or loose on bottom. In still or slow flowing water   *Bombina*, Fire-bellied Toads (p. 60)

   W. and S. Iberia. Eggs dark above, whitish below, about 1½–2 mm, capsule about 7 mm. Attached to plants or stones in clumps of 10–15, usually in still water
                              Pleurodeles waltl, Sharp-ribbed Salamander (p. 38)

W. Italy. Eggs brown above, paler below, about 2 mm, capsule about 5 mm. Laid in clumps of 10–15 on twigs, stones etc. in clean, running water
Salamandrina terdigitata, Spectacled Salamander (p. 35)
Eggs whitish or pale buff, capsule about 3–7 mm. Laid singly among stones in cool, running water
Pyrenees, Corsica and Sardinia,
Euproctus, Brook Salamanders (p. 38)
W. Iberia. *Chioglossa*, Golden-striped Salamander (p. 35)
All areas. Eggs brown or whitish above, capsule typically longer than broad. Usually laid singly, often carefully wrapped in leaves of plants in still water *Triturus*, Newts, **5**

5. S.W. Europe. Eggs pale, greenish-white. Relatively large, about 2 mm, capsule about 4.5 mm maximum diameter
Triturus marmoratus, Marbled Newt (p. 42)
Not Iberia or S.W. France. Eggs pale, yellowish white. Relatively large, about 2 mm, capsule about 4.5 mm maximum diameter *Triturus cristatus*, Warty Newt (p. 43)
Eggs pale brownish or grey-brown, or greyish above. Smaller about 1.5 mm or a little more, capsule about 3 mm maximum diameter other *Triturus* species, smaller Newts (p. 46)

6. W. Europe only. Eggs large and pale without obvious gelatinous capsule, about 3.5–4 mm. Laid in strings, each egg attached to the next by a narrow connector. Usually seen wrapped round hind legs of adult males, or in water when empty *Alytes*, Midwife Toads (p. 63)
Eggs dark, laid in long gelatinous strings.
Bufo, Typical Toads, **7**
Eggs about 1.5–2.5 mm. Laid in thick band often wrapped around the stems of water plants; may smell fishy and sometimes breaks into sections **8**
Eggs pale brownish above, yellowish below, about 1.5 mm, capsule 3–4 mm. Laid in small clumps, about the size of a walnut *Hyla*, Tree Frogs (p. 74)
Eggs brown or black above, about 1.5–3 mm, capsule about 6–12 mm. Laid in large, often amorphous clumps
Rana, Typical Frogs, **9**

7. Eggs 1.5–2 mm; black all over, often in three or four rows when strings are free in water, two rows when gently stretched *Bufo bufo*, Common Toad (p. 72)
Eggs 1–1.5 mm; black, often in three or four rows when strings are free in water; two rows gently when stretched
Bufo viridis, Green Toad (p. 74)

Eggs 1–1.5 mm, black above, paler below; often two rows when strings are free in water, one row when gently stretched
Bufo calamita, Natterjack (p. 73)

8. Eggs blackish   *Pelodytes punctatus*, Parsley Frog (p. 71)
   Eggs grey or brown   *Pelobates*, Spadefoots (p. 67)

9. *Rana*, Typical Frogs
   The eggs of these species are often difficult to identify with certainty. Range and habitat are often helpful.
   N. Italy. Eggs laid in a floating layer about one egg thick and 30–150 cm across. Either attached to weeds or free
   Rana catesbeiana, American Bullfrog (p. 87)
   Eggs laid in irregular clumps several eggs thick   **10**

10. Eggs laid in floating clumps; black with small, pale spot on lower surface, about 2–3 mm, capsule 8–10 mm
    Rana temporaria, Grass Frog (p. 78)
    Eggs usually laid beneath surface   **11**

11. *Rana lessonae*, Pool Frog (p. 85), *Rana esculenta*, Edible Frog (p. 86); *Rana ridibunda*, Marsh Frog (p. 85). Eggs brown above, yellowish below, about 1.5 mm diameter, capsule 7–8 mm
    Rana arvalis, Moor Frog (p. 80). Eggs blackish above, lower third or half is whitish, 1.5–2 mm, capsule 7–8 mm
    Rana dalmatina, Agile Frog (p. 80). Eggs blackish-brown above, lower half whitish, 2–3 mm, capsule 9–12 mm
    Rana latastei, Italian Agile Frog (p. 81). N. Italy. Eggs blackish-brown above, lower third whitish, 1.5–2 mm, capsule 6–7 m
    Rana graeca, Stream Frog (p. 82), *Rana iberica*, Iberian Frog (p. 83). Spawn not well known

Identification of Amphibian Larvae

Most European amphibians have free-living aquatic larvae, which are often called tadpoles (strictly, this word applies only to the larvae of frogs and toads but it is commonly used for those of newts and salamanders as well). Newt and salamander larvae are long-bodied, with feathery gills and they develop their forelegs before the hind ones. In contrast, the tadpoles of frogs and toads have rounded bodies, the gills are not visible externally, except in the early stages of development, and their hindlegs develop before the forelimbs. They also have rather specialised mouths with a horny beak bordered by several rows of labial teeth. Because the gills are enclosed, they are aerated by a stream of water that enters via the mouth and leaves through an opening in the body-wall, the spiracle.

The main features that are helpful in the identification of tadpoles are shown in the Figs. on p. 231 and p. 236; the mouth of a typical frog or toad larva is also illustrated (Fig. p. 236). Tadpoles are best examined in a small transparent plastic bag, although they should not be kept in this for very long. A lens is very useful in checking most characters but, in the few cases where mouth parts need to be examined (which should only be attempted on dead tadpoles), a dissecting microscope is needed. As with amphibian eggs, habitat, species range and presence of adult animals nearby can be helpful clues in identification. The tadpoles of some groups (e.g. Brown Frogs and the smaller newts) are all similar yet rather variable. They are therefore sometimes difficult to identify, especially as there

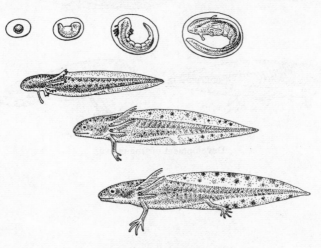

Development of newt tadpole

229

is often insufficient knowledge of the amount of variability to be expected. Like most adult amphibians, tadpoles can change the intensity of their colouring quite rapidly. Stages in the development of a newt and a frog tadpole are shown in Figs., p. 229 and below).

Neoteny. Sometimes tadpoles do not change (metamorphose) into the adult form. Instead they retain larval characteristics and, in the case of some newts and salamanders, they may even breed in this condition. In some species, only the neotenous larval form is known and normal adults do not exist. The Olm (*Proteus anguinus*) is one of these permanent larvae. Neoteny occurs occasionally in many species of amphibians, and is most frequent in highland areas where the water contains relatively little nutriment. However it is also found in other situations and is sometimes associated with albinism. The condition is relatively common in the Alpine Newt (*Triturus alpestris*), which has some completely neotenous populations in W. Yugoslavia. Neotenous tadpoles usually grow much larger then normal ones and they may also take on some adult characters. Both these features are useful in identifying them.

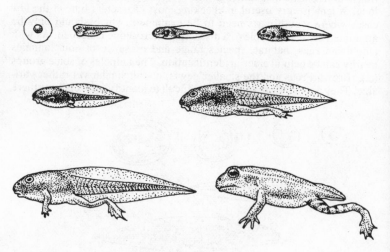

Development of frog tadpole

Identification of Newt and Salamander Larvae

A few species do not have free-living tadpoles. These are the Alpine Salamander (*Salamandra atra*), apparently Luschan's Salamander (*S. luschani*) and the Cave Salamanders (*Hydromantes*). Sizes given are for large larvae, just before metamorphosis; the illustrations depict animals at this stage. Fig., below shows some of the features important for identification; to make this easier, newt and salamander tadpoles are dealt with in three geographical groups. Tail and crest shape are often quite variable within species. Young tadpoles may not have their full complement of toes.

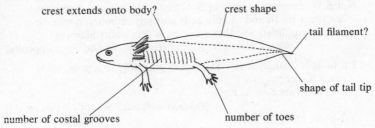

Some features to check when identifying salamander and newt tadpoles

Key

ALL AREAS EXCEPT IBERIA, THE PYRENEES, CORSICA AND SARDINIA

E. Adriatic coastal area only. Very long-bodied and very pale, with not more than two toes on the hind feet. Usually in subterranean waters (or more rarely in their surface outlets).
Proteus anguinus, Olm (p. 54)

W. Italy only. Up to 3 cm. Tail tip rounded. Four toes on hind feet, even in well developed larvae (not five as in other species). Usually in cool, flowing water
Salamandrina terdigitata, Spectacled Salamander (p. 35 and Fig., p. 233)

Up to 6.5 cm. Tail tip blunt or rounded, upper crest usually extends at least a short distance onto body. Head broad and rounded (when viewed from above). Distance between nostrils much greater than distance from nostril to eye. Often a light spot at the base of each leg. Found in clean, often flowing water   *Salamandra salamandra*, Fire Salamander, (p. 33 and Fig., p. 233)

Not S.W. and S. France. Up to 8 cm (usually smaller but rarely less than 5 cm when fully developed). Undamaged tail tapers gradually to a long filament. Crest extends far forwards on back. 15 or 16 costal grooves between fore and hindlimbs. Brownish with no green colouring; often large dark spots present on borders of tail. Usually in still or slow-flowing water *Triturus cristatus*, Warty Newt (p. 43 and Fig., opposite)

W., S.W. and central France. Tadpoles like those of *T. cristatus*, but only 12 or 13 costal grooves between fore and hindlimbs and usually at least a tinge of green in coloration
    Triturus marmoratus, Marbled Newt (p. 42 and Fig., opposite)

Not S.W. France, S. Italy or S. Greece. Up to 5 cm. Tail does not taper much and usually ends abruptly although it may be obtusely pointed and there may be a very short filament
    Triturus alpestris, Alpine Newt (p. 46 and Fig., opposite)

Up to 4 cm (usually less). Tail tapers gradually to a point without a filament.
Not S. France or S. Italy
    Triturus vulgaris, Smooth Newt (p. 47)
Not E. areas or Italy.
    Triturus helveticus, Palmate Newt (p. 51 and Fig., opposite)
S. and central Italy only   *Triturus italicus*, Italian Newt (p. 52)

Carpathian and Tatras mountains. Tail shape variable (rounded or obtusely pointed). Often intermediate in appearance between the tadpoles of *T. vulgaris* and *T. alpestris* (with which it may occur). Just before metamorphosis, there may be two rows of light spots on the back
    Triturus montandoni, Montandon's Newt (p. 47)

IBERIA AND THE PYRENEES

W. Iberia only. Up to 4.5 cm. Body very long, tail-tip rounded, crest does not extend onto body. Found in clear, flowing water.   *Chioglossa lusitanica*, Golden-striped Salamander
    (p. 35 and Fig., opposite)
Pyrenees only. Up to 6 cm. Tail-tip blunt or rounded, crest only extends a short distance onto body. Head narrow, and not rounded (when viewed from above), over 1½ times longer than wide. Found in cold, often flowing water.
    Euproctus asper, Pyrenean Brook Salamander
    (p. 38 and Fig., opposite)

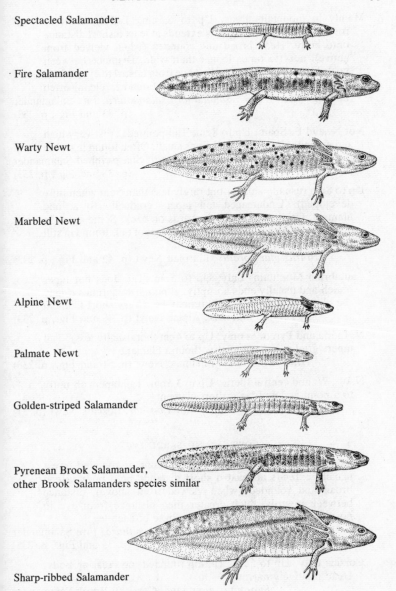

Spectacled Salamander

Fire Salamander

Warty Newt

Marbled Newt

Alpine Newt

Palmate Newt

Golden-striped Salamander

Pyrenean Brook Salamander,
other Brook Salamanders species similar

Sharp-ribbed Salamander

Mainly in mountain areas. Up to 6.5 cm. Tail-tip blunt or rounded, upper crest usually extends at least a short distance onto body. Head broad and rounded (when viewed from above), not 1½ times longer than wide. Distance between nostrils much greater than distance from nostril to eye. Often, a light spot at the base of each leg. Found in clean, often flowing water *Salamandra salamandra*, Fire Salamander
(p. 33 and Fig., p. 233)

Not N. and E. Spain. Up to 8 cm. Tail pointed, crest very high and extends almost to head. Eyes small. Often found in turbid lowland waters. *Pleurodeles waltl*, Sharp-ribbed Salamander
(p. 38 and Fig., p. 233)

Up to 8 cm (usually smaller but rarely less than 5 cm when fully developed). Undamaged tail tapers gradually to a long filament. Crest extends far forwards on back. Some green in colouring and large dark spots on borders of tail. Found in still or slow-flowing water
Triturus marmoratus, Marbled Newt (p. 42 and Fig., p. 233)

Cantabrian Mountains only. Up to 5 cm. Tail does not taper much and usually ends abruptly, although sometimes it may be obtusely pointed and there may be a very short filament
Triturus alpestris, Alpine Newt (p. 46 and Fig., p. 233)

N. Iberia and Pyrenees only. Up to 4 cm (but usually less). Tail tapers gradually to a point without a filament
Triturus helveticus, Palmate Newt (p. 51 and Fig., p. 233)

N.W., W. and central Iberia. Up to 3.5 cm. Tail tapers abruptly to a point and ends in a short filament
Triturus boscai, Bosca's Newt (p. 51)

CORSICA AND SARDINIA

Corsica only. Up to 6.5 cm. Tail tip blunt or rounded, crest usually extends at least a short distance onto body. Head broad and rounded (when viewed from above), distance between nostrils much greater than distance from eye to nostril. Often a light blotch at the base of each leg
Salamandra salamandra, Fire Salamander
(p. 33 and Fig., p. 233)

Corsica only. Up to 5 cm. Tail-tip rounded, no crest on body. Head relatively narrow.
Euproctus montanus, Corsican Brook Salamander
(p. 39 and Fig., p. 233)

Sardinia only. Up to 5 cm. Tail-tip often pointed, crest usually extends at least a short distance onto body. Head relatively narrow. The only free-living salamander or newt larva on Sardinia   *Euproctus platycephalus*, Sardinian Brook Salamander

(p. 39 and Fig., p. 233)

Identification of Frog and Toad Larvae

Sizes given are for large larvae with well-developed hind legs. The illustrations depict the tadpoles at this stage; Figs., below show some of the features important for identification. Tail and crest shape are often quite variable within species.

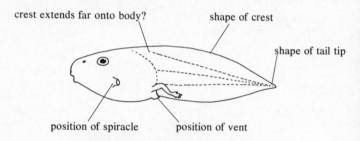

Some features to check when identifying frog and toad tadpoles

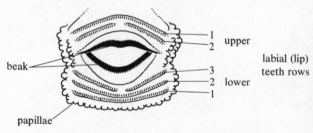

Mouth of frog or toad tadpole

Key

1. Spiracle on mid-line of belly   **2**
   Spiracle on left flank   **3**

2. Iberia etc., Tyrrhenian area, Sicily, Malta. Up to about 3.5 cm. Spiracle centrally placed on underside. Tail over 1½ times body length, not very deep; tail tip rounded. A polygonal network of fine black lines often visible (with lens) on crests

         Discoglossus, Painted Frogs (p. 62 and Fig., opposite)
NOTE: *D. pictus* and *D. sardus* can be separated by range (see Maps 23 and 24)

Painted Frog

Fire-bellied Toad

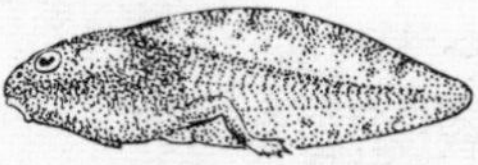

Midwife Toad

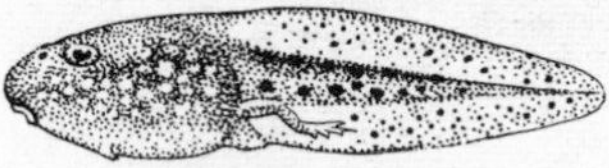

Common Toad

Green Toad

Common Tree Frog

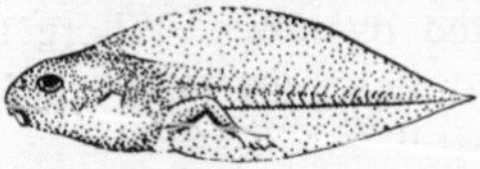

Stripeless Tree Frog

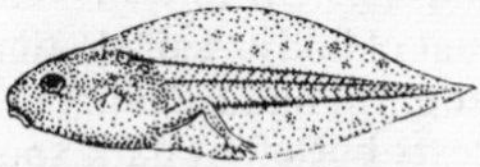

Parsley Frog

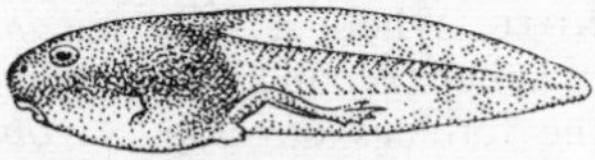

Western Spadefoot

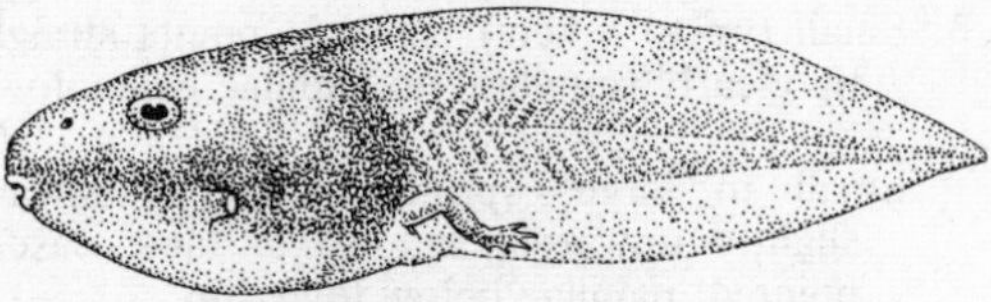

American Bullfrog

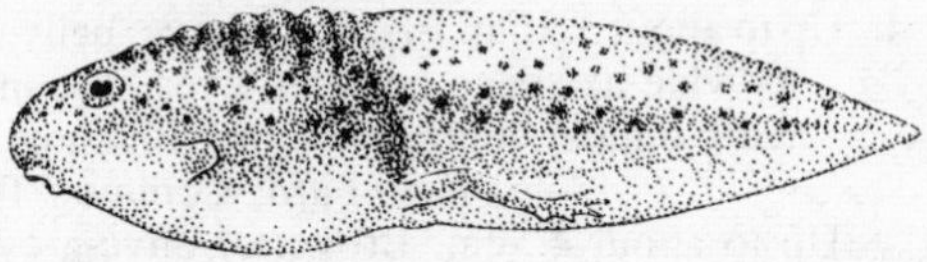

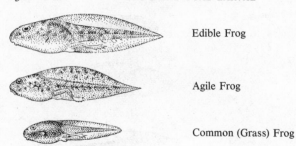

Edible Frog

Agile Frog

Common (Grass) Frog

Not Iberia or most Mediterranean islands (except N.E. Sicily). Up to about 5cm. Spiracle placed slightly towards back of body. Tail less than 1½ times body length, deep; tail tip bluntly pointed or rounded. Numerous intersecting dark lines often visible (with lens) on crests

Bombina, Fire-bellied Toads (p. 60 and Fig., p. 237)

NOTE: *B. bombina* and *B. variegata* can sometimes be separated by range. Where they occur together, mouth shape may help: the mouth is triangular in *B. bombina* and more oval in *B. variegata*.

W. Europe. Up to 8 or 9cm. Spiracle placed slightly towards front of body. Tail 1½ times body length or more, often fairly deep; tip bluntly pointed or rounded. No fine black lines on crests but often dark spots or blotches.

Alytes, Midwife Toads (p. 63 and Fig., p. 237)

NOTE: Where *A. obstetricans* and *A. cisternasii* are found together (W. and central Iberia), they can be separated once the forelegs develop: *A. obstetricans* has three tubercles on the palm, while *A. cisternasii* has two.

3. Small (up to 4.5cm); spiracle points straight backwards; tail tip clearly rounded; no papillae below lower lip

Bufo, Typical Toads, **4**

Small to large; spiracle points backwards and at least slightly upwards; tail tip in most cases at least bluntly pointed; papillae below lower lip **5**

4. Up to about 3.5cm. Blackish above, belly very dark grey. Mouth as wide as space between eyes. Second row of upper labial teeth almost continuous, or with short break

Bufo bufo, Common Toad (p. 72 and Fig., p. 237)

Up to about 4.5cm. Brown or olive-grey above, belly greyish

white. Mouth nearly as wide as space between eyes. Second row of upper labial teeth often broken in middle

Bufo viridis, Green Toad (p. 74 and Fig., p. 237)

Up to about 2.5cm. Blackish above, belly dark grey, often with bronzy spots; may have light stripe on back. Mouth often only half as wide as space between eyes. Second row of upper labial teeth with wide gap in middle

Bufo calamita, Natterjack (p. 73)

5. Upper crest extends forwards almost to level of eyes, which are on sides of head. Usually golden-olive above and white below. Very fast and fish-like   *Hyla*, Tree Frogs, **6**

Upper crest does not extend almost to level of eyes, which tend to be towards top of head   **7**

6. Muscular part of tail plain or spotted, and there may be a short stripe at base. Second row of upper labial teeth with a narrow gap in middle

Hyla arborea, Common Tree Frog (p. 75 and Fig., p. 237)

Muscular part of tail with a dark stripe above and below. Second row of upper labial teeth with a broad gap in middle

Hyla meridionalis, Stripeless Tree Frog (p. 78 and Fig., p. 237)

7. Vent on mid-line   **8**

Vent opens towards lower edge of tail-fin, on its right side

Rana, Typical Frogs,   **9**

8. Up to about 6cm. Tail rather blunt; beak white with a black edge.

Pelodytes punctatus, Parsley Frog (p. 71 and Fig., p. 237)

Up to 16cm or even more. Tail sharply pointed; beak black.

Pelobates, Spadefoots (p. 67 and Fig., p. 237)

Range is useful in distinguishing the three species. *P. cultripes* has a relatively shorter tail than the others.

9. The tadpoles of Typical Frogs (*Rana*) are all similar and all rather variable, so they are difficult to identify with certainty. As with other difficult groups, range is sometimes a helpful clue to identity.

Rana catesbeiana, American Bullfrog (p. 87 and Fig., p. 237). N. Italy only. Up to 16cm. Olive green above, belly whitish. Tail tip clearly pointed.

Rana esculenta, Edible Frog (p. 86 and Fig., opposite), *Rana lessonae*, Pool Frog (p. 85). Up to about 7.5cm (usually smaller). Olive, olive-brown or olive grey above (often green in the later stages), belly white. Tail tip clearly pointed.

Rana ridibunda, Marsh Frog (p. 85). Up to about 9cm

(sometimes more but usually less). Generally like tadpole of *R. esculenta*.

Rana arvalis, Moor Frog (p. 80). Up to about 4.5 cm. Brown above, belly greyish, sometimes large dark spots on upper crest. Tail-tip usually clearly pointed.

Rana dalmatina, Agile Frog (p. 80 and Fig., p. 238). Up to 6 cm. Pale brown or rufous above with darker spots, belly white with gold spottings. Often some dark spots on upper crest, which is fairly high and tapers abruptly to a very pointed tail tip.

Rana latastei, Italian Agile Frog (p. 81). N. Italy only. Up to about 4.5 cm. Rather like tadpole of *R. dalmatina*, but crest lower. Brown above, belly whitish, often some dark spots on upper crest.

Rana temporaria, Common (Grass) Frog (p. 78 and Fig., p. 238). Up to about 4.5 cm. Brown to black above, belly grey or black. Tail tip usually blunt.

Rana graeca, Stream Frog (p. 82) and *R. iberica*, Iberian Frog (p. 83). Similar to *R. temporaria*, but crest higher and usually blotched.

Internal Characters

In the species texts, identifications have been made using only external characters, but in some difficult groups, differences in skeleton may sometimes be helpful in confirming identities of dead animals.

NEWTS (*Triturus*). Two of the bones on each side of the skull, the frontal and the squamosal, often have projections that may meet to form a structure called the *fronto-squamosal arch*. Sometimes the arch is completely bony, but often it is interrupted in the middle or is entirely absent. Among European species, the structure usually varies as follows (Fig., below):

Arch completely bony: *T. helveticus, T. boscai*
Arch present but interrupted: *T. vulgaris, T. italicus*
Arch completely bony *or* interrupted: *T. montandoni.*
Arch very reduced: *T. alpestris, T. marmoratus*
Arch absent: *T. cristatus*

  This feature is most useful in identifying newts apparently intermediate between *T. vulgaris* and *T. helveticus*.

N.B. The differences listed above are true for adults. Juveniles of all species often lack a complete arch.

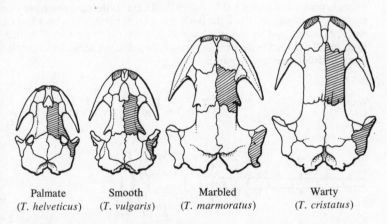

| Palmate | Smooth | Marbled | Warty |
| (*T. helveticus*) | (*T. vulgaris*) | (*T. marmoratus*) | (*T. cristatus*) |

Newts showing differences in development of frontosquamosal arch

GREEN LIZARDS (*Lacerta* part I). In N. Spain, occasional animals may be found that are not clearly either the Green Lizard (*Lacerta viridis*) or Schreiber's Green Lizard (*L. schreiberi*). In such cases checking the skull may help. In *L. schreiberi*, the postorbital and postfrontal bones (Fig., below) form a single unit throughout life, whereas in *L. viridis* they are separate, except in some old animals. The bones are best examined from underneath.

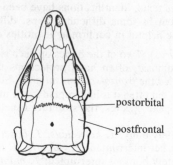

— postorbital

— postfrontal

Skull of Green Lizard

SMALL LACERTAS (*Lacerta* part II and *Podarcis*).
European Rock, Meadow and Viviparous Lizards (*Lacerta* part II) can be distinguished from Wall Lizards (*Podarcis*) by the shape of the vertebrae in the base of the tail. In both groups, the first 4–6 vertebrae of the tail have a simple projection on each side, but in Wall Lizards the next few have two pairs of projections of which the back one is longer and points backwards. Rock, Meadow and Viviparous Lizards may have a single pair of projections on all tail vertebrae, or if any have two pairs, the back one is shorter than the front pair and is parallel to it.

Wall Lizard

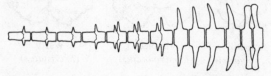

Rock, Meadow and Viviparous Lizards

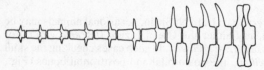

Basal tail vertebrae of Small Lacertas

GLOSSARY

Many terms not included in this glossary are explained in the preliminary remarks at the beginning of the sections on the main animal groups (pp. 29, 55, 88, 101, 183).

Aestivation. A period of inactivity during the summer months.

Albino (hence albinism). An animal in which dark pigment fails to develop so that it appears white or pinkish. Albinism occurs as a rare variation in many species.

Amplexus. The sexual embrace of amphibians. It occurs in all European frogs, toads and salamanders but not newts. In frogs and toads the male grasps the female just behind the arms in some species, and around the loins in others.

Anal Gland. A paired gland situated in the base of the tail of many snakes and opening into the vent. Anal glands often produce a foul-smelling secretion that is ejected when the snake is frightened.

Autotomy. The ability to shed a part of the body either spontaneously or when it is grasped by an attacker. In Europe many lizards and one salamander are capable of autotomizing the tail if it is held. In most cases a new tail is grown afterwards.

Balkans. Used here for the whole of S.E. Europe, north to Yugoslavia, S. Hungary and Romania.

Bridge. The part of the shell of tortoises, terrapins and turtles that joins the upper and lower sections.

Canthus (pl. *canthi*; abbreviation of *canthus rostralis*). A slight ridge separating the top and side surfaces of the snout in some amphibians and reptiles. Typically it runs from the front corner of the eye to the general region of the nostril.

Carapace. Upper section of the shell of tortoises, terrapins, and turtles.

Cloaca. The cavity into which the contents of the intestine, reproductive glands and kidneys discharge their products in reptiles and amphibians. The cloaca empties through the vent.

Cloacal Swelling. The swollen area around the vent in many newts and salamanders.

Collar. A transverse fold of skin on the lower surface of the neck in some lizards; it is usually covered with enlarged scales (see e.g. Fig., p. 104).

Constriction. Method of killing prey used by some snakes – in Europe, the Sand Boa (*Eryx*) and Rat Snakes (*Elaphe*). The victim is held very tightly by coils of the body so that breathing and often the action of the heart are prevented.

Costal Grooves. Vertical grooves on the flanks of some salamanders, newts and their larvae. They correspond to the position of the ribs. Differences in the number of grooves between the fore and hind limbs can be important in the recognition of newt tadpoles, especially *Triturus cristatus* and *T. marmoratus* (see p. 232).

Crepuscular. Active at twilight.

Crest. The flexible cutaneous structure that develops on the tail and back of male newts in the breeding season. It is believed to be important both as a respiratory structure and a recognition feature that helps females to identify males of their own species.

Display. A conspicuous and usually ritualised pattern of behaviour that is capable of affecting the behaviour of other animals at which the display is directed.

Diurnal. Habitually active by day.

Dorsal. To do with the upper side of the body. In lizards and snakes, **dorsal scales** usually include those on the sides as well.

Dorsolateral Fold. A ridge running from the side of the head to the groin in some frogs (see e.g. Fig., p. 55).

Dry-stone walls. Walls constructed by piling natural, undressed stones without the use of mortar. They contain numerous crevices and hollows beloved of many reptiles and some amphibians.

Emarginate. Used here to describe an arrangement where the edge of a scale cuts into the otherwise smooth margin of a larger one. See, for example, Fig., p. 162.

Endemic. Restricted to a particular region, and (in some cases) originating there.

Fang. An enlarged, hollow or grooved tooth, which acts as a means of injecting venom into prey or an attacker.

Femoral Pores. A series of pores on the underside of the thigh of many lizards (Fig., p. 104), normally better developed in males than females. Their function is uncertain.

Gill. A respiratory organ located in the neck region that functions in water. Gills may be external and feathery in salamander larvae and young frog and toad larvae, or enclosed, as in older frog and toad larvae.

Herpetology. The study of reptiles and amphibians.

Hibernation. An extended period of rest, immobility or torpor during the winter. Hibernation occurs in most European amphibians and reptiles, including all the more northern ones in which it is often very prolonged. See also p. 16.

Hybrid. An individual animal that is the offspring of parents of different species.

Iberia. Used here for the Iberian Peninsula, i.e. Portugal and Spain; Andorra and the French Pyrenees are often included.

Iris. The often brightly coloured and circular area of the eye surrounding the pupil.

Jizz. (Originally a term used by American bird-watchers.) The combination of subtle and usually indefinable features that is often the easiest way of identifying and separating closely related species. Successful use of jizz depends on having some experience of the animals concerned. It should not be relied on too much until the observer has developed this familiarity.

Karst. Limestone formations with characteristic pattern of erosion typified by deep hollows, crevices and caves.

Labial. Of the lips. In reptiles, a scale that borders the lips.

Larva. A specialised stage in the life history of many animals including most European amphibians, the eggs of which give rise to a free-living aquatic form that finally changes (metamorphoses) to produce the adult stage.

Lateral. To do with the sides.

Lichenous. Used to describe markings which have irregular, poorly defined edges, rather like lichens.

Lumbar. Used here for the region of the back just in front of the hind limbs.

Melanism (hence melanistic, melanic). A condition in which an animal has an unusually large amount of dark pigment so that it appears black or blackish. Melanism occurs in many small-island populations of Wall Lizards, but also sporadically in many other species.

Metamorphosis. The rapid changes that occur in amphibians when a larva (tadpole) assumes the form of an adult animal. In newts and salamanders the most obvious sign is the disappearance of the feathery gills. In frogs and toads it is the development of the forelegs and the rapid loss of the tail.

Metatarsal Tubercle. A prominent tubercle on the hind foot of many frogs and toads (see e.g. Fig., p. 86).

Montane. Living in mountainous country.

Morph. See p. 15.

Nasolabial Groove. A narrow groove running from the nostril to the edge of the upper lip in plethodontid salamanders, i.e. in Europe *Hydromantes* (Fig., p. 30).

Neoteny. A condition in which a larva (e.g. tadpole) fails to metamorphose but may grow to a large size and sometimes achieve sexual maturity. Neoteny occurs sporadically in many salamanders and newts. Neotonous frog tadpoles are rare and cannot breed. See also p. 230.

Nuptial Pads. Rough, and usually dark, areas of skin found on many frogs and toads and some salamanders. Nuptial pads develop to their full extent during the breeding season and are believed to help males maintain their grip on females. In frogs and toads they are often situated on the thumb, but other fingers may be involved and some species have rough areas present on the belly, toe-web or forearm.

Ocelli (sing. *ocellus*). Eye-like spots that often occur in the patterns of reptiles, especially lizards. Ocelli are approximately round with a contrasting border (see e.g. Pl. 22). **Ocellated.** With ocelli.

Paratoid Gland. Swelling on head and neck, situated behind the eye and present in many amphibians, particularly Typical Toads (*Bufo*) and Salamanders (*Salamandra*), see e.g. Fig., p. 72. In these animals the paratoid glands produce a noxious secretion that deters predators.

Plastron. Lower section of the shell of tortoises, terrapins and turtles.

Reticulated. Used to refer to patterns made up of lines and blotches interconnected in a net-like fashion (see e.g. Pls. 26 and 27).

Salp. A soft-bodied, floating marine animal related to sea-squirts. A common food of some marine turtles.

Scree. Slope, usually in a mountain area, composed of stones that have fallen from higher ground. **Boulder Scree.** Scree made up of large rocks. Screes contain many crevices and are consequently good habitats for reptiles and amphibians.

Scrub. Used here for a wide variety of vegetable communities where there is a fairly dense, although often interrupted, low growth.

Spade. Enlarged metatarsal tubercle present on the hind foot of Spadefoot toads and used for digging.

Species. See p. 14.

Spectacle. Permanent transparent covering of the eye found in snakes and some lizards.

Spermatophore. A gelatinous mass containing spermatazoa, produced by male newts and salamanders and taken up by the females.

Spiracle. The small opening in the body wall of frog and toad tadpoles that leads from the gill chamber (Fig., p. 236). The enclosed gills are bathed in a stream of water that enters through the mouth and leaves through the spiracle.

Spur. Any pointed, projecting structure on the limbs, especially the hind ones. Among European species used for the conical horny scales on the back of the thighs of some tortoises (e.g. *Testudo graeca*) and for the projection on the hind limb of some male Brook Salamanders (*Euproctus*).

Subarticular Tubercles. Tubercles situated under the joints of the fingers and toes.

Subspecies. See p. 15.

Tadpole. In its narrow sense the larva of a frog or toad, but also often used, as here, for the larvae of newts and salamanders.

Tubercle. A small well-defined, sometimes pointed swelling on the skin or an enlarged usually pointed scale.

Tyrrhenian Region. The islands lying in and around the Tyrrhenian Sea, e.g. Corsica, Sardinia, Monte Cristo, Giglio, and sometimes also Elba and Iles d'Hyères.

Uniform. Of a single colour; lacking contrasting markings.

Vent. The external entrance/exit of the cloaca (q.v.).

Ventral. To do with the underside. **Ventral scales** are the belly scales of lizards and snakes. See p. 184 for a more precise definition of snake ventrals.

Vertebral. Used here for the area over the vertebral column (spine) when describing scaling or pattern.

Vocal Sac. See p. 18.

Wart. Used for any well-defined, raised area on the skin of amphibians.

Web. The thin sheet of skin joining the hind toes of many European frogs and toads and some salamanders and newts.

BIBLIOGRAPHY

1. General accounts, or those dealing with particular species.

BOULENGER, G. A. 1897–98. *The Tailless Batrachians of Europe* (2 vols). Ray Society, London. Still the best general account of European frogs and toads. Some names outdated: *Bombinator = Bombina*; *Rana agilis = R. dalmatina*.

BOULENGER, G. A. 1913. *The Snakes of Europe*. Methuen, London. A good general account. Some names outdated: *Coluber = Elaphe*; *C. leopardinus = E. situla*; *Zamenis = Coluber*; *Z. gemonensis = C. viridiflavus*, *C. gemonensis* and *C. jugularis*; *Z. dahlii = C. najadum*; *Tarbophis = Telescopus*; *Coelopeltis = Malpolon*; *Tropidonotus = Natrix*; *T. viperinus = N. maura*.

BRONGERSMA, L. D. 1967. *British Turtles, Guide for the Identification of Stranded Turtles on British Coasts*. British Museum (Natural History), London.

BRONGERSMA, L. D. 1972. *European Atlantic Turtles*. Zoologische Verhandelingen. E. J. Brill, Leiden. A detailed account of turtles stranded, or observed in Atlantic waters.

FREYTAG, G. E. 1954. *Der Teichmolch*. Ziemsen, Wittenberg, Lutherstadt. An illustrated account of the Smooth Newt (*Triturus vulgaris*) and other central European species.

FREYTAG, G. E. 1955. *Feuersalamander und Alpensalamander*. Ziemsen, Wittenberg Lutherstadt. A general account of *Salamandra salamandra* and *S. atra*.

FROMMHOLD, E. 1964. *Die Kreuzotter*. Ziemsen, Wittenberg Lutherstadt. A general account of the Adder (*Vipera berus*).

HEILBORN, A. 1949. *Der Frosch*. Ziemsen, Wittenberg Lutherstadt. A general account of central European Brown Frogs (*Rana temporaria, R. dalmatina*, and *R. arvalis*).

MERTENS, R. and WERMUTH, H. 1960. *Die Amphibien und Reptilien Europas*. Verlag W. Kramer, Frankfurt. The standard checklist. Lists all subspecies recognised at time of publication.

GLASS H. and MEUSEL, W. 1969. *Die Süsswasserschildkröten Europas*. Ziemsen, Wittenberg Lutherstadt. A general account of European terrapins.

PETZOLD, H. G. 1971. *Blindschleiche und Scheltopusik*. Ziemsen, Wittenberg Lutherstadt. A general account of *Anguis* and *Ophisaurus*.

SAVAGE, R. M. 1961. *The ecology and life history of the Common Frog (Rana temporaria temporaria)*. I. Pitman, London.

SCHREIBER, E. 1912. *Herpetologia Europaea* (2nd Ed.). G. Fischer, Jena. A good general account, if rather old.

STEWARD, J. W. 1969. *The Tailed Amphibians of Europe*. David & Charles, Newton Abbot. A general account.

STEWARD, J. W. 1971. *The Snakes of Europe*. David & Charles, Newton Abbot. A general account.

THORN, R. 1968. *Les Salamandres d'Europe, d'Asie et d'Afrique du Nord*. Lechavalier, Paris. A good concise account; considerable detail of habits, breeding etc.

TRUTNAU, L. 1975. *Europäische Amphibien und Reptilien*. Belser Verlag, Stuttgart. Contains photographs of many species.

2. Regional accounts

Albania

KOPSTEIN, F. and WETTSTEIN, O. 1920. Reptilien und Amphibien aus Albanien. *Verh, zool.-bot. Ges. Wien*, 70: 387-409.

Austria

EISELT, J. 1961. *Catalogus Faunae Austriae*. 21: *Amphibia, Reptilia*. Springer-Verlag, Wien.

Belgium

WITTE, G. F. DE. 1948. *Faune de Belgique. Amphibiens et Reptiles* (2nd ed). Musée Royal d'Histoire Naturelle de Belgique, Bruxelles.

Bulgaria

BESKOV, V. and BERON, P. 1964. *Catalogue et Bibliographie des Amphibiens et des Reptiles en Bulgarie*. Acad. Bulgar. Sci., Sofia.

BURESCH, I. and ZONKOV, J. Untersuchungen über die Verbreitung der Reptilien und Amphibien in Bulgarien und auf der Balkanhalbinsel. *Izv. tsarsk. prirodonauch. Inst. Sofia*. (German summaries.)
1. Tortoises and Lizards, 1933: 150–207
2. Snakes, 1934: 106–188
3. Salamanders and newts, 1941: 171–237
4. Frogs and toads, 1942: 68–154.

Czechoslovakia

LAĆ, J. 1968. *Obojzivelniky ad Plazy*. Stavovce Slovenska I, Bratislava. (In Slovak.)

Denmark

SHIØTZ, A. 1971. Danske Padder. *Natur og Museum,* 15 (1): 1-23. Amphibians.

SØAGER, O. 1971. Faunaundersøgelsen 1970/71. *Nordisk Herpetologisk Forening*, 1971:57-66.

Finland

LANGERWERT, B. 1975. Reptielen en amfibieën in Finland. *Lacerta* 34 (1): 4-7. (In Dutch.)

France

ROLLINAT, R. 1934. *La Vie des Reptiles de la France Centrale.* Librairie Delagrave, Paris.

ANGEL, F. 1946. *Faune de France. Reptiles et Amphibiens.* Lechavalier, Paris.

FRETEY, J. 1975. *Guide des reptiles et batraciens de France.* Hatier, Paris.

Great Britain and Ireland

ARNOLD, H. R. 1973. *Provisional atlas of the amphibians and reptiles of the British Isles.* Nature Conservancy.

LEVER, C. 1977. *The naturalised animals of the British Isles.* Hutchinson, London.

SMITH, M. A. 1973. *British Amphibians and Reptiles* (5th Ed.). Collins, London.

TAYLOR, R. H. R. 1963. The distribution of amphibians and reptiles in England and Wales, Scotland and Ireland and the Channel Isles: a revised survey. *Brit. Journ. Herpetol.* 3: 95–115.

Greece

WERNER, F. 1938. Die Amphibien und Reptilien Griechenlands. *Zoologica 94*: 1–117, Stuttgart.

WETTSTEIN, O. 1953, 1957. Herpetologia aegaea. *Sitz-Ber. Österr. Akad. d. Wiss., math.-naturw. Kl., Wien* 162: 651-833. *166*: 123-164.

Germany

DURINGEN, B. 1897. *Deutschlands Amphibien und Reptilien.* Creutz'sche Verlagsbuchhandlung, Magdeburg.

MERTENS, R. 1947. *Die Lurche und Kriechtiere des Rhein-Main-Gebietes.* Kramer, Frankfurt.

MERTENS, R. 1968. *Kriechtiere und Lurche.* Kosmos, Stuttgart.

FROMMHOLD, E. 1965. *Heimische Lurche und Kriechtiere.* Ziemsen, Wittenberg Lutherstadt.

Hungary

FEJÉRVÁRY-LANGH, A. M. 1943. Beiträge und Berichtigungen zum Amphibien-Teil des ungarischen Faunenkataloges. *Fragmenta Faunistica Hungarica* 6: 42–58. Reptilien-Teil: 81–98.

Italy

CAPOCACCIA, L. 1968. *Anfibi e Rettili.* Mondadori, Milano.

TORTONESE, E. and LANZA, B. 1968. *Pesci, Anfibi e Rettili.* Aldo Martello Editore, Milano.

BRUNO, S. 1970. Anfibi e Rettili di Sicilia. *Atti della Accad. Gioenia di Scienze naturali in Catania*. 7th Ser. 2: 1–144.

BRUNO, S. 1973. Anfibi d'Italia: Caudata. *Natura, Milan*, 64: 209-450.

Netherlands

BUND, C. F. van de. 1964. De verspreiding van de reptielen en amphibieën in Nederland. *Lacerta 22*: 1–72.

Poland

BERGER, L., JASKOWSKA, J. and MLYNARSKI, M. 1969. Plazy i gadi. *Kat. Fauny Polski (Catalogus Faunae Poloniae)*. 39: 1–73.

Portugal

CRESPO, E. G. 1972. Amphíbios de Portugal Continental das colecções do Museu Bocage. *Arquivos do Museu Bocage* (2nd Ser) 3 (8): 203–303.

CRESPO, E. G. 1972. Répteis de Portugal Continental das colecções do Museu Bocage. *Arquivos do Museu Bocage* (2nd Ser) 3 (17): 447–612.

Romania

FUHN, I. 1960. *Fauna R.P. Romîne. Amphibia*. Acad. RPR, Bucureşti.

FUHN, I. and VANCEA, S. 1961. *Fauna R.P. Romîne. Reptilia*. Acad. RPR, Bucureşti.

FUHN, I. 1969. *Broaşte, şerpi, şopîrle*. Editura ştiînţifica. Bucureşti.

Spain

SALVADOR, A. 1974. *Guia de los anfibios y reptiles españoles*. Instituto Nacional para la Conservacion de la Naturaleza.

Sweden

GISLÉN, T. and KAURI, H. 1959. Zoogeography of the Swedish Amphibians and Reptiles. *Acta Vertebratica*, 1: 193–397. Almqvist and Wiksell, Stockholm. (In English.)

CURRY-LINDAHL, K. 1975. Groddjur och kräldjur i färg. Awe/ Gebers, Stockholm.

Switzerland

GROSSENBACHER, K. and BRAND, M. 1973. *Schlüssel zur Bestimmung der Amphibien und Reptilien der Schweiz*. Naturhistorisches Museum, Bern.

GROSSENBACHER, K. 1975. *Verzeichnis der herpetologischen Literatur aus der Schweiz*. Naturhistorisches Museum, Bern.

USSR

TERENT'EV P. V. and CHERNOV, S. A. 1965 (trans). Key to Amphibians and Reptiles. Israel Program for Scientific Translation, Jerusalem. (In English.)

BANNIKOV, A. G., DAREVSKII, I. S. and RUSTAMOV, A. K. 1971. Zemnovodnye i Presmykayshchie SSR. Izdatel'stvo "Mysl". Moscow.

Yugoslavia

RADOVANOVIC, M. 1951. *Vodozemcí i gmízavci naše zemlje.* Belgrade.

POZZI, A. 1966. Geonomia e catalogo ragionato degli anfibi e dei rettili della Jugoslavia. *Natura*, Milano. 57: 5–55.

3. Recordings of frog and toad calls

ROCHE, J.-C. 1965. *Guide sonore du Naturaliste, 2: Batraciens.* J.-C. Roche.

WEISSMAN, C. 1971. *Danske Padder.* Naturhistorisk Museum, Århus, Denmark.

BOSWALL, J. (in press). *A field guide to amphibian voices of Europe.* Swedish Broadcasting Corporation, Stockholm.

DISTRIBUTION MAPS

The maps show the areas where a particular species can be expected to occur. However, within these areas, it will only be found in suitable habitats, so the relevant section on **Habits** in the text must be checked before deciding whether the species is likely to be encountered at a particular locality. Additional information about distribution may be found in the appropriate section on **Range**.

In the maps, question marks indicate doubtful areas of distribution and small arrows are used to make very small parts of the range more conspicuous. In the Aegean Sea, the presence of a species in some or all the islands of the Cyclades is shown by a pointer (thus ◄).

When using the maps remember that accuracy varies. This is due to a number of causes. For some countries relatively up-to-date information on distribution is available but for others it is scant or very diffuse and hard to locate. In some places, known localities for a given species are widely separated and it is difficult to tell whether this really represents a broken range, or whether insufficient observations have been made in the area. Another problem concerns retreating species: several forms are no longer found in parts of their original range, but the old records for these areas may never have been refuted. Account is taken of large, well-established introductions but small-scale ones and those of short duration are ignored.

However, on the whole, omissions in the maps are probably fairly minor and if a species is apparently encountered very far outside its marked range, this will most likely be due to misidentification. In such cases, the animal in question should be checked very carefully against both key and texts. If you are convinced that an extension in range is involved, your record (supported by a detailed description and if possible photograph, or even the animal itself) should be checked by a reputable herpetological society or a museum.

In the captions below each map there are two sets of numbers. The first, in **bold** type, refer to plate numbers where the species is illustrated. The second, in ordinary type, refer to text pages where it is described.

1. *Salamandra salamandra*
Fire Salamander **1**, 33

2. *Salamandra atra*
Alpine Salamander **1**, 34

3. *Salamandra luschani*
Luschan's Salamander **2**,
34

4. *Salamandrina terdigitata*
Spectacled Salamander
1, 35

5. *Chioglossa lusitanica*
Golden-striped
Salamander **1**, 35

6. *Pleurodeles waltl*
Sharp-ribbed Salamand
2, 38

7. *Euproctus asper*
Pyrenean Brook
Salamander **2**, 38

8. *Euproctus montanus*
Corsican Brook
Salamander **2**, 39

9. *Euproctus platycephalu*
Sardinian Brook
Salamander **2**, 39

254

0. *Triturus marmoratus*
Marbled Newt **3**, 42

11. *Triturus cristatus*
Warty Newt **3**, 43

12. *Triturus alpestris*
Alpine Newt **5**, 46

3. *Triturus montandoni*
Montandon's Newt
5, 47

14. *Triturus vulgaris*
Smooth Newt **4**, 47

15. *Triturus helveticus*
Palmate Newt **4**, 51

6. *Triturus boscai*
Bosca's Newt **4**, 51

17. *Triturus italicus*
Italian Newt **5**, 52

18. *Hydromantes genei*
Sardinian Cave
Salamander **1**, 53

19. *Hydromantes italicus*
Italian Cave Salamander
1, 53

20. *Proteus anguinus*
Olm **2**, 54

21. *Bombina variegata*
Yellow-bellied Toad
9, 60

22. *Bombina bombina*
Fire-bellied Toad **9**, 61

23. *Discoglossus pictus*
Painted Frog **6**, 62

24. *Discoglossus sardus*
Tyrrhenian Painted Frog
6, 62

25. *Alytes obstetricans*
Midwife Toad **6**, 63

26. *Alytes cisternasii*
Iberian Midwife Toad
6, 66

27. *Pelobates cultripes*
Western Spadefoot
7, 67

28. *Pelobates fuscus*
Common Spadefoot
7,67

29. *Pelobates syriacus*
Eastern Spadefoot **7**,70

30. *Pelodytes punctatus*
Parsley Frog **6**,71

31. *Bufo bufo*
Common Toad **8**,72

32. *Bufo calamita*
Natterjack **8**,73

33. *Bufo viridis*
Green Toad **8**,74

34. *Hyla arborea*
Common Tree Frog
9,75

35. *Hyla meridionalis*
Stripeless Tree Frog
9,78

36. *Rana temporaria*
Common Frog **10**,78

257

37. *Rana arvalis*
    Moor Frog **10**, 80

38. *Rana dalmatina*
    Agile Frog **11**, 80

39. *Rana latastei*
    Italian Agile Frog **11**, 8

40. *Rana graeca*
    Stream Frog **11**, 82

41. *Rana iberica*
    Iberian Frog **11**, 83

42. *Rana ridibunda*
    Marsh Frog **12**, 85

43. *Rana lessonae*
    Pool Frog **12**, 85
    and *Rana esculenta*
    Edible Frog **12**, 86

44. *Rana catesbeiana*
    American Bullfrog
    87

45. *Testudo hermanni*
    Hermann's Tortoise
    13, 91

258

46. *Testudo graeca*
Spur-thighed Tortoise
13,91

47. *Testudo marginata*
Marginated Tortoise
13,92

48. *Emys orbicularis*
European Pond Terrapin
14, 93

49. *Mauremys caspica*
Stripe-necked Terrapin
14, 93

50. *Tarentola mauritanica*
Moorish Gecko **15**, 108

51. *Hemidactylus turcicus*
Turkish Gecko **15**, 109

52. *Phyllodactylus europaeus*
European Leaf-toed
Gecko **15**, 109

53. *Cyrtodactylus kotschyi*
Kotschy's Gecko
15,110

54. *Agama stellio*
Agama **16**,110

55. *Chamaeleo chamaeleon*
Mediterranean
Chameleon **16**, 111

56. *Algyroides*
nigropunctatus
Dalmatian Algyroides
18, 115

57. *Algyroides moreoticus*
Greek Algyroides
18,118

58. *Algyroides fitzingeri*
Pygmy Algyroides
18,118

59. *Algyroides marchi*
Spanish Algyroides
18,118

60. *Ophisops elegans*
Snake-eyed Lizard
17,119

61. *Psammodromus algirus*
Large Psammodromus
17, 120

62. *Psammodromus*
hispanicus
Spanish
Psammodromus **17**,121

63. *Acanthodactylus*
erythrurus
Spiny-footed Lizard
17,122

64. *Eremias arguta*
Eremias **17**,122

65. *Lacerta lepida*
Ocellated Lizard
20,**22**,130

66. *Lacerta schreiberi*
Schreiber's Green Lizard
20,**22**,131

67. *Lacerta viridis*
Green Lizard **21**,**22**,131

68. *Lacerta trilineata*
Balkan Green Lizard
21,**22**,132

69. *Lacerta agilis*
Sand Lizard **19**,**22**,134

70. *Lacerta vivipara*
Viviparous Lizard
23,137

71. *Podarcis muralis*
Common Wall Lizard
23,138

72. *Lacerta monticola*
Iberian Rock Lizard
24,141

73. *Podarcis hispanica*
Iberian Wall Lizard
24,142

74. *Podarcis bocagei*
Bocage's Wall Lizard
24,143

75. *Lacerta perspicillata*
Moroccan Rock Lizard
25,147

76. *Podarcis lilfordi*
Lilford's Wall Lizard
25,150

77. *Podarcis pityusensis*
Ibiza Wall Lizard **25**,150

78. *Lacerta bedriagae*
Bedriaga's Rock Lizard
26,152

79. *Podarcis tiliguerta*
Tyrrhenian Wall Lizard
26,153

80. *Podarcis sicula*
Italian Wall Lizard
27,155

81. *Podarcis wagleriana*
Sicilian Wall Lizard
27,158

82. *Podarcis filfolensis*
Maltese Wall Lizard
26,158

83. *Lacerta horvathi*
Horvath's Rock Lizard
28,163

84. *Lacerta mosorensis*
Mosor Rock Lizard
28,163

85. *Lacerta oxycephala*
Sharp-snouted Rock
Lizard **28**,164

86. *Podarcis melisellensis*
Dalmatian Wall Lizard
28,165

87. *Lacerta praticola*
Meadow Lizard **29**,168

88. *Lacerta graeca*
Greek Rock Lizard
30, 169

89. *Podarcis taurica*
Balkan Wall Lizard
29,170

90. *Podarcis erhardii*
Erhard's Wall Lizard
31,171

263

91. *Podarcis
peloponnesiaca*
Peloponnese Wall
Lizard **30**,172

92. *Podarcis milensis*
Milos Wall Lizard
31,173

93. *Anguis fragilis*
Slow Worm **33**,175

94. *Ophisaurus apodus*
European Glass Lizard
33,175

95. *Ablepharus kitaibelii*
Snake-eyed Skink **32**,
178

96. *Chalcides ocellatus*
Ocellated Skink **32**,179

97. *Chalcides bedriagai*
Bedriaga's Skink
32,180

98. *Chalcides chalcides*
Three-toed Skink
32,180

99. *Ophiomorus
punctatissimus*
Greek Legless Skink
33,181

264

00. *Blanus cinereus*
Amphisbaenian
33,182

101. *Typhlops vermicularis*
Worm Snake **34**,188

102. *Eryx jaculus*
Sand Boa **34**,189

03. *Malpolon
monspessulanus*
Montpellier Snake
34,190

104. *Coluber hippocrepis*
Horseshoe Whip
Snake **34**,191

105. *Coluber algirus*
Algerian Whip Snake
35,194

06. *Coluber najadum*
Dahl's Whip Snake
35,194

107. *Coluber viridiflavus*
Western Whip Snake
35,195

108. *Coluber gemonensis*
Balkan Whip Snake
35,196

109. *Coluber jugularis*
Large Whip Snake
35,196

110. *Elaphe situla*
Leopard Snake **36**,197

111. *Elaphe quatuorlineata*
Four-lined Snake
36,198

112. *Elaphe longissima*
Aesculapian Snake
36,199

113. *Elaphe scalaris*
Ladder Snake **36**,200

114. *Natrix natrix*
Grass Snake **37**,201

115. *Natrix maura*
Viperine Snake **37**,203

116. *Natrix tessellata*
Dice Snake **37**,204

117. *Coronella austriaca*
Smooth Snake **38**,204

266

118. *Coronella girondica*
Southern Smooth
Snake **38**, 205

119. *Macroprotodon
cucullatus*
False Smooth Snake
38, 206

120. *Telescopus fallax*
Cat Snake **38**, 207

121. *Vipera ursinii*
Orsini's Viper **39**, 215

122. *Vipera berus*
Adder **39**, 217

123. *Vipera aspis*
Asp Viper **39**, 40, 218

124. *Vipera latasti*
Lataste's Viper **40**, 219

125. *Vipera ammodytes*
Nose-horned Viper
40, 222

126. *Vipera xanthina*
Ottoman Viper **40**, 223

INDEX

In this index, the first numbers given refer to pages where the main descriptive texts are to be found. **Bold** numbers refer to the colour plates, *italic* numbers to the maps.